FINANCIAL ASTROLOGY

Almanac 2025

Trading & Investing Using the Planets

M.G. Bucholtz, B.Sc, MBA, M.Sc.

A WOOD DRAGON BOOK

Financial Astrology Almanac 2025
Trading & Investing Using the Planets

Copyright © 2024 by M.G. Bucholtz

Published by:
Wood Dragon Books
Box 429, Mossbank, Saskatchewan, Canada, S0H 3G0
http://www.wooddragonbooks.com

ISBN: 978-1-990863-80-6 (Paperback)
ISBN : 978-1-990863-79-0 (eBook)

Contact the author at: supercyclereport@gmail.com or visit www.investingsuccess.ca

DEDICATION

To the many traders and investors who, at some visceral level, suspect there is more to the financial market system than P/E ratios and analyst recommendations.

You are correct. There is more. Much more. Rooted in astronomical and astrological timing, the markets are a rich tapestry of interwoven cycles. This book will add a whole new dimension to your trading and investing activities.

DISCLAIMER

All material provided herein is based on material gleaned from mathematical and astrological publications researched by the author to supplement his own trading. This publication is written for those who actively trade and invest in the financial markets and who are looking to incorporate astrological phenomena and esoteric math into their market activity. While the material presented herein has proven reliable to the author in his personal trading and investing activity, there is no guarantee this material will continue to be reliable into the future.

The author and publisher assume no liability whatsoever for any investment or trading decisions made by readers of this book. The reader alone is responsible for all trading and investment outcomes and is further advised not to exceed his or her risk tolerances when trading or investing in the financial markets.

TABLE OF CONTENTS

INTRODUCTION

Many traders and investors think company press releases, media news opinions, quarterly earnings reports, and analyst targets drive stock prices and major index movements. I disagree.

I believe price action is driven by human emotion. Psychologists describe six emotions: happy, sad, fear, disgust, anger, and surprise. I have a shorter list. I believe fear and greed are the two classes of emotion that influence the financial markets. When we are greedy, we run towards the market. We buy, buy, buy. When we are fearful, we run away from the market. We sell, sell, sell.

I believe the emotions of fear and greed are particularly influenced by events in our cosmos such as changes in the declination of Venus, Mars, and Moon, angular aspects between orbiting planets, transits past key points in natal first trade horoscopes, perihelion and aphelion occurrences of Mercury and Venus, and Mercury retrograde events.

I further believe that of all the celestial bodies, the Moon is the most influential. In 1937, New York-based astrologer Louise McWhirter penned a book entitled *The McWhirter Theory of Stock Market Forecasting.* In her book she made clear that the Moon orbiting past certain degree points of the NYSE natal horoscope wheel could trigger price responses on the Dow Jones Average. My observations over the past dozen years indicate she was correct in her assertions.

Overlap and weave together these celestial phenomena and the result will be the ups and downs of price that characterize a stock chart, a commodity price chart, or the chart of a major index. The average trader or investor who remains fixated on media releases and analyst opinions ignores this rich tapestry of planetary influence.

Distances of planets from the Sun, changes in planetary declination, and movement of the Moon are all *astronomy* type events. The question that must be dispensed with is—why is the term *astrology* used in the title of this publication? Why is this book not entitled the Financial Astronomy Almanac?

Webster's dictionary states that: *astronomy is concerned with the study of objects outside the earth's atmosphere.* Webster's further says that: *astrology is the divination of how planets influence our lives.*

Years ago, when I first began writing these annual Almanacs, I thought about using the word *astronomy.* However, the community of people who apply the study of cosmic events to the financial markets call themselves financial astrologers. So, in keeping with that usage, I have maintained the use of the term *astrology* in the title of my annual publications.

When I began to embrace financial astrology in 2012, it was a monumental shift for me. My educational background includes an Engineering degree, an MBA degree, and a M.Sc. degree. My approach to financial astrology and to the markets in general is thus heavily slanted towards Fibonacci mathematics, quantum science, and cyclical planetary events.

My approach also entails the use of technical chart indicators to help identify changes in price trend. Trend changes that occur at the same time as a planetary event get my attention quickly. For example, trend changes that occur at Fibonacci price retracements of 48.6%, 61.8%, or 78.6% tend to be significant. Trend changes that occur at quantum price lines are always powerful events. Trend changes that occur at planetary retrograde events, declination extrema, or elongation maxima also tend to be significant.

I cannot emphasize enough the importance of following the price trend when trading and investing. So strong is my conviction towards the trend, in 2023 I released a book entitled *Follow the Trend–When to Buy and When to Sell*. Of all the trend indicators discussed in the book, the *Ergodic Oscillator* and the *True Strength Index* are particularly powerful. Both were developed by trader and mathematician William Blau in the 1980s. In addition, the *Stochastic* chart indicators created by Martin Pring and George Lane are also potent. In this edition of the Almanac, I have included a chapter to further explain how to use these various chart indicators.

The *Financial Astrology Almanac 2025* is structured around long cycles, medium cycles, and shorter cycles. A long cycle of planetary activity that overlaps and interweaves with time is the Jupiter/Saturn Gann Master Cycle which unfolds over two decades of heliocentric planetary movement. Threaded through the fabric of this Master Cycle is another long cycle, the McWhirter 18.6-year cycle which aligns to the movement of the North Node through the signs of the zodiac. This nodal cycle broadly defines overall economic activity. As the Node progresses through the zodiac, aspects to major outer planets can exacerbate (or mitigate) the tenor of economic activity.

On a more moderate timeframe, the repeated cyclical movement of Venus and Mars above and below the ecliptic plane aligns to swing highs and swing lows on commodity futures and equity indices. Events of Mercury or Venus being retrograde often align to trend reversals on stocks and equity indices. A similar observation holds for both Mercury and Venus being at easterly and westerly elongation extremes, superior conjunctions, inferior conjunctions, perihelion, and aphelion. Medium-term cycles also arise from key annual celebratory events delineated in the Hebrew lunar-based calendar, including the seven-year Shemitah cycles.

On a shorter timeframe, the movement of the Moon through the signs of the zodiac is a powerful phenomenon. Times when the Moon is *Void of Course* align to expressions of notable volatility on equity indices. The cycle from one New Moon to the next can also be seen to have a bearing on the New York Stock Exchange (NYSE), especially when the Moon transits past 14 degrees of Cancer and 24 degrees of Pisces. These degree positions mark the location of the Ascendant and Mid-Heaven respectively on May 17, 1792 when the NYSE was founded. The importance of these degree positions precedes the NYSE. The Moon was at 14 of Cancer on the morning of April 30, 1789 when George Washington was sworn in as America's first President.

Also on a shorter timeframe, the movement of Sun, Mars, Venus, and Moon past key points in the natal first trade horoscope of a particular financial exchange can be seen as having a strong correlation to volatile price reactions. W.D. Gann is reported to have paid attention to such movements past key points of the April 1848 natal horoscope wheel of the Chicago Board of Trade and the April 1871 natal horoscope for the New York Cotton Exchange. How exactly human emotion is tied to the planetary placements at the founding date of a commodity exchange remains a mystery to me. In fact, human emotion changing at planetary transits of natal horoscope points fuels my sense of awe for what I deem to be a higher power that guides the Universe.

A human emotional connection to the cosmos predates the founding of financial exchanges. Consider the beliefs of the Cree First Nations people in Alberta, Canada. They hold sacred the story of the Pleiades star cluster, visible in the constellation Taurus. One day, Sky Woman spotted a far-away planet and expressed a desire to visit it. Spider Woman, who lived amongst the stars of the Pleiades, spun a web so that Sky Woman could reach the far-off planet. The far-off planet was Earth. Mankind originates with Sky Woman and her visit to Earth. I am often humbled when I look at stock market reactions as Sun, Venus, and Mars transit conjunct to the Pleiades star cluster in Taurus.

Consider the beliefs of the ancient Egyptians with respect to the star Sirius. I am humbled when I look at stock market reactions during periods of the year when Sirius is rising in the early morning sky or setting in the evening sky.

Ancient civilizations as far back as the Babylonians also recognized planetary activity. Their high priests observed changes in the emotions of the people and correlated these changes to movements of Mercury, Venus, Mars, Jupiter, and Saturn in the heavens. They assigned to these planets the names of the various deities revered by the people. They also identified and named various star constellations in the heavens and divided the heavens into twelve signs. This was the birth of *astrology* as we know it today. After reading this Almanac, you too may have reason to pause and ponder the power of the cosmos. You may well find yourself thinking that a higher power guides the Universe.

Stories of traders benefiting from planetary activity are also not new. In the early 1900s, esoteric thinkers such as the famous Wall Street trader W.D. Gann reportedly made handsome monetary gains when he realized that cycles of astrology bore a striking correlation to financial market price action. Gann is most famous for identifying the Saturn/Jupiter cycle which he labelled the Gann Master Cycle. He followed the cyclical activity of Jupiter and Neptune when he traded Wheat and Corn futures. He also delved deep into square root math which led him to develop his *Square of Nine* approach to trading. The concept of price squaring with time is also a Gann construct. Today many traders and investors attempt to emulate Gann but they do so in a linear fashion, looking for repetitive cycles on the calendar. What they are missing is the astrology component, which must be interpreted using a zodiac wheel.

In the 1930s, Louise McWhirter greatly illuminated the connection between the stock market and planetary cycles. She identified an 18.6-year cyclical correlation between the general state of the American economy and the position of the North Node of the Moon in the zodiac. Her methodology extended to include the transiting Moon passing by key points of the 1792 natal birth horoscope of the New York Stock Exchange. She also identified a correlation between price movement of a stock and those times when transiting Sun, Mars, Jupiter and Saturn made hard aspects to the natal Sun position in the stock's natal birth (first trade) horoscope. [1]

The late 1940s saw mathematical modelling applied to the stock market when astrologer Garth Allen (a.k.a. Donald Bradley) created his *Siderograph Model* based on aspects between the various transiting planets. Each aspect as it occurs is given a sinusoidal weighting as the orb (separation) between the planets varies. Bradley's model was obscured in the aftermath of the 2008 financial crisis when the Federal Reserve started injecting massive amounts of liquidity into the financial system. Now that excess liquidity has stopped flooding the system and the Federal Reserve has embarked on balance sheet reduction, Bradley's model again has the potential to be a powerful indicator of trend changes on the S&P 500. [2]

As the 1950s dawned, academics at institutions like Yale and Harvard came to dominate discussions of the financial markets. In my opinion, financial astrology was in danger of becoming too well known about. The power players on Wall Street could not tolerate this reality so they engaged academia to help. Talk of planetary events influencing financial markets was quickly replaced by academic constructs like *Modern Portfolio Theory* and the *Efficient Market Hypothesis*. These models promoted the idea that investing was for the long term and that investors should buy, hold, and forget about the interim ups and downs of the market. The academics were successful. Financial astrology faded away from every day discourse. These academic models persisted for several decades to follow until coming under severe scrutiny first with the 2000 tech bubble meltdown and again with the 2008 sub-prime mortgage collapse that nearly derailed the global economy.

The failure of these models to predict these market shocks brought financial astrology to the fore again. Since the events of 2008, the application of planetary science to the stock market has been made more user friendly. The software designers at Australian company Optuma now have an impressive financial astrology platform built into their *Optuma* charting program. This is the software I have used to generate the charts in this Almanac. Software designers at U.S. firm Astrolabe developed *Solar Fire Gold* which I use to generate horoscope wheels to help me determine what planetary aspects lay ahead.

You have probably experienced the effects of the planets on the financial market without even realizing it. Think back to the dark days of late 2008 when there was genuine concern over the very survival of the financial market system. This timeframe was the end of an 18.6-year cycle of the North Node traveling around the zodiac. To high-level, power-players in the financial system who understood astrology, this period was a prime opportunity to feast off the fear of the investing public and the anxiety of government officials who were standing at the ready with lucrative bailout packages. The S&P 500 low in March 2009 came at a confluence of a Mars and a Neptune quantum point. (Mars and Neptune are deemed to be the planetary rulers of the New York Stock Exchange.) The March 2009 low on the S&P 500 also aligned perfectly to the start of Venus being retrograde.

Think back to August 2015 and the S&P 500 selloff that the financial media did not see coming. This selloff started at a confluence of three events: Venus being retrograde, the appearance of Venus as a Morning Star after having been only visible as an Evening Star for the previous 263 days, and the close conjunction of Venus and Jupiter (a once in 26-month cyclical event).

Remember the early days of 2016 when Mercury was retrograde and the S&P 500 hit a rough patch? Remember the weakness of June 2016 when Venus emerged from conjunction to become visible as an Evening Star?

Do you recall the dire predictions for financial market calamity following the 2016 election of Donald Trump to the White House? When the S&P 500 instead powered higher, analysts were flummoxed. What they failed to realize was that Venus had made its declination minima right at the time of the American election. Venus declination minima events bear a striking correlation to changes of trend on US equity markets.

What about the early days of 2018 when fear once again gripped the system? Venus was at its declination minimum. The S&P 500 reached another turning point in the first week of October 2018 when Venus was again at a declination low. Add the fact that Venus turned retrograde at the same time and the fear starts to make sense. The S&P 500 sold off sharply into mid-December before starting to recover. Sun was conjunct Saturn at this recovery point which correlates strongly to trend changes on equity markets. The North Node had also just changed zodiac signs, an event which further aligns with trend changes.

The S&P 500 hit a sudden rough patch in early August 2019 when the Federal Reserve cut interest rates due to overnight repurchase agreement (repo) market liquidity concerns. At the time, Mercury had just finished retrograde and Moon had just transited a key point on the NYSE 1792 natal horoscope.

US equity markets peaked in late February 2020 and went into total spasm in March 2020 when fears of the potential for a viral pandemic were stirred up. At the time, Mercury was retrograde and Mars had just made its declination minimum. Venus was at the same degree of declination it had been in 1792 when the NYSE was founded.

Remember the confusion surrounding the November 2020 election of Joe Biden to the White House? The day of the election, Mercury finished being retrograde, and heliocentric Jupiter and Saturn were exactly at 0-degrees of separation. To have these two specific events occur on the day of the election is a rarity. The events concerning the validity of this election will be hotly debated for years to come.

The events of late 2021 reminded us all again of the power of planetary events. As 2021 was ending, both the Nasdaq 100 and S&P 500 equity markets were peaking. Mercury was approaching its greatest easterly elongation. Venus was retrograde and also was approaching its inferior conjunction. Mercury would soon turn retrograde. Mars was approaching its declination minimum. This was a powerful concentration of cosmic energy bearing down on human emotion. The powerful players (whoever they were) took full advantage, pushing the markets into a downtrend through aggressive selling. Individual investors (whose emotions were rattled by the cosmic events) panicked and started selling which fed into the downtrend. By June 2022, the selling had caused a full 20% decline across equity markets.

The period September 2021 to September 2022 was a Shemitah Year in the Hebrew faith (a one-in-seven-year occurrence). I predicted at the outset that this Shemitah Year would deliver some headline events. And sure enough, headlines were created when Russia invaded Ukraine, inflation surged, gasoline prices at the pump jumped, and Europe stumbled into an energy crisis. True to form for a Shemitah year, North American markets recorded a significant bottom in October 2022 just after the Shemitah year ended.

North American equity markets then rallied into July 2023 before hitting resistance. A Fibonacci 38.2% retracement of this rally took the S&P 500 to a swing low in October 2023 just as Venus was at its declination maximum. The markets then rallied into late March 2024 before hitting resistance just as Mercury turned retrograde.

After a Fibonacci 23.6% retracement on the S&P 500 and a Fibonacci 38.2% retracement on the Nasdaq 100, a rally began which took these indices to a resistance point in July 2024 when Mars transited past the Pleiades point at 27 Taurus. Also at this time, Venus was becoming visible as the Evening Star, having just completed Superior Conjunction.

As I wrote this manuscript in August 2024, the S&P 500 and the Nasdaq 100 were exhibiting short-term bearish behavior. August 2 and August 5 were particularly harsh days with these indices selling off 5% fueled by Mercury having turned retrograde on August 5.

Despite what I deem to be an obvious correlation between market price action and human emotion, the North American mainstream media steadfastly refuses to embrace cosmic events as valid tools for timing the markets. Perhaps this is because the average investor on the street is not supposed to know about this correlation. It remains my opinion that there are powerful players in the major financial centres of the globe who *do* embrace planetary cycles and transits. Knowing that planetary aspects and cycles influence human emotion, these power players use these occurrences to their advantage to make money in up-trending markets. They also use their short-selling prowess at these cyclic events to induce trend reversals on markets. As the price trend turns and markets start to fall, these players profit from their short positions while average investors experience emotional angst and sleepless nights knowing the markets are trending down and working against them. "Who are the powerful players that use astrology to move markets?" is a question that burns in my mind. Is it a select group at J.P. Morgan? Is it a group in a dark-panelled office in London? I will likely never know.

Cosmic events continue to unfold as time marches on. People who view the markets through the lens of analyst opinions and media blather will be unable to appreciate this cosmic activity hidden in plain view. They will ride an emotional roller coaster as their financial planners tell them that investing is for the long-term and not to worry. On the other hand, investors who are able to identify and appreciate cosmic activity will be able to take steps to protect themselves and profit accordingly.

This Almanac (which is my twelfth such annual publication) is designed to provide the reader with a new perspective on the financial markets. I sincerely hope that the material presented herein will help you take your trading and investing activity to a new level. I further hope this Almanac will help you better navigate all the market events that 2025 has in store.

Note from the Author: I am also the author of several other astrology books and publish a bi-weekly subscription-based newsletter called *The Astrology Letter*. Through all of my written efforts, I hope to encourage people to embrace the events in our cosmos as valuable tools to aid in trading and investing decision making.

CHAPTER ONE

Fundamentals

The Sun is at the center of our solar system, with the Earth, Moon, planets and other asteroid bodies completing the planetary system. In addition to the Sun and Moon, there are eight celestial bodies relevant to the financial markets. These planets are: Mercury, Venus, Mars, Jupiter, Saturn, Uranus, Neptune, and Pluto.

Figure 1-1 illustrates these various bodies and their spatial relation to the Sun. Mercury is the closest to the Sun while Pluto is the farthest away.

Their distances from the Sun (in astronomical units (au), where 1 au is approximately 150 million km) are: Mercury (0.39 au), Venus (0.79 au), Mars (1.5 au), Jupiter (5.2 au), Saturn (9.54 au), Uranus (19.2 au), Neptune (30.06 au), and Pluto (39 au). Close examination of ratios of these distances to one another shows a close alignment to the Fibonacci sequence. For example, the ratio of the Venus distance to the Mercury distance is the Fibonacci number 2. The ratio of the Jupiter distance to the Mercury distance is the Fibonacci number 13. The ratio of the Pluto distance to the Mercury distance is the Fibonacci number 89. (1)

Price retracements that align to Fibonacci ratios, and spatial relations between planets that align to the Fibonacci sequence are both humbling phenomena that lead me to the observation – as above, so below.

The Ecliptic and the Zodiac

The various planets and other asteroid bodies rotate 360-degrees around the Sun following a path called the *ecliptic plane*. As shown in Figure 1-2, Earth and its Equator are slightly tilted (approximately 23.45-degrees) relative to the ecliptic plane.

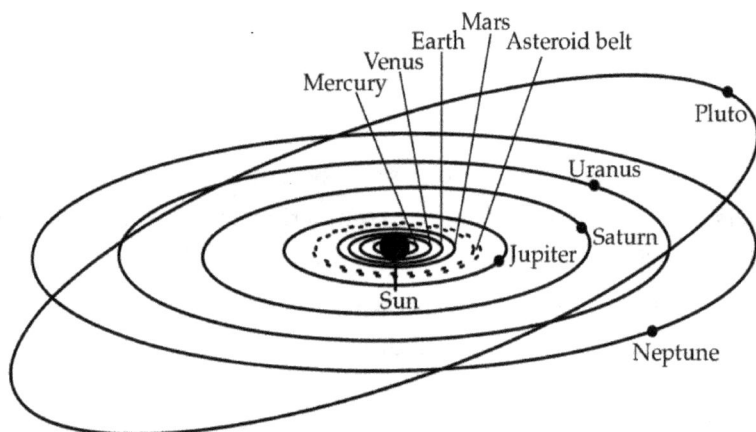

Figure 1-1
The Planets

Projecting the Earth's equator into space produces the *celestial equator plane*. There are two points of intersection between the ecliptic plane and celestial equator plane. Mathematically, this makes sense as two non-parallel planes must intersect at two points. These points are commonly called the *vernal equinox* (occurring at March 20th) and the *autumnal equinox* (occurring at September 20th).

The starting point (or zero-degree point) of the zodiac wheel occurs in the sign Aries at the vernal equinox. The vernal equinox is when, from our vantage point on Earth, the Sun appears at 0-degrees Aries. The Sun at this location is more commonly referred to as the *first day of spring*. The autumnal equinox is when, from our vantage point on Earth, the Sun appears at 180-degrees from the vernal equinox (0-degrees of Libra). Sun at 0-degrees of Libra is more commonly referred to as the *first day of autumn*.

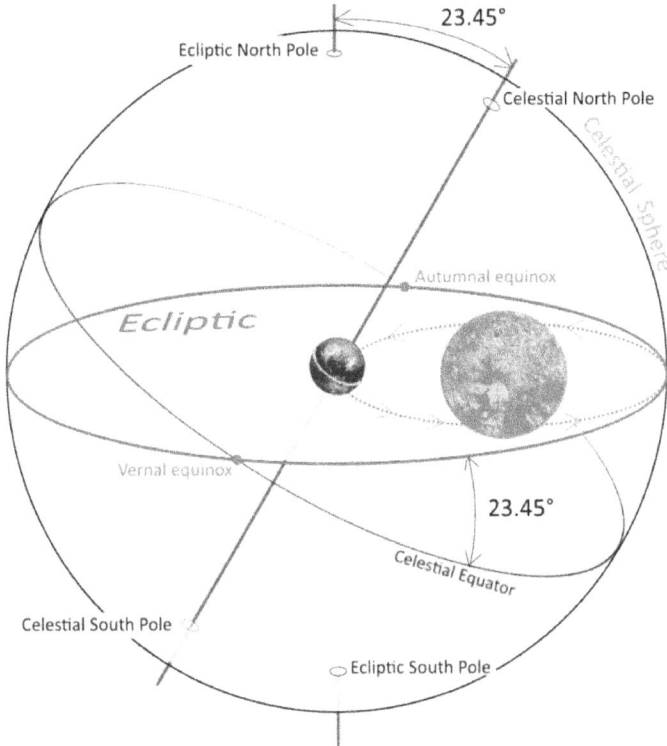

Figure 1-2
The Ecliptic

The Glyphs

Dividing the ecliptic plane into twelve equal sections of 30-degrees results in what astrologers call the *zodiac* or the *zodiac wheel*. Ancient civilizations looking skyward identified patterns of stars called *constellations* that aligned to these twelve zodiac divisions. The twelve portions of the zodiac have names such as Aries, Cancer, and Leo. (If these names sound familiar, they should. You routinely see all twelve names in the daily horoscope section of your morning newspaper.)

Figure 1-3 illustrates the symbols that appear in the twelve segments of a zodiac wheel. The twelve segments are more properly called *signs*; the symbols are called *glyphs*. The various planets are also denoted by glyphs, as shown in Figure 1-4.

Figure 1-3
The Zodiac Wheel

Geocentric and Heliocentric Astrology

The terms *synodic* and *sidereal* help define the two distinct varieties of astrology – geocentric and heliocentric.

In *geocentric* astrology (synodic), the Earth is the vantage point for observing the planets as they pass through the signs of the zodiac.

In *heliocentric* astrology (sidereal), the Sun is the vantage point for observing the planets as they pass through the signs of the zodiac. An observer positioned on the Sun would also see the orbiting planets making aspects with one another.

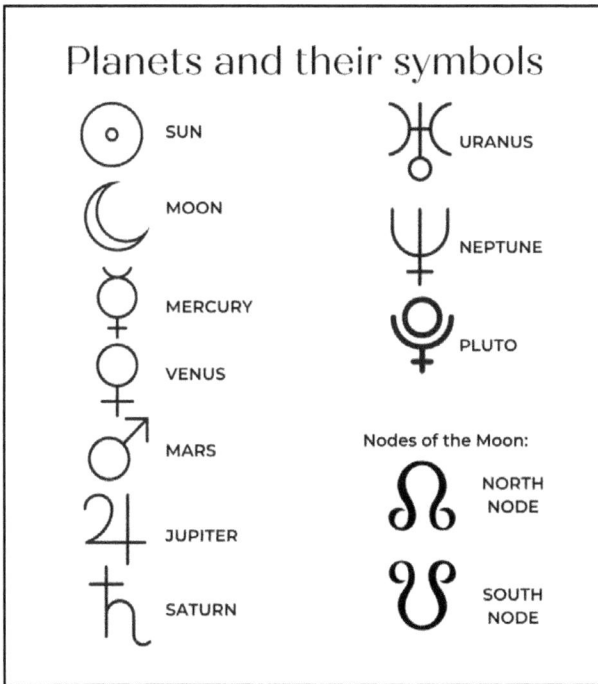

Figure 1-4
The Glyphs

Declination

As the various celestial bodies make their respective journeys around the Sun, they can be seen to move above and below the ecliptic plane. This movement is termed *declination*. Celestial bodies experience declinations of up to about 25-degrees above and below the ecliptic plane. Declination occurs as a result of the Sun's force of gravitational pull on a planet. The larger outer planets (Jupiter, Saturn, Neptune, Uranus and Pluto), owing to their size and distance from the Sun, experience declination changes that are slower to evolve. The smaller inner planets (Mercury, Venus, Mars) exhibit more amplitude in their declination patterns.

Declination is often incorrectly described by financial astrology writers and bloggers. The **correct** way of describing declination is with heliocentric data. An observer situated on a fixed reference point of the Sun will be able to see the various planets moving above or below the ecliptic plane. Attempting to describe declination using geocentric data is misleading because an Earth-bound observer is trying to observe the other planets moving relative to the ecliptic plane while he is moving as the planet Earth moves above or below the ecliptic.

As this Almanac will illustrate, changes in the declination of a celestial body (most notably Mars and Venus) can affect the financial markets. W.D. Gann believed that the dates Venus and Mars return to the same declination level they were at when a stock or a commodity future first started trading (first trade date/natal declination level) influence price trend changes.

The Moon

Just as the planets orbit 360-degrees around the Sun, the Moon orbits 360-degrees around the Earth. The Moon orbits the Earth in a plane of motion called the *lunar ecliptic plane*. This plane is inclined at about 5-degrees to the ecliptic plane as Figure 1-5 shows. The Moon orbits Earth with a slight elliptical pattern in approximately 27.3 days, relative to an observer located on a fixed frame of reference such as the Sun. This time period is known as a *sidereal month*. However, during one sidereal month, an observer located on Earth (a moving frame of reference) will revolve part way around the Sun. Because of this added movement, the Earth-bound observer will see a complete orbit of the Moon around the Earth in approximately 29.5 days. This 29.5-day period of time is known as a *synodic month* or more commonly a *lunar* month.

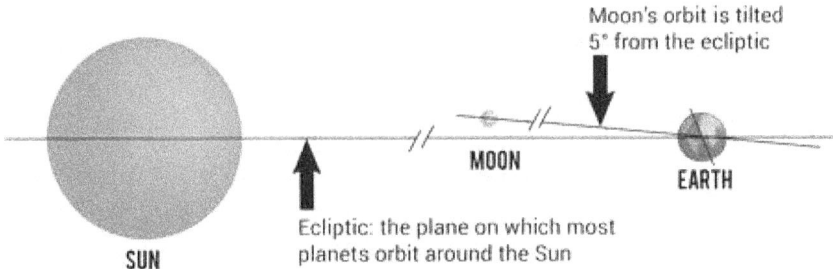

Figure 1-5
Lunar Orbit

Moon Void of Course (VOC)

The Moon moves through a sign of the zodiac about every 2.3 days. Often, there will be a short period of time just before the Moon enters a new sign where it makes no aspects to any of the planets in the zodiac. This brief timeframe is referred to as *Moon Void of Course* (VOC). It is not uncommon to see emotions temporarily become heightened and markets become jittery at these VOC events. In a given month, the Moon will be VOC approximately 12 times. In order for VOC to affect equity markets, the VOC event must occur between Monday and Friday, must be more than four hours in duration, and must occur during NYSE trading hours. I disregard any VOC events outside these parameters. The net result is that in a typical month there might be up to four VOC events that affect the markets.

The Nodes

A mathematical construct related to the Moon, and central to financial markets, is the *Nodes*. The Nodes are the points of intersection between the Earth's ecliptic plane and the Moon's ecliptic plane. In astrology, typically only the North Node is referred to. The North Node forms the basis for the McWhirter Method (which will be discussed in Chapter 3).

Synodic and Sidereal Cycles

The concepts of synodic and sidereal extend beyond the Moon to include all the planets. To an earth-bound observer, a synodic time period is the time between two successive planetary occurrences. For example, how many days does it take for Sun passing Pluto on the zodiac wheel to Sun again passing Pluto? To a Sun-bound observer (a fixed frame of reference), a sidereal time period is the number of days (or years) it takes for a planet to orbit the Sun. The data in Figure 1-6 presents synodic and sidereal times.

PLANET	SYNODIC PERIOD	SIDEREAL PERIOD
Mercury	116 days	88 days
Venus	584 days	225 days
Mars	780 days	1.9 years
Jupiter	399 days	11.9 years
Saturn	378 days	29.5 years
Uranus	370 days	84 years
Neptune	368 days	164.8 years
Pluto	367 days	248.5 years

Figure 1-6
Synodic and Sidereal Data

Dividing the Zodiac

As the Earth rotates on its axis once in every 24 hours, an observer situated on Earth will detect an apparent motion of the constellation stars that define the zodiac. To better define this motion, astrologers apply four cardinal points to the zodiac, almost like the north, south, east and west points on a compass. These cardinal points divide the zodiac into four quadrants. The east point is termed the *Ascendant* and is often abbreviated *Asc*. It is located at the 9:00 o'clock position on the Zodiac wheel. The west point is termed the *Descendant* and is often abbreviated *Dsc*. It is located at the 3:00 o'clock position. The south point is termed the *Medium Coeli* (Latin for *Mid-Heaven*) and is often abbreviated *MC* or *MH*. It is located at the top of the zodiac wheel. The north point is termed the *Imum Coeli* (Latin for *bottom of the sky*) and is abbreviated IC. It is located at the 6:00 o'clock position. The two cardinal points most often referred to this Almanac are the Ascendant and the Mid-Heaven.

Retrograde

The term *retrograde* is taken from the Latin expression *retrogradus* which means "backward step".

From our vantage point on Earth, we describe the position of the planets relative to one of the twelve constellations in the sky. There will be three (occasionally four) times during a year when Earth and Mercury pass by each other (Mercury retrograde). There will be one time (occasionally two times) per year when Earth and Venus pass each other (Venus retrograde). There will be one time every two years when

Earth and Mars pass each other (Mars retrograde). In the case of a faster-moving planet starting to lap past slower-moving Earth, we can observe the faster-planet's position relative to one of the star constellations in the sky. Owing to the different orbital speeds of Earth and the faster planet, there will be a period of time when we see the faster planet in what appears to be the previous constellation. For example, we might start off seeing Mercury against the star constellation of Gemini. As Mercury begins to lap past Earth, we will see Mercury against the star constellation of Taurus. As Mercury passes by Earth, we will see Mercury again in Taurus. Of course, Mercury has not physically reversed course and moved backwards. This is an optical illusion created by the different orbital speeds of Mercury and Earth.

These brief illusory periods are what astrologers call *retrograde* events. To ancient societies, retrograde events were of great significance as human emotion was often seen to be changeable at these events.

Retrograde events involving Mercury, Venus, and Mars very often lead to short term price trend changes developing. Is it possible that our DNA is hard-wired such that we feel agitated at retrograde events? Does this emotional agitation compel us to buy or sell on the financial markets?

Elongation and Conjunction

From an observer's vantage point on Earth, there will also be times when planets are at maximum angles of separation from the Sun. These events are what astronomers refer to as *maximum easterly* and *maximum westerly* elongations. These events definitely have a correlation to trend changes on the markets.

Mercury and Venus are closer to the Sun than is the Earth. From our vantage point on Earth, there will be times when Mercury and Venus are situated between the Earth and the Sun. There will also be times when the Sun is between the Earth and Mercury or Venus. On the zodiac wheel, the times when Mercury or Venus are in the same zodiac sign and degree as the Earth are what astronomers call *conjunctions*.

An *inferior conjunction* occurs when Mercury or Venus is between Earth and the Sun.

A *superior conjunction* occurs when the Sun is between Earth and Mercury or Venus. Figure 1-7 illustrates the concept of elongation and conjunction.

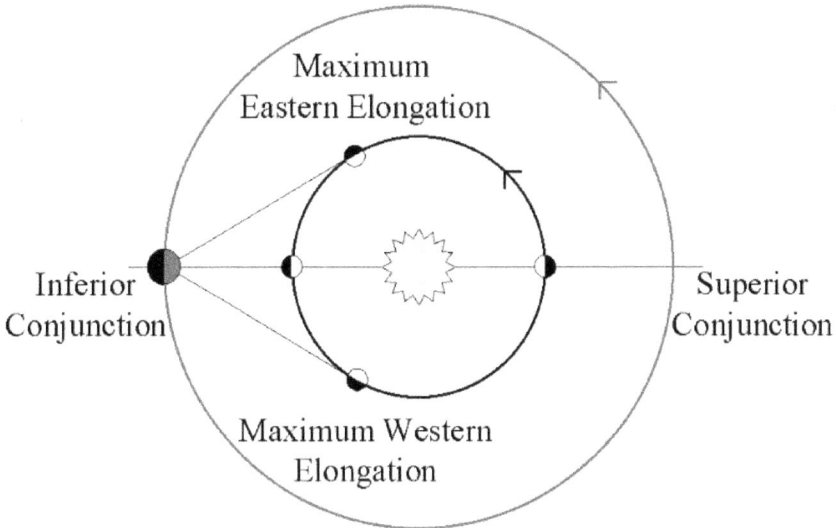

Figure 1-7
Superior and Inferior Conjunction

When applying these events to interpreting stock and index price charts, Mercury conjunctions are left out. Mercury moves around the Sun in 116 geocentric days. Its superior and inferior conjunctions thus occur frequently and my back-testing has shown these events are not effective tools to use.

Inferior conjunction events occur on either side of retrograde events. For example, Venus was retrograde from July 22, 2023 to September 3, 2023. Its exact Inferior Conjunction was recorded on August 13, 2023. The peak on the S&P 500 and Nasdaq 100 in early August 2023 was directly connected to these Venus phenomena which disturbed human emotion. As unsettled investors began selling, the trend on these indices changed to negative. The negative sentiment remained intact until late-October 2023 when Venus was at its declination maximum. Such are the intricacies of the cosmos and their effects on human emotion and the markets.

After Venus has been at inferior conjunction, it will be visible in the early morning hours as the *Morning Star.*

After it has been at superior conjunction, it will be visible just before sunset as the *Evening Star.*

Venus was at Superior Conjunction on March 28, 2013 (8 Aries), October 25, 2014 (1 Scorpio), June 6, 2016 (16 Gemini), January 8, 2018 (18 Capricorn), August 14, 2019 (20 Leo), March 26, 2021 (6 Aries), October 22, 2022 (28 Libra), and June 4, 2024 (15 Gemini).

Venus was at Inferior Conjunction on June 6, 2012 (15 Gemini), January 11, 2014 (21 Capricorn), August 15, 2015 (22 Leo), March 25, 2017 (4 Aries), October 26, 2018 (3 Scorpio), June 3, 2020 (14 Gemini), January 8, 2022 (19 Capricorn), and August 2023 (20 Leo).

If one plots consecutive superior conjunction events (or consecutive inferior conjunction events) on a zodiac wheel, the plotted points can be joined to form a 5-pointed star called a pentagram. Such is the elegance and mystique of the cosmos.

Helion Events

From an observer's vantage point on Earth, there will also be times when Mercury and Venus are closest to or farthest away from the Sun. Times of being closest to the Sun are termed *perihelion* events. Times of being farthest away from the Sun are termed *aphelion* events.

Venus has an orbit that is only slightly elliptical. When Venus is nearer to the Sun (107.4 million kms away), it is moving at about 35 km/second. When Venus is farthest from the Sun (109 million kms away), it is moving at about the same 35 km/second. Despite this small separation (109 versus 107.4 million kms), Venus helion events can be seen to have an effect on human emotion and the markets.

Mercury has an eccentric orbit in which its distance from the Sun will range from 46 million km to 70 million km. When Mercury is nearer to the Sun (46 million kms away), it is moving at its fastest (56.6 km per second). When Mercury is farther from the Sun (70 million km away), it is moving slower (38.7 km per second). [2] Mercury helion events can be seen to have an effect on human emotion and the markets.

Aspects

Owing to the different times for the planets to each orbit the Sun, an observer situated on Earth will see the planets making distinct angles (called *aspects*) with one another and also with the Sun. An observer situated on the Sun, will see the planets making distinct angles (called *aspects*) with one another and also with the Earth. The aspects that are commonly used in mundane astrology are 0, 30, 45, 60, 90, 120, 150 and 180-degrees. In financial astrology, it is common to refer to only the 0, 90, 120 and sometimes 180-degree aspects. In this Almanac, aspects discussed will be those as seen from the vantage point of Earth.

Data

To identify these aspects, astrologers often use Ephemeris tables. For geocentric astrology, the *New American Ephemeris for the 21ˢᵗ Century* is commonly used. For heliocentric astrology, the *American Heliocentric Ephemeris* is a good resource.

As an alternative to using an Ephemeris book of tabular data, quicker aspect determination can be made using software. An excellent software program is *Solar Fire Gold* produced by software company Astrolabe. I also use the *Optuma* software program. This brilliant piece of software, developed in Australia, allows the user to generate end-of-day price charts for equities and commodities and then overlay various planetary aspects and cyclical planetary occurrences onto the charts. As your journey into trading and investing using the planets deepens, you might be tempted to spend the money to acquire one or both of these software programs.

Cosmobiology

The big question then is – how does planetary activity trigger human emotion? The answer to this question resides in a field of study called *Cosmobiology*. This field is not new. In fact, it was pioneered in Germany in the late 1920s by H.A. Strauss who was interested in finding the relation between the planets and man. Strauss's work was followed up by the late Reinhold Ebertin who published several books on the subject. [3] As you peruse this Almanac, I encourage you to give thought to the emotional connection between man and the planets.

Having looked at the basics of astrology, let's next engage in a deeper exploration of events of the cosmos and how these events can impact financial markets.

CHAPTER TWO

Trend Changes

In previous editions of this Almanac, I have included a paragraph advising readers that planetary cyclical events should be acted on if a price trend change is also visible on the stock, commodity future, or index being studied. Discussions with people who have purchased previous Almanacs, or who subscribe to my newsletters, have revealed that the subject of trend change needs more focus in my written offerings. This chapter focuses on price trend and illustrates how technical chart indicators can be used to help determine when the price trend changes.

Financial market software/data platforms come programmed with a variety of *moving averages* ranging from *simple* to *exponential* to *smoothed*.

On a given trading day, the *simple moving average* is the mathematical average of the past *'n'* price bars on a price chart of a stock, commodity, or futures contract. The next day, the calculations discard the first value in the data series and add the most recent data point. An *exponential moving average* is similar to a simple moving average, except the mathematical calculation underlying the exponential average places greater weight (emphasis) on the more recent of the 'n' data points.

There is considerable flexibility in determining how many data points to use in the average calculation. On a daily chart, I regard a 200-bar moving average to be indicative of the broader trend. I regard a 50-bar moving average to be indicative of the shorter-term trend. The trend can be deemed to be changing from bearish to bullish when price moves up and through a moving average. Similarly, the trend is turning bearish when price moves below a moving average.

A *smoothed moving average* is an average of an average. Suppose an 18-day moving average has been calculated using n=18 price bars. After a longer period of time has elapsed, suppose an 18-day moving average of a series of 18-day moving average data points is calculated. This smoothed moving average reduces the variability of the data points and helps traders better identify trend directions.

Market data platforms also come programmed with a variety of *stochastic* and *oscillator* functions. Stochastic and oscillator functions compute the price range of data over a specified period of time. The price at a given day is then expressed as a percentage of this data range. I have a preference for the *Ergodic Oscillator* and the *True Strength Index*, both developed in the 1990s by trader and mathematician William Blau. Not every data platform will provide the Ergodic Oscillator, but the True Strength Index will likely be a standard offering on most software programs.

Consider the example of energy producer Devon Energy (NYSE: DVN) in Figure 2-1. As of early August 2024, the prevailing trend was bearish with price beneath the 200-day average and the 50-day average. Notice how the price reached a peak in April 2024. At this April inflection point, the True Strength Index was overextended, signaling that a trend change could occur. Venus was passing the Devon Energy 1988 natal Mars, while Moon was passing the 1988 natal Moon and the natal Ascendant. This is the sort of setup I remain alert for when following individual stocks.

Since recording its price peak in April 2024, notice that the price of DVN has steadily declined. Although there have been some minor rallies along the way that all align to astrology events, attempting to chase these rallies would have been futile as the True Strength Index never did get above the 'zero' level, meaning the trend has remained bearish. An example of this is the sharp reversal recorded on August 5. Mars was conjunct the 1988 natal Ascendant, but even that was not enough to shake DVN out of its bearish trend. Likewise, Venus passing by the 1988 natal Sun on September 5 did not shake the stock out of its bearish trend.

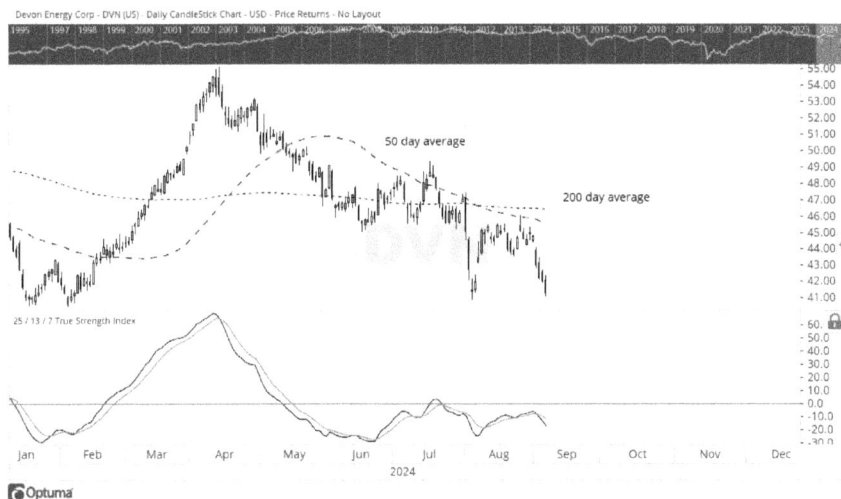

Figure 2-1
Devon Energy (NYSE:DVN)

I also use the *Slow Stochastic Oscillator*. This oscillator function was developed by famed market trader George Lane in the early 1960s. The oscillator function comprises an *indicator line* (% K line) and a *signal line*. (% D line). The indicator line crossing over the signal line generates a buy signal. I pay particular attention to these crossovers when they occur at an oscillator value less than 20. When the oscillator surpasses its upper boundary value of 80 and then turns and crosses beneath this level, a sell signal is triggered.

Figure 2-2 illustrates price action on data analytics company Palantir (Nasdaq:PLTR).

Figure 2-2
Palantir (Nasdaq:PLTR)

The price chart has been fitted with the Slow Stochastic indicator at a 21/5 setting. This means an oscillator function (% K line) is calculated based on 21 bars of data. A 5-bar average of this oscillator is then calculated (% D line).

In late May 2024, price began to rally and by June 5 had moved above the 50-day average. At this same time, the stochastic crossed above its lower boundary at the '20' level. The %K line had also crossed above the %D line. A trader buying the stock at this point would have realized nearly a $7 per share gain by mid-July, 2024. So, why did a buy signal emerge in late May? Moon was conjunct the Palantir September 30, 2020 natal Moon. As price moved above its 50-day average, Mars was conjunct the natal Mars location. This example nicely illustrates that taken together with planetary aspects to the natal horoscope, an indicator such as the Slow Stochastic can help a trader or investor focus in on a suitable buying opportunity. Looking further at the price chart, one can see a sharp sell-off in the first few days of August. Mercury was about to turn retrograde which rattled the entire equity market complex. In the case of Palantir, Moon had just passed the natal Mid-Heaven and Sun was about to make an exact conjunction to the Mid-Heaven. A trader paying close attention to the price chart would have hopefully been out of any positions around July 23 when the Stochastic broke beneath its upper boundary of '80'. A few days prior, the %K line had crossed beneath the %D line as well to give advance warning of a coming trend change. At this same time, Venus was passing the natal Mid-Heaven.

This Palantir example was purely a random selection on my part. My experiences have shown time and again that trend changes on stocks and market indices mark changes in market participant emotion. We seem to be hard wired to respond to planetary aspects to stock natal horoscope charts. This response is then reflected in the chart technical indicators such as stochastics and strength indices.

To delve deeper into the mathematics of the trend, I encourage you to get a copy of my 2023 publication *Follow the Trend.* I explore a wide variety of trend indicators as well as Fibonacci mathematics to help the reader more thoroughly grasp the concept of price trend.

CHAPTER THREE

Long Cycles

The price charts of equity market indices are an overlapping array of long and short cycles. This chapter examines the long cycles that influence equity markets in North America.

The Gann Master Cycle

W.D. Gann closely followed the cycles of Jupiter and Saturn. To an observer situated on the fixed (heliocentric) vantage point of the Sun, Jupiter can be seen orbiting the Sun in about 12 years and Saturn in just over 29 years. Gann interpreted these orbital cycles one step further and noted that every 19.86 years, heliocentric Jupiter and Saturn were at conjunction (separated by 0-degrees) in a particular sign of the zodiac. This 19.86-year time span is what he called the *Master Cycle*.

The curious feature of the Master Cycle is that the occurrence of the Jupiter/Saturn conjunction does not always align precisely with a change of trend. Interfering in the background are geopolitical events and Central Bank policy decisions. However, the trend always will change. Consider the following examples:

☼ The market weakness in late 1901 aligned to a conjunction of these two outer planets. But following this conjunction event, the Dow Jones remained bearish and did not reach a definitive turning point low until late 1903 when the two planets were 45-degrees apart.

☼ In 1920, the U.S. economy encountered a recession. In August 1921, Jupiter and Saturn reached conjunction. After conjunction, the Dow Jones started to rally higher almost as if on cue. The 1929 market peak was not related to Jupiter and Saturn being 0-degrees conjunct. They were 120-degrees apart (trine aspect) at the time. The Dow Jones severely re-tested the 1921 lows in 1932 when the two planets were exactly 150-degrees apart.

☼ In late 1940, Jupiter and Saturn again were at conjunction. Geopolitics weighing on human emotion meant the Dow Jones did not record a definitive low until early 1942 when the two planets were 30-degrees apart.

☼ In April 1961, Jupiter and Saturn again were at conjunction. The Dow Jones eventually reached a turning point low in mid-1962 when the two planets were 22.5-degrees apart.

☼ In the Spring of 1981, Jupiter and Saturn recorded a conjunction event. The actual market peak came a few months ahead of the exact conjunction when the two planets were 1-degree apart. The ensuing bearish trend lasted until August 1982 when the Dow Jones recorded a turning point low that evolved into a massive bull market run that endured until the next conjunction event in June 2000.

☼ In June of 2000, Jupiter and Saturn recorded a conjunction event. The market peak had already been recorded in January when the two planets were still 8-degrees apart. Following this June 2000 conjunction and the start of a new Master Cycle, it would not be until October 2002 that the bearish trend abated and the Dow Jones reached a turning point low. The market then remained bullish until 2007.

✿ In November 2020, heliocentric Saturn and Jupiter again made their 0-degree conjunction right at the time of the US Presidential election. But the market had already recorded a significant low point several months beforehand–in late March when the two planets were 12-degrees apart (which technically is close to being within orb of a conjunction event). This particular turning point will long be remembered as the COVID panic selloff.

✿ The next Saturn-Jupiter conjunction event will occur in December of 2040. If you are examining this manuscript in 2040, you might have seen the overall trend change several months before or several months after this conjunction date.

3-Cycle Spans of Time

Triple recurrences of the Gann Master Cycle can have a repetitive impact on geopolitics and on the financial markets. For example, *heliocentric* Jupiter and Saturn were conjunct in April 1961 in the latter part of the sign of Capricorn. The 1981 conjunction occurred in the sign of Libra. The June 2000 conjunction occurred in the sign of Taurus. The November 2020 conjunction occurred at 0-degrees Aquarius, a mere 7-degrees from where the 1961 conjunction had occurred. This seems to imply that after a 3 Master Cycle time span, history can start to rhyme again. Consider the following examples of such recurrences.

✿ The US equity market recorded its post-1929 crash low in 1932. Forward 3 cycles, and 1982 marked the start of what would be a major bull market.

- ✿ The year 1937 marked an interim peak on the US stock market. Forward 3 cycles, and an interim peak followed by the 1997 Asian currency crisis comes into focus.
- ✿ A low was recorded on the market in 1942. Forward 3 cycles to 2002 and a similar event occurred.
- ✿ A low was again recorded in 1949. Forward 3 cycles, and the March 2009 lows make an appearance.
- ✿ Late 1961 marked a turning point on the market. Add 3 cycles, and late 2021 likewise presented a turning point.
- ✿ From a low in late 1962 the US market rallied briskly into late 1965. **This pattern seems to imply that late 2022 to late 2025 could see a generally positive tone to the equity market. However, expect volatility to be a factor along the way.**

It is further interesting to note that the 3-cycle pattern can sometimes be seen outside of the financial markets. Consider that construction on the Pentagon building in Washington commenced on September 11, 1941. Three cycles later on September 11, 2001 the Pentagon was the target of a major terrorist attack.

Early 1965 saw the first US ground troops land in Vietnam. This marked the start of what would be a decade-long simmering conflict. Add 3 cycles and ask the question—will 2025 see geopolitical events occurring that set the stage for a multi-year simmering conflict? As I finish this manuscript in September 2024, the Israel-Hamas conflict certainly has potential to spread throughout the Middle East. The first F-16 fighter jets have also arrived in Ukraine. This conflict is now in a new chapter with Ukrainian forces making offensive incursions into Russia territory.

The 18.6-Year Cycle

In addition to the Gann Master Cycle, there exists another long cycle that has a powerful impact on the financial markets (and the global real estate market as well).

This cycle was first written about in the late 1930s by a mysterious figure called Louise McWhirter. [1] I say *mysterious* because in all my research I have neither come across any other writings by her nor have I found reference to her in other manuscripts. I am almost of the opinion that the name was a pseudonym for someone seeking to disseminate astrological ideas while remaining anonymous.

McWhirter focused on the fact that the Moon orbits the Earth in a plane of motion called the *lunar ecliptic*. The planetary ecliptic plane not being parallel to the lunar ecliptic plane means the two planes must intersect at two points. The two points are termed the *North Node* and *South Node*. These two nodal points are opposite one another in the zodiac wheel. Common practice among practitioners of astrology is to focus only on the North Node.

McWhirter recognized that the transit of the North Node of the Moon around the zodiac wheel takes 18.6 years and that the Node progresses in a backwards (retrograde) motion through the zodiac signs.

Through examination of copious amounts of economic data provided by Leonard P. Ayers of the Cleveland Trust Company, McWhirter was able to conclude that when the North Node moves through certain zodiac signs, the economic business cycle reaches a low point. When the Node is passing certain other signs, the business cycle is at its strongest.

This line of thinking is still with us today. A notable authority embracing this economic cycle is British economist Fred Harrison. In his published works, he discusses this long economic cycle going back to the Industrial Revolution in the 1700s. But to maintain respect in academic circles, he stops just shy of stating a connection to the zodiac and the North Node. Two of his notable publications are *Power in the Land* and *Boom Bust 2010.*

McWhirter was able to discern the following from the Cleveland Trust data:

○ As the Node enters Aquarius, the low point of economic activity is reached
○ As the Node leaves Aquarius and begins to transit through Capricorn and Sagittarius, the economy starts to return to normal
○ As the Node passes through Scorpio and Libra, the economy is functioning above normal
○ As the Node transits through Leo, the high point in economic activity is reached
○ As the Node transits through Cancer and Gemini, the economy is easing back towards normal
○ As the Node enters the sign of Taurus, the economy begins to slow
○ As the Node enters Aquarius, the low point of economic activity is reached and a full 18.6-year cycle is completed.

McWhirter further observed some secondary factors that could influence the tenor of economic activity in a *good* way, regardless of which sign the Node was in at the time:

○ Jupiter being 0-degrees conjunct to the Node
○ Jupiter being in Gemini or Cancer
○ Pluto being at a favorable aspect to the Node.

McWhirter also observed some secondary factors that can influence the tenor of economic activity in a *bad* way, regardless of which sign the Node was in at the time:

- ✿ Saturn being 0, 90, or 180-degrees to the Node
- ✿ Saturn in Gemini or Cancer
- ✿ Uranus in Gemini
- ✿ Uranus being 0, 90 or 180-degrees to the Node
- ✿ Pluto being at an unfavorable aspect to the Node.

In early 2020, the North Node was in the sign of Cancer. The economy was gently easing, in alignment with McWhirter's predictions. None of the above mentioned secondary bad factors were in play. But yet along came the COVID panic which sent markets into a tailspin. One has to wonder if this pandemic was foisted upon the markets by manmade efforts and not planetary forces.

The COVID pandemic was met head-on with massive government stimulus to prevent a full-blown economic crisis. The Node entered Taurus in early 2022 and the economy started to encounter stiff headwinds emboldened by strained supply chains, rising inflation, a flattening yield curve, and a Russian invasion of Ukraine. Market strategists soon started talking about recession.

In late March 2022, Saturn formed a hard, 90-degree square aspect to the Node. In alignment with McWhirter's findings, this 90-degree square event negatively impacted the already slowing economy. Waves of selling pressure across equity markets lasted into late June 2022. Saturn turned retrograde on June 4, 2022. As it did, the reins of power were handed off to Uranus which then started its march towards a conjunction with the Node. The exact conjunction of Uranus to Node occurred on July 30. Once this exact conjunction was complete, Uranus and Node slowly drifted apart, maintaining a 3-to-4-degree unfavorable separation which still qualified as a conjunction. The negative tenor from this conjunction created another wave of weakness on equity markets that persisted into October 2022.

In late 2022 as I penned the 2023 Almanac manuscript, the Node was at 13 degrees of Taurus and was poised to enter Aries in mid-2023. Pluto would form an unfavorable, hard, square aspect to the Node in April 2023.

I suggested this Pluto square aspect would stimulate talk of economic weakness among the financial media. I further noted that in May 2023, Jupiter would form a conjunction to the Node, possibly allaying fears of a recession. By 2023 year-end, Pluto would be moving away from its conjunction with the Node, erasing any fears of recession. As I completed the final edits on my manuscript in late October 2023, I noted that talk of recession by analysts and the financial media had abated. The naysayers who were forecasting a hard landing and a recession in 2023 had pushed their gloomy ideas off into late 2024.

What the economic naysayers did not realize was that for 2024, there were no unfavorable aspects of Saturn or Pluto to the Node. In May 2024, Jupiter entered the sign of Gemini; a favorable event for the broader economy according to McWhirter.

Jupiter will remain in Gemini until early June 2025 giving a generally positive tone to the economy. Jupiter will then move into the sign of Cancer, which according to McWhirter is still positive. However, along the way Saturn will muddy the waters in the April-May 2025 period as it records a 0-degree aspect to the Node.

Despite Jupiter imparting favorable influence on the economy in 2025, the Node will enter the sign of Pisces in February 2025–a reminder that the 18.6-year cycle is getting long in the tooth; late in the ballgame.

By August 2026, the Node will be in Aquarius to mark the end of the 18.6-year cycle. I will not be surprised to see another financial crisis in late 2026 and into 2027 that rivals the one in 2008.

There is one more cyclical event that troubles me. I hate to think about it, but it bears discussion. In 2026, Uranus will be in Gemini and also at a hard 90-degrees to the Node. This astro positioning warns of a negative economic time. It also warns of possible war. The 1776 natal horoscope for the USA has Uranus in the sign of Gemini. By mid-2027 Uranus will be exactly conjunct to the 1776 Uranus natal position at 8 degrees of Gemini. Uranus takes 84 years to travel one time through the zodiac. Subtract Uranus cycles from the year 2027 and past dates aligning to World War II, the US Civil War, and the War of Independence all come into focus. One need not look too hard to see how fragile the global geopolitical situation is. The seeds for a 2027 catastrophe may already have been sown, as the October 2023 events involving Israel, Gaza, and Iranian-backed terrorist groups have illustrated. The ongoing Ukraine situation will fan the flames.

To sum up,

- ☼ **The McWhirter 18.6-year cycle suggests the economy is on a slowing trajectory with Node in Aries. A full-blown financial crisis will manifest in late 2026 – early 2027.**
- ☼ **For 2025, the economy should remain generally resilient with Jupiter in Gemini until mid-2025 and in Cancer thereafter. However, the overall 18.6 year cycle being in late innings will mean a volatile market scenario.**

CHAPTER FOUR

Medium Cycles

Periodogram Cycles

In the late 1800s, British mathematician Sir Arthur Schuster studied solar sun spots. Schuster was a mathematical pioneer and he used the work of French mathematician Jean Baptiste Joseph Fourier to analyze the sunspot data. Fourier's method allowed Schuster to convert the time series data points into a frequency function. The use of Fourier mathematics to analyze a time series of data points is today called *spectral density analysis*. An algorithm to process time series data, such as a stock or index price chart, so as to identify the dominant frequencies is called a *Periodogram function*. The Optuma software platform comes complete with a Periodogram function.

On a weekly chart of the S&P 500, the dominant frequency of the data is 28 price bars. This frequency has been overlaid on the S&P 500 weekly chart in Figure 4-1. Note how the July 2024 significant market peak is aligned to the mid-point of a 28-bar cycle. By the time this publication goes to press, the current 28-bar cycle will have concluded in mid-October and another cycle will have started.

Late April 2025 will mark the end of the 28-bar cycle.
Mid to late October 2025 will see the end of the following cycle.

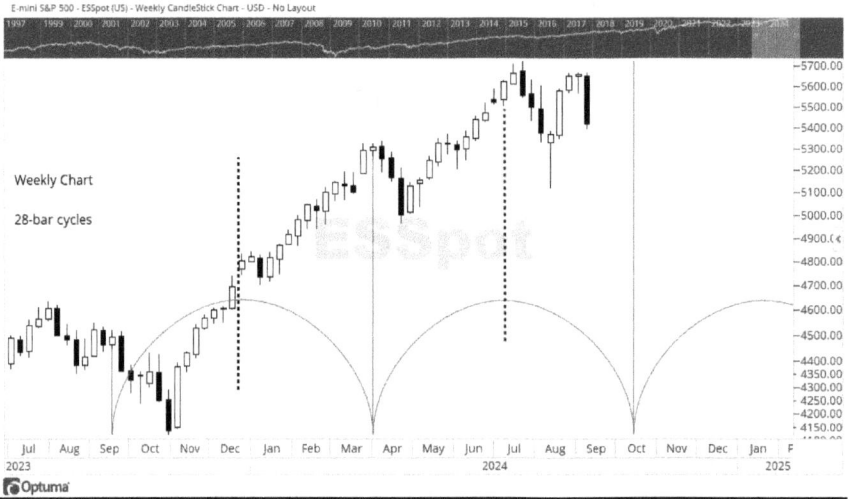

Figure 4-1
S&P 500 Dominant Frequency

On a weekly chart of the Nasdaq 100, the dominant frequency of the data is 26 price bars. This frequency has been overlaid on the Nasdaq 100 weekly chart in Figure 4-2. Note how the October 2023 low aligned to the end of one of these cyclical intervals. In mid-July 2024, at the crest/mid-point of one of these cyclic intervals, greed turned to fear and loathing as institutional investors decided to adjust their exposure to the big-name tech stocks that had been driving the Nasdaq 100. Mid-October 2024 will see the end of the current 26-bar cyclic interval.

Late April 2025 will see the end of the next 26-bar cycle.
Mid to late October 2025 will see the end of the following cycle.

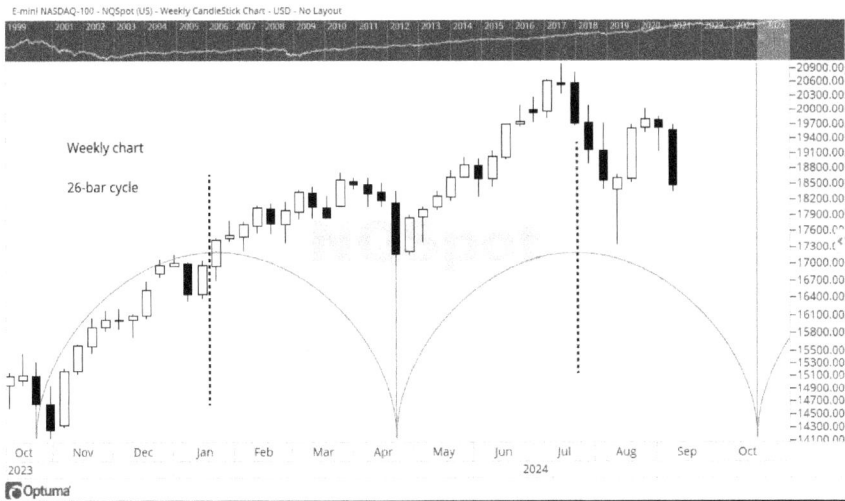

Figure 4-2
Nasdaq 100 Dominant Frequency

Currency and Commodity Periodogram Cycles

Commodity futures contracts and currency futures contracts also exhibit cycles than can be discerned with the Periodogram algorithm. Some of these commodities have a dominant daily-chart cycle while some have a dominant weekly-chart cycle.

For example, Gold futures have a dominant daily chart cycle of 40-bars. For 2025, start projecting 40-bar cycles from December 23, 2024.

Silver futures have a dominant daily chart cycle of 48-bars. For 2025, start projecting this cycle from a start point of November 12, 2024.

Copper futures a dominant weekly chart cycle of 46-bars. For 2025, start projecting this cycle from October 11, 2024 which is the mid-point of a cycle that will end on March 21, 2025.

Platinum futures have a dominant daily chart cycle of 106-bars. For 2025, start projecting these cycles from a start point of December 5, 2024.

Wheat futures have dominant daily chart cycle of 81-bars. For 2025, start projecting this cycle from a start point of December 11, 2024. There is a secondary cycle of 38-bars. For 2025, start identifying this secondary cycle from January 15, 2025.

Corn futures have a dominant daily chart cycle of 265-bars. For 2025, start projecting this cycle from a start point of September 4, 2024.

Soybean futures have dominant daily chart cycle of 163-bars. For 2025, start projecting the 163-bar cycle from October 22, 2024.

WTI Crude Oil futures have dominant weekly chart cycles of 33-bars and 53-bars. For 2025, start projecting the 33-bar cycle from a start point of September 27, 2024. Start projecting the 53-bar cycle from May 3, 2024.

Natural Gas futures have a dominant weekly cycle of 73-bars. For 2025, start projecting this cycle from a start point of September 6, 2024.

The US Dollar has dominant daily chart cycles of 80-bars and 127-bars. For 2025, start projecting the 80-bar cycle from a start point of November 29, 2024. Start projecting the 127-bar cycle from October 23, 2024.

Professor Weston's Cycles

In 1921, a mysterious person from Washington, D.C. using the name Professor Weston wrote a paper in which he analyzed decades of past price data for the Dow Jones Average. Who exactly Weston was, will likely never be known; another one of those figures who emerged to write his ideas down before vanishing into the ether.

His work was based on the premise that the Dow Jones price data was comprised of a series of interwoven, overlapping cycles. He applied Fourier mathematics to the data to delineate the dominant cycles. His analysis revealed a 10-month, 14-month, 20-month and 28-month cycle pattern. Note the harmonic relationship with 14-months being half of 28-months and 10-months being half of 20-months. Using the OPTUMA software, I have been able to demonstrate that these 10, 14, 20, and 28-month cycle intervals are indeed still evident on a monthly chart of the Dow Jones Average.

Perhaps Weston knew W.D. Gann personally. Perhaps he just knew of him. In any case, Weston followed the 20-year Gann Master Cycle of Jupiter and Saturn.

Weston further broke this long cycle into two components of 10 years each.

His Fourier mathematical analysis showed that investors can expect:

- ☼ a 20-month market cycle to begin in November of the 1st year of the 10-year cycle
- ☼ another 20-month cycle to begin in November of the 5th year of the 10-year cycle
- ☼ 28-month cycles to begin in July of the 3rd and 7th years of the 10-year cycle
- ☼ a 10-month cycle to begin in November of the 9th year of the 10- year cycle
- ☼ a 14-month cycle to begin in September of the 10th year of the 10-year cycle.

To put this into perspective, a new Gann Master Cycle began on November 1, 2020 as heliocentric Jupiter and Saturn made a 0-degree aspect. The entire cycle will run until December 2040.

Following Weston's methodology for the first half of the overall Master Cycle (2020 to 2031):

- ☼ the first 20-month cycle will start in November 2020 and go to until July 2022
- ☼ a 28-month cycle will run from July 2022 through November 2025
- ☼ a 20-month cycle will run from November 2025 through July 2027
- ☼ a 28-month cycle will run July 2027 through November 2029
- ☼ a 10-month cycle will then run from November 2029 through September 2030
- ☼ lastly, a 14-month cycle will last until November 2031.

We are now in the 28-month cycle that will terminate at or near November 2025.

Weston also postulated that in the various years of a 10-year segment of the overall Master Cycle, there would be market maxima as listed in Figure 4-3.

Weston calculated these events using cycles of Venus. He argued that the 16th harmonic of a 10-year period (120 months) was actually the heliocentric time it takes for Venus to orbit the Sun ($120 \times 30 / 16 = 225$ days). Back-testing has shown that these dates should be taken with a time span of perhaps +/- 3 weeks. In other words, a November maxima might manifest in mid-October or perhaps in mid-November.

YEAR OF CYCLE	MAXIMA	MAXIMA
1	March	October
2		May
3	January	September
4	April	November
5	May	November
6		June
7	January	September
8		June
9	April	
10	February	August

Figure 4-3

Weston's Secondary Cycles

Within the new Master Cycle that began in November 2020, Weston's work cautions investors to be alert for market maxima:

✡ in April and November 2024
✡ in May and November 2025.

As I pen this manuscript in August 2024, I note that the S&P 500, Nasdaq 100, and Dow Jones Average all recorded a swing high in April 2024 which led to a 5% sell-off.

Shemitah 7-Year Cycles

Just as intriguing as Weston's cycles are medium-term cycles steeped in religious doctrine that intersect with financial market turning points. One religious concept is that of *Shemitah* which is rooted in the Hebrew Bible.

I first learned of Shemitah from the writings of Rabbi Jonathan Cahn. [1][2][3] On the surface, Cahn appears to be an average, ordinary Rabbi from New Jersey, USA. But behind the scenes, he has done a masterful job of applying Shemitah to the financial markets. His books include: *The Harbinger, The Book of Mysteries,* and *The Paradigm.*

As Cahn explains:

In the book of Exodus (Chapter 23, verses 10-11), it is written: *You may plant your land for six years and gather its crops. But during the seventh year, you must leave it alone and withdraw from it.*

In the book of Leviticus (Chapter 25, verses 20-22), it is written: *And if ye shall say: "What shall we eat the seventh year? Behold, we may not sow, nor gather in our increase"; then I will command My blessing upon you in the sixth year, and it shall bring forth produce for the three years. And ye shall sow the eighth year, and eat of the produce, the old store; until the ninth year, until the produce come in, ye shall eat the old store.*

Breaking these Biblical statements down into simple-to-understand terms means that every 7th year something will happen in the geopolitical sphere and on the financial markets.

The first Shemitah year in the modern State of Israel was 1951-52. Subsequent Shemitah years have been 1958–59, 1965–66, 1972–73, 1979–80, 1986–87, 1993–94, 2000–01, 2007–08, 2014-15, and 2021-2022. The next Shemitah year will be 2028-2029.

Shemitah years can be grinding and difficult for market participants. The most recent Shemitah year concluded in September 2022. During this Shemitah year, Russia invaded Ukraine; the price of crude oil surged; the price of gasoline at the pump rose smartly; fertilizer prices for farm operators jumped, food prices inflated; inflation reached the 8% level; the Federal Reserve ceased its liquidity injections into the financial system; BitCoin got pummeled, and the equity markets sagged from January through September.

A Shemitah year starts in the month of Tishrei (the first month of the Jewish civil calendar) and ends in the month of Elul. This timeframe on the Gregorian calendar will roughly run from September to the following September. The website **www.chabad.org** will help identify the exact dates. Although the next Shemitah year will be in 2029, I thought it best to include this discussion in this Almanac so that readers who are new to my writings are at least aware of the Shemitah concept.

Sacred Dates and Kabbalah Cyclic Intervals

According to Rabbi Cahn, in addition to the Shemitah year, there are certain annual dates from the Hebrew calendar that can have a strong propensity to align with swing highs and lows on the New York Stock Exchange. While these dates actually comprise shorter-term cycles, I will discuss them in this chapter while still on the topic of Rabbi Cahn.

He advises to pay close attention to six particular dates from the Hebrew calendar:

- ✿ The 1st day of the month of Tishrei marks the start of the Jewish civil calendar, much like January 1 marks the start of the Gregorian calendar.
- ✿ The 1st day of the month of Nissan marks the start of the Jewish sacred year.
- ✿ The 3rd important date is the 9th day of the month of Tammuz which marks the date when Babylon destroyed the Temple at Jerusalem in 586 BC.
- ✿ The 4th date is the 9th day of Av. Calamitous events have beset the Jewish people on the 9th of Av throughout history. In particular, Cahn tells of the mass expulsion of Jewish people from Spain in 1492. As this expulsion was going on, a certain explorer with three ships was about to set sail on a voyage of discovery. That explorer sailed out of port on August 3,

1492 which was one day after the 9th of Av. That explorer was Christopher Columbus.

☼ The 5th key date in the Jewish calendar is Shemini Atzeret (the Gathering of the Eighth Day). This date typically falls somewhere in late September through late October in the month of Tishrei. It follows the 7-day Sukkot celebratory period and marks a time of bonding with God.

☼ The 6th key date is Yom Kippur which falls on the 10th day of Tishrei. On the Gregorian calendar, this event lands in late September or early October.

The website **www.chabad.org** allows one to quickly scan back over a number of years to pick off these important dates. My back-testing has shown a correlation between equity market performance and these dates. The correlation is valid enough that I recommend traders and investors pay attention to these dates.

For 2024, these critical dates fell as follows: 1st of Nissan on April 9, the 9th of Tammuz on July 15, the 9th of Av on August 13, the 1st of Tishrei on October 3, 10th of Tishrei on October 12th and Shemini Atzeret from October 23-25.

The S&P 500 turned bearish on April 2 just before the 1st of Nissan and fell 250 points. July 16 (one day after the 9th of Tammuz) marked a swing high on the S&P 500 and the onset of bearish sentiment. The 9th of Av (August 13) saw the S&P 500 rocket higher by over 90 points, which underscores the importance of these dates. The 10th of Tishrei (October 12th) saw the S&P surge to close at the 5,900 level. The day before this sacred date, the price of Gold snapped what was looking to be a bearish move and surged higher. The first trading day after this sacred date saw price declines on the 10-Year Treasury Note futures come to a halt. October 23rd saw the S&P 500 decline decidedly with an intraday range of 92 points.

For 2025, these critical dates will fall as follows:

- ✡ **1ˢᵗ of Nissan on March 30**
- ✡ **9ᵗʰ of Tammuz on July 5**
- ✡ **9ᵗʰ of Av on August 3**
- ✡ **1ˢᵗ of Tishrei on September 23**
- ✡ **10ᵗʰ of Tishrei on October 2**
- ✡ **Shemini Atzeret from October 13-15.**

In addition to cycles related to religious doctrine, cycles related to Kabbalah mathematics are also intriguing. A 2005 article in *Trader's World* magazine [4] suggested that W.D. Gann might have been given knowledge of Jewish mysticism based on Kabbalah doctrine. Gann apparently had connections to a New York personality named Sepharial who is said to have taught Gann about astrology and esoteric matters.

The Kabbalah centers around the Hebrew Alef-bet (alphabet). The Hebrew Alef-bet comprises 22 letters. In Kabbalistic methodology, these letters are assigned a numerical value. Starting with the first letter, values are 1, 2, 3, 4, 5, 6, 7, 8, 9, 10, 20, 30, 40, 50, 60, 70, 80, 90, 100, 200, 300, and 400.

There are many mathematical techniques that can be applied to parsing the Alef-bet. One in particular involves taking the odd-numbered letters and the even numbered letters and assigning their appropriate numerical values.

The numerical value (sum total) of the Alef-bet is 1495. The sum total of the odd-numbered letters is 625. The sum total of the even numbered letters is 870.

- ✡ 625/1495 = 42%. Taking a circle of 360-degrees, 42% is 150.5 degrees.

- ✿ 870/1495 = 58%. Taking a circle of 360-degrees, 58% is 209.5 degrees.
- ✿ Kabbalists are also well aware of phi as it pertains to the Golden Mean. Phi is famously known as 1.618.
- ✿ 1/phi = 61.8%. Taking a circle of 360-degrees, 61.8% is 222.5 degrees.
- ✿ 1 − (1/phi) = 38.2%. Taking a circle of 360-degrees, 38.2% is 137.5 degrees.

From a significant price low (or high) starting point, one can examine price charts for time intervals when a heliocentric planet advances 137.5, 150.5, 209.5, or 222.5-degree amounts. My back-testing has shown that Venus and Mars heliocentric advances are very apt to align to market turning points.

To illustrate, consider the significant low in March 2009 on the S&P 500 as a start point. Applying the above described 137.5-degree ratio, what emerges is the discovery that 11 years after the March 2009 lows, one of the Venus 137.5-degree advancements of heliocentric Venus landed on the March 2020 lows.

Extending these various degree intervals forward from the March 2009 lows reveals many correlations to swing points on the S&P 500 chart. For example, from the October 2022 swing lows on the S&P 500, Venus 209.5-degree intervals align to the October 2023 swing low and the July 2024 swing high.

Application of Venus and Mars intervals is not limited to equity markets. These intervals can be applied to commodity price charts too. From the March 2022 swing pivot point on Gold futures at $2072 per ounce, Mars intervals of 137.5, 150.5, 209.5 and 222.5-degrees can be seen aligning to pivot points in 2023 and 2024.

Consider also the April 2020 negative price anomaly on WTI Oil futures. Extending Mars and Venus heliocentric intervals of 137.5, 150.5, 209.5, and 222.5-degrees from this point, shows an alignment to several swing pivot points.

Consider too, the Soybean market. From the June 2022 significant price high, heliocentric Mars and Venus intervals of 137.5, 150.5, and 209.5-degrees can be seen aligning to various swing highs and lows.

To assist you in identifying some *heliocentric* intervals in 2025:

- ✿ For the S&P 500 in 2025 (using a start point of October 13, 2022), the first Venus intervals to appear in 2025 will be January 23 (222.5-degrees), February 3 (150.5-degrees), February 5 (137.5-degrees), and May 3 (209.5 degrees).
- ✿ For the Nasdaq in 2025 (using a start point of October 13, 2022), the first Venus intervals to appear in 2025 will be February 2 (150.5-degrees), February 15 (137.5-degrees), and April 14 (209.5-degrees).
- ✿ For WTI Oil in 2025 (using a start point of April 2020), Mars intervals will occur January 5 (150.5-degrees), April 25 (137.5-degrees), and October 20 (209-degrees).
- ✿ For Gold in 2025 (using a start point of March 8, 2022), the Mars degree intervals will occur: April 11 (150.5-degrees), October 11 (137.5-degrees), and June 10 (209.5-degrees).
- ✿ For Soybeans in 2025 (using a start point of June 9, 2022), the Mars degree intervals will occur: July 6 (137.5-degrees), September 26 (150.5-degrees), and December 8 (209.5 degrees).
- ✿ For Soybeans in 2025 (using a start point of June 9, 2022), the first Venus degree intervals will occur: January 2 (150.5-degrees), January 7 (137.5-degrees), February 4 (222.5-degrees), and April 19 (209.5-degrees).

✧ For the US Dollar Index in 2025 (using a start point of September 27, 2022), the Mars degree intervals will occur: January 31 (222.5-degrees), August 27 (150.5-degrees), and September 16 (137.5-degrees).

✧ For the US Dollar Index in 2025 (using a start point of September 27, 2022), the first Venus intervals will occur: January 7 (222.5-degrees), January 19 (150.5-degrees), and February 11 (137.5-degrees).

Beyond these examples, for a particular market index, currency, or commodity, identify a key high or low point. With heliocentric data in hand, count forward the requisite number of degrees (137.5, 150.5, 209.5 or 222.5) and see where the next intervals manifest. Not every single interval will necessarily align to a significant price inflection point. However, the correlation between these degree intervals and inflection points is robust enough that they cannot be ignored.

CHAPTER FIVE

Shorter Cycles

Venus Cosmic Occurrences

Cycles of Venus play a key role in anticipating trend changes on equity and commodity markets.

Venus orbits the Sun in 225 days relative to an observer standing at a fixed venue like the Sun. This is its *heliocentric* orbital time.

To an observer situated on Earth (a moving frame of reference), Venus appears to take 584 days to orbit the Sun. This is its *geocentric* orbital time.

Conjunctions

During this 584-day geocentric orbital period, there will be a period of time when Venus is situated between Earth and Sun. This is its *Inferior Conjunction.* As Venus slowly moves out of this conjunction, it will become visible in the early morning hours as the *Morning Star.*

During its 584-day geocentric orbital period, there will be a period of time when the Sun is situated between Venus and Earth. This is its *Superior Conjunction*. As it moves out of this conjunction, it becomes visible in the evening before sunset as the *Evening Star*.

To ancient civilizations, seeing Venus both in the morning and also in the evening over a 584-day span of time must have been unsettling. Is it possible that the human species is hard-wired to react to this behavior of Venus? Price reactions on the financial markets tend to support this hypothesis.

The patterns of Venus are further intriguing. Multiplying the 584-day geocentric cycle by 5 yields a value of 2920. Dividing 2920 by the 365-day orbital period of Earth yields a value of 8. The ratio of the Venus geocentric orbital period to the orbital period of Earth is thus a 5:8 ratio. Multiplying eight by five yields 40, a symbolic number cited frequently in Biblical texts. Dividing 5 by 8 gives 62.5% which is close to the Fibonacci ratio of 61.8%.

Venus was at Superior Conjunction on March 28 2013 (8 Aries), October 25, 2014 (1 Scorpio), June 6, 2016 (16 Gemini), January 8, 2018 (18 Capricorn), August 14, 2019 (27 Leo), March 26, 2021 (6 Aries), October 22, 2022 (4 Libra), and June 4, 2024 (15 Gemini).

If one plots these groups of superior conjunction events on a zodiac wheel, it becomes evident that they can be joined to form a 5-pointed star called a pentagram.

Venus was at Inferior Conjunction on June 6, 2012 (15 Gemini), January 11, 2014 (21 Capricorn), August 15, 2015 (22 Leo), March 25, 2017 (4 Aries), October 26, 2018 (3 Scorpio), June 4, 2020 (13 Gemini), and January 9, 2022 (18 Capricorn), and August 13, 2023 (20 Leo).

These conjunction degree points can also be plotted and when joined will form a pentagram. Such are the mysteries of our cosmos.

Consider the following Venus events in the context of the financial markets:

- ✿ The Inferior Conjunction event on June 4, 2020 delivered a 200- point drop on the S&P 500. But the Federal Reserve came to the rescue with more fiat liquidity to save the markets from steeper decline.
- ✿ The Superior Conjunction event of March 26, 2021 was immediately preceded by the Dow Jones dropping 1100 points (high to low) over six trading sessions.
- ✿ The Venus Inferior Conjunction on January 9, 2022 confirmed that the trend had indeed changed on equity markets. The Federal Reserve vowed that it was intent on raising rates. Emotion on Wall Street boiled over.
- ✿ The Venus Superior Conjunction on October 22, 2022 came a handful of days after the critical low that spelled the end of the 2022 bear market. This timeframe also yielded chaos in the UK as newly minted Prime Minister Lizz Truss resigned.
- ✿ Leading up to the Venus Inferior Conjunction on August 13, 2023, the S&P 500 reached a swing high point on August 1. The inferior conjunction event intensified the weakness by hastening the price decline.
- ✿ Venus was again at Superior Conjunction on June 4, 2024. Both the Nasdaq 100 and the S&P 500 were looking vulnerable to a trend change at this time, but the superior conjunction triggered human emotion and these two indices instead pushed higher making valuations even more stretched.

Venus will be at Inferior Conjunction again March 23, 2025. Venus will be Superior Conjunction again on January 6, 2026.

Declination

As Venus orbits around the Sun in the ecliptic plane, it moves above and below the plane and records *declination maxima* and *minima*. Declination maxima and minima play key roles in price trend changes on financial markets. As noted in an earlier chapter, one must be careful when using astrology software as many programs default to displaying declination as a geocentric phenomenon.

Consider the following Venus declination events:

- ✪ The Venus declination minimum in early September, 2021 was followed by a 200-point drawdown on the S&P 500. A brief recovery attempt followed that lasted into early January 2022 but failed to hold as Venus entered Inferior Conjunction and then maximum declination.
- ✪ Venus at declination minimum in early December 2022 marked the start of a 300-point retreat on the S&P 500.
- ✪ Venus at declination maximum in late March 2023 marked the general start of a rally that endured until August 2023. Emotion was so fixated on the market moving higher that the Venus declination minimum event in July failed to interrupt the trend.
- ✪ November 6, 2023 saw Venus at its declination maximum again. In the days leading up to this event, both the Nasdaq 100 and the S&P 500 recorded a swing low inflection point.
- ✪ Venus was at its declination minimum on February 27, 2024. Shortly after this event, the Nasdaq 100 and S&P 500 recorded 6% drawdowns.
- ✪ Venus was at its declination minimum again on October 9, 2024.

Retrograde

Another cyclical event pertaining to Venus is its *retrograde* events. From our vantage point on Earth, we describe the position of Venus relative to one of the twelve star constellations in the sky. There will be one time per year when Earth and Venus pass by each other. Owing to the different orbital speeds of Earth and Venus, as faster-moving Venus laps past Earth, there will be a period of time when we see Venus in the previous constellation to where it was just prior to starting to pass by Earth. For example, we might start off seeing Venus against the star constellation of Gemini. As Venus begins to lap past Earth, we will see Venus against the star constellation of Taurus. As Venus passes by Earth, we will see Venus again in Gemini. Of course, Venus has not physically reversed course and moved backwards. This is an optical illusion created by the different orbital speeds of Venus and Earth.

These brief illusory periods of backwards motion are what astrologers call *retrograde events*. To ancient societies, retrograde events were of great significance as human emotion was often seen to be highly changeable at those times. It is also curious to note that Venus retrograde periods last around 40 days. This time period is often cited in Biblical texts.

There is a curiously strong correlation between equity markets and Venus retrograde. Sometimes Venus retrograde events encompass a sharp market inflection point. Sometimes a market peak or bottom will follow closely behind a retrograde event. Sometimes a peak or bottom will immediately precede a retrograde event. I believe human emotion is hardwired to retrograde events of Venus. When a Venus retrograde event is approaching, one must use a suitable chart technical indicator to determine if the price trend is changing.

The last time Venus was retrograde was from July 22 to September 3, 2023. The onset of retrograde triggered a trend change that ended up shaving 2000 points off the Nasdaq 100 and 500 points off the S&P 500.

Knowing that the potential exists for sizeable moves, aggressive traders can avail themselves of these retrograde correlations. Less aggressive investors may simply wish to place a stop loss order under their positions to guard against sharp price pullbacks.

Venus will again be retrograde from March 2, 2025 through April 12, 2025.

This event potentially ties to the Professor Weston suggestion of a market maxima in May 2025.

The influence of Venus also extends beyond just the equity markets. Commodities can also be influenced.

Consider the price of Gold:

- ✿ In early 2022 just as the Venus retrograde event started, Gold prices started to trend higher, gaining over $200 per ounce.
- ✿ In August 2023, Venus was again retrograde. Two days before the retrograde event, Gold failed to maintain its momentum above the 50-day average. The trend changed to bearish and the price began to decline.

Consider too the price of Oil and the price of Wheat:

- ✿ As the Venus retrograde event started in early 2022, Oil prices started to trend higher, moving from $67 per barrel to $130 per barrel.

- ✪ The Venus retrograde event in August 2023 amounted to a trap for many Oil futures traders. Mid-way through the retrograde event, Oil prices started falling. After a $6 per barrel drawdown, Oil prices suddenly rebounded leaving short sellers scrambling to cover their positions.
- ✪ As the Venus retrograde event in early 2022 wrapped up, Wheat prices started to rally, moving from $7 per bushel to $13 per bushel.
- ✪ In August 2023, as Venus turned retrograde Wheat prices started to tumble. By the time the retrograde event was complete, Wheat prices had declined by $2 per bushel.

Aphelion and Perihelion

As noted in Chapter One, even though the difference in distance from the Sun is small between aphelion and perihelion, there does seem to be an effect on human emotion at these extrema.

On March 20, 2024 Venus was at aphelion. In the days that followed, the S&P 500 could not push any higher and finally on April 1, human emotion gave way and the S&P 500 faded by 5%.

On July 9, 2024 Venus was at perihelion. In the days that followed, the S&P 500 pushed only marginally higher before human emotion gave way to a near 10% decline.

For 2025:
- ✪ **Venus will be at Perihelion on February 19 and October 2.**
- ✪ **Venus will be at Aphelion on June 12.**

Elongation

Related to Venus's orbit is its *elongation*. As discussed earlier in Chapter One, elongation refers to the angle between a planet and the Sun, using Earth as a reference point. Figure 5-1 illustrates the concept of elongation. Times when Venus is at its greatest elongation can have a notable impact on human emotion. For example, on March 24, 2020 Venus was at its greatest easterly elongation. This date marked the bottom after the COVID panic selloff. On October 23, 2023 Venus was at its greatest westerly elongation. This date marked the end of a 3-month period of weakness on the equity markets.

For 2025:
- ☼ **Venus will be at its greatest easterly elongation January 10**
- ☼ **Venus will be at its greatest easterly elongation June 1.**

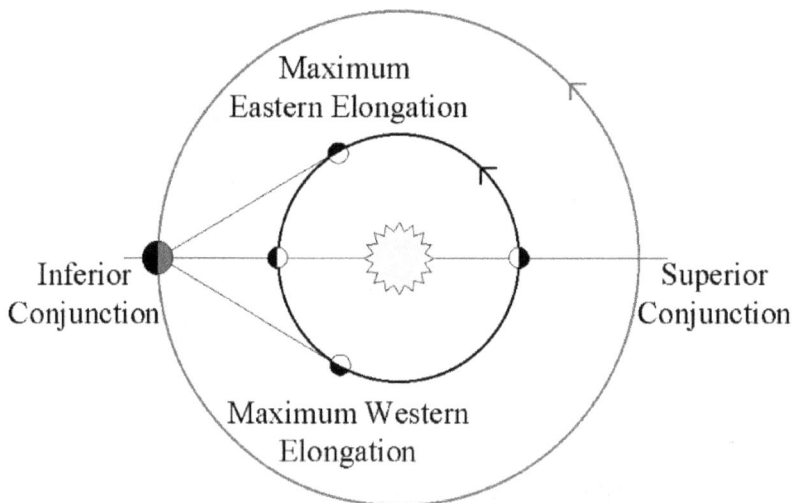

Figure 5-1
Superior and Inferior Conjunction

Mercury Cosmic Events

Mercury is the smallest planet in our solar system. It is also the closest planet to the Sun. As a result of its proximity to the powerful gravitational pull of the Sun, Mercury moves very quickly, completing one heliocentric cycle of the Sun in 88 days.

Aphelion and Perihelion

As noted in Chapter One, Mercury helion occurrences seem to affect human emotion and also the financial markets.

For example, in 2020, Mercury was at perihelion just as the equity markets were reaching a peak ahead of the COVID panic selloff. Emotions were running high as perihelion approached and investors then went into full panic mode at the thought of a respiratory virus sweeping the globe. The selloff abated in late March just as Mercury was nearing aphelion. Somehow the approaching aphelion event calmed investor emotion.

Mercury perihelion and aphelion events do not always seamlessly correlate to all market inflection points as in this 2020 example. Nevertheless, past market performance suggests these dates should be anticipated by traders and investors.

In 2023, Mercury was at perihelion at: January 8, May 4, September 5, and December 22. Aphelion dates were: March 10, July 2, and October 26.

The January 8 perihelion event aligned to a consolidation bottom on the S&P 500. Days after the May 4 event, the S&P 500 started to rally in earnest. The September 5 event aligned to the sudden end of a countertrend rally attempt. December 22 marked only an interim pause in a significant rally that would continue into March 2024.

The March 10 aphelion event marked a swing pivot low. The July 2 event was rather insignificant. The October 26 event marked a significant swing low.

In 2024, Mercury was at perihelion: April 15, August 15, and December 5. Several days after the August 13 event, the S&P 500 exhibited another drawdown.

In 2024, Mercury was at aphelion: February 20, June 14, and October 8. The February and October events had little impact. This manuscript will be getting published as the October event comes and goes.

> **For 2025:**
> ☿ **Mercury will be at aphelion January 19, and July 14.**
> ☿ **Mercury will be at perihelion March 4, May 31, August 27, and November 23.**

Elongation

Mercury too experiences maximum easterly and westerly elongation points. Times when Mercury is at these greatest elongation points bear a strong correlation to short-term turning points on financial markets.

In 2024, Mercury was at its greatest easterly elongation March 24, July 22, and November 16. The March event marked a change of trend that saw the S&P 500 shave off 5% of its value in the weeks that followed. Several days prior to the July event, the S&P 500 recorded a peak and a trend change.

In 2024, Mercury was at its greatest westerly elongation January 12, May 9, September 4, and December 24. The January event aligned to the start of a rally that continued until late March. The May event aligned to the start of another rally event.

For 2025,
- ☿ **Mercury will be at its greatest easterly elongation March 8, July 4, and October 29.**
- ☿ **Mercury will be at its greatest westerly elongation April 21, August 19, and December 7.**

Retrograde

There will be three (occasionally four) times during a year when Earth and Mercury pass by each other. Owing to the different orbital speeds of Earth and Mercury, as Mercury starts to lap past Earth there will be a period of time when we see Mercury in what appears to be the previous constellation. For example, just as Mercury starts to lap past Earth, we might start off seeing Mercury against the star constellation of Gemini. As Mercury continues to lap past Earth, we will see Mercury against the star constellation of Taurus. As Mercury finally passes by Earth, we will see Mercury again in Taurus. Of course, Mercury has not physically reversed course and moved backwards. This is an optical illusion created by the different orbital speeds of Mercury and Earth.

To ancient societies, retrograde events were of great significance as human emotion was often seen to be volatile at these events. Mercury retrograde events have been popularized by modern-day classical astrologers. They tell people not to sign important contracts during Mercury retrograde, not to cross the street, not to leave their houses and so on. While I tend to ignore this mundane talk, I have noticed a striking correlation between financial market behavior and Mercury retrograde events. Somehow human emotion is hard-wired to the apparition of the planet appearing to move backwards in the heavens.

Sometimes Mercury retrograde events encompass a sharp market inflection point. Sometimes a market peak or bottom will follow closely behind a retrograde event; sometimes a peak or bottom will immediately precede a retrograde event. Mercury retrograde events can be highly unpredictable as to when the impact on a financial instrument will appear.

Knowing that a Mercury retrograde event is approaching, traders and investors should remain alert for indications of a trend change using chart technical indicators.

Figure 5-2 illustrates three Mercury retrograde events from late 2023 through August 2024 overlaid on a chart of the S&P 500.

The late 2023 event resulted in the S&P 500 trending sideways in a consolidation pattern. The April 2024 event marked a drawdown on the S&P 500. The onset of the August 2024 event marked a sudden intra-day reversal and a complete change in human emotion.

Figure 5-2
S&P 500 and Mercury retrograde

Mercury retrograde events can sometimes be seen influencing commodity markets. For example, Figure 5-3 illustrates a Wheat futures price chart overlaid with Mercury retrograde events from late 2023 through August 2024.

The late 2023 event aligned to the start of a 5-month period of bearish price sentiment. The April 2024 event saw a powerful rally get underway just before the retrograde event ended. The August event saw emotion turn even more bearish, sending Wheat prices to four-year lows.

Figure 5-3
Mercury retrograde and Wheat futures

For 2025, Mercury will be:
- ☿ **retrograde from March 15 through April 6**
- ☿ **retrograde from July 18 through August 10**
- ☿ **retrograde from November 9 through November 28.**

Pleiades Aspects

Another short-term phenomenon involves the *Pleiades*–a cluster of stars situated in the constellation of Taurus. On the geocentric zodiac wheel, the position of 27 degrees Taurus aligns with the Pleiades star cluster.

The Pleiades are sometimes called the *Seven Sisters*. Many cultures from around the world have mythological tales that incorporate the Pleiades. For example, the Cree indigenous people of western Canada regard the Pleiades as a hole in the sky from which they came. As the story goes, Sky Woman spotted Earth and expressed a desire to visit the planet. With help from Spider Woman, who spun a web, Sky Woman was able to complete her journey to planet Earth.

Figure 5-4
Gold Price and Transits of the Pleiades

The chart in Figure 5-4 depicts daily price action on Gold futures. The chart has been overlaid with Mars, Venus and Sun transiting past the Pleiades at 27 Taurus. The Sun and Venus transits took place in the third week of May, 2024. The Mars transit took place mid-July.

Notice on Figure 5-4 that these transits align to price spike patterns. Human emotion was evidently stirred up by these Pleiades transits, both of which aligned to price drops of near $100 per ounce.

The chart in Figure 5-5 depicts daily price action on WTI Crude Oil futures. The chart has been overlaid with Mars, Venus and Sun transiting past the Pleiades at 27 Taurus. The Sun and Venus transits in May 2024 aligned to a $4 per barrel price drawdown. The transit of Mars in July 20924 aligned to a more substantive price drop.

Figure 5-5
WTI Crude Oil Price and Transits of the Pleiades

In 2025:
- ☉ **Sun will pass the Pleiades point between May 14 and May 22**
- ☉ **Venus will pass the Pleiades point in Taurus between June 29 and July 6**
- ☉ **Mars will *not* pass the Pleiades point in 2025.**

Sirius Rising and Setting

Sirius is the brightest star in our night sky and is situated near 13 degrees of Cancer. Its brightness in the night sky likely explains why ancient civilizations held it in such reverence. Its synodic patterns were also revered by the ancients. The Egyptians timed the planting of their crops to the rising of Sirius in the early morning sky. The ancient Romans held sacrificial ceremonies that coincided with the appearance of Sirius in the night sky. In ancient Persian mythology, Sirius was revered as the rain-maker divinity.

This ancient reverence makes me wonder if humans are still emotionally hard wired to the appearance of Sirius. For latitudes in North America, Sirius can be seen setting in the southwest evening sky in April and rising in the early morning sky in mid-August. Back-testing shows that markets can be prone to increased volatility in the April and August time frames.

Synodic Cycles

As discussed in an earlier chapter, planetary movements can be examined in terms of synodic cycles (geocentric) and sidereal cycles (heliocentric).

The time it takes from Venus recording a conjunction with Sun until that same conjunction occurs again is 584 days. Mars takes 780 days from a Sun/Mars conjunction to the next Sun/Mars conjunction. Sun/Saturn conjunctions are 376 days apart. Sun/outer planet conjunctions take 367 to 399 days.

Synodic cycles involving celestial bodies such as Sun, Mercury, and Venus relative to slower moving bodies such as Pluto, Saturn, and Jupiter are of particular interest in identifying trend turning points on equity and commodity markets. A trailblazer in correlating this synodic behavior to the markets was the late American financial astrologer, Jeanne Long. (1)

As an example, Figure 5-6 illustrates Oil prices and the Sun-Pluto synodic cycle. The aspects overlaid on this chart are 0, 90, 120, and 180-degrees. All aspects have been drawn to within orb (+/-5 degrees of exact alignment). These aspects can be seen aligning to price pivot points.

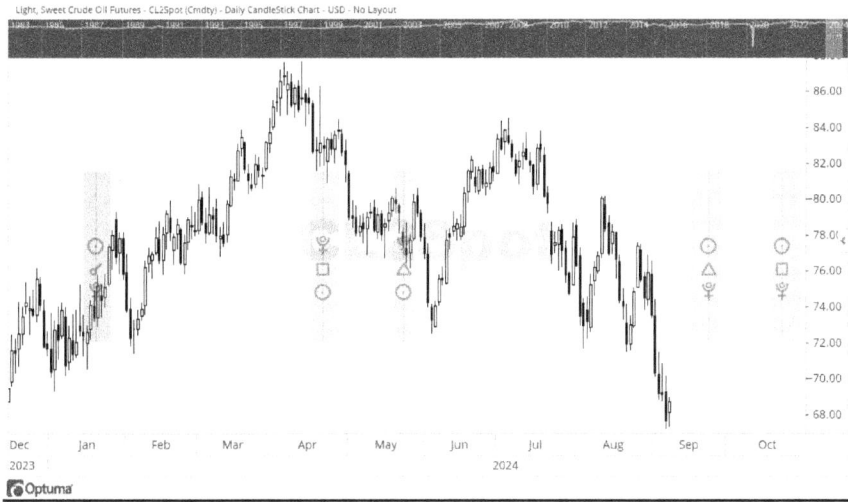

Figure 5-6
Sun-Pluto aspects and Oil prices

Figure 5-7 illustrates Silver prices in the context of aspects between Venus and Jupiter. The aspects overlaid on this chart are 0, 90, and 120 degrees. All aspects have been drawn to within orb (+/-5 degrees of exact alignment). These aspects can be seen aligning to swing high and swing low pivot points.

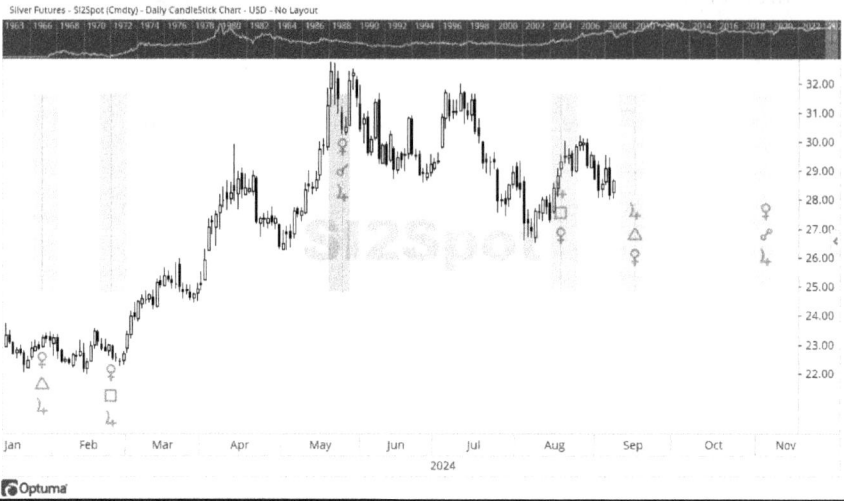

Figure 5-7
Venus-Jupiter aspects and Silver prices

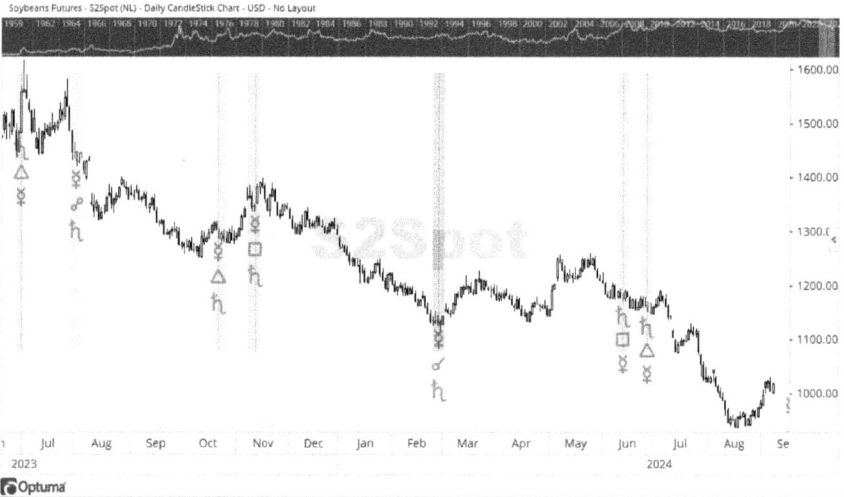

Figure 5-8
Mercury-Saturn aspects and Soybeans

Figure 5-8 illustrates aspects between Mercury and Saturn from mid-2023 through mid-2024 in the context of Soybean futures. Aspects in mid-2023 led to a prolonged price decline that continues at this time of writing. A conjunction aspect in late February triggered a $0.70 per bushel rally ($3500 per contract) which then faded. As was stressed earlier in this book, chasing price reactions at planetary events when the prevailing trend is against you is not wise. A 120-degree trine event in late June aligned to the resumption of the price drawdown.

In addition to Jeanne Long's excellent work from years ago, back-testing has shown that:

- heliocentric Jupiter-Neptune aspects influence trend changes on Wheat and Corn
- Mercury-Saturn aspects influence short term trend changes on Euro, British pound, Australian dollar, Canadian dollar currency futures, Corn futures, and Meat futures (Live cattle, Feeder cattle, Lean hogs)
- Mercury-Jupiter aspects influence Wheat futures, 10-Year Treasury Notes, and 30-Year Bonds
- Sun-Neptune aspects influence Gold futures and Coffee futures
- Sun-Pluto aspects influence Copper, Cocoa, and Sugar futures
- Sun-Jupiter aspects influence the Nasdaq.

For 2025, the above-described aspects will occur on following dates:

PLANETARY PAIR	ASPECT	DATES
Sun-Pluto	0 degrees	January 15-26
	60 degrees	March 19-28
	90 degrees	April 18-28
	120 degrees	May 19-29
	180 degrees	July 20-31

PLANETARY PAIR	ASPECT	DATES
Sun-Pluto	120 degrees	September 21-29
	90 degrees	October 20-28
	60 degrees	November 18-29

PLANETARY PAIR	ASPECT	DATES
Sun-Jupiter	120 degrees	January 27-February 4
	90 degrees	February 25-March 7
	60 degrees	March 30-April 11
	0 degrees	June 17-June 30
	60 degrees	September 5-18
	90 degrees	October 11-22
	120 degrees	November 12-22

PLANETARY PAIR	ASPECT	DATES
Sun-Neptune	60 degrees	January 12-21
	0 degrees	March 14-24
	60 degrees	May 17-May 25
	90 degrees	June 18-27
	120 degrees	July 19-29
	180 degrees	September 19-28
	120 degrees	November 18-27
	90 degrees	December 11-27

PLANETARY PAIR	ASPECT	DATES
Venus-Jupiter	90 degrees	January 10-January 19
	60 degrees	February 13-March 10
	60 degrees	May 29 - June 11
	0 degrees	August 6- August 16
	60 degrees	October 4 - October 12
	90 degrees	October 29-November 7
	120 degrees	November 22-December 1
	180 degrees	October 28-November 8
	120 degrees	December 14-24

PLANETARY PAIR	ASPECT	DATES
Mercury-Saturn	60 degrees	January 14-January 21
	0 degrees	February 23-February 27
	0 degrees	March 30 – April 16
	60 degrees	May 23-May 28
	90 degrees	June 6 – June 11
	120 degrees	June 23-July 1
	120 degrees	August 6 – August 15
	180 degrees	September 15-September 21
	120 degrees	October 22-October 29
	90 degrees	December 26-December 31

PLANETARY PAIR	ASPECT	DATES
Mercury-Jupiter	120 degrees	February 1-February 6
	90 degrees	February 18-February 21
	60 degrees	March 9-March 16
	60 degrees	May 2-May 9
	0 degrees	June 6 - June 11
	60 degrees	September 10-September 15
	90 degrees	September 28-October 4
	120 degrees	October 20-October 27
	120 degrees	November 19-November 30

The Bradley Model

Planetary aspect cycles pre-date the work of Jeanne Long. In 1946, astrologer Donald Bradley (2) defined a model based on *geocentric* pairings of planets. In his model, as a pair of planets approach one another and come to within 15-degrees separation, a sinusoidal weighting is applied to the separation. At a 15-degree separation the weighting assigned is zero. At a 0-degree separation (planets are conjunct) the weighting is 10. Bradley's model also included a variable defined as the mathematical average of the declination of Venus and Mars. Running the model on a daily basis generates a plot with many inflection points. The image in Figure 5-11 illustrates the Bradley Model plot for 2025.

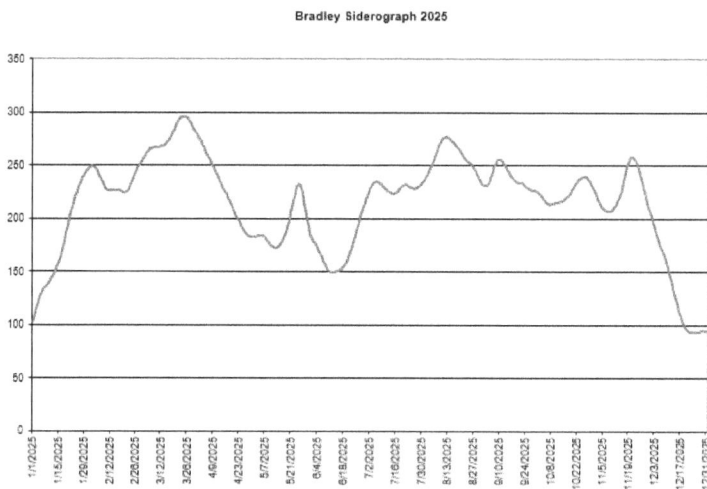

Figure 5-9
Bradley Model Plot

Many people mis-interpret the Bradley Model. They take the slope of the model to mean the S&P 500 price trend will have the same slope. That is, they feel the market should rise when the Bradley plot is sloping higher. I have come to realize that the most effective way to interpret the model is to focus on the inflection points in the output plot.

An inflection point, when the slope of the plot suddenly changes, has a very strong correlation to price changes on the S&P 500. I take this as evidence that planetary pairings affect the human emotions of fear and greed, both of which propel financial markets.

In 2024, the trend reversal on the S&P 500 in late March was identified by an inflection point on the Bradley Model. The swing low on April 22 was marginally apparent on the Bradley Model. The Bradley Model showed a major inflection around July 1, 2024. The S&P 500 crested 2 weeks later. A slightly identifiable aberration in the plot in early August 2024 aligned to the sharp reversal on the S&P 500. An inflection point in early November aligned to the S&P 500 surging to the 6000 level.

I am not overly impressed with how the Bradley Model held up in 2024. Certainly, prior years have had a more robust correlation to the S&P 500. If 2025 proves to have a weak correlation, I may have to reconsider the use of the Bradley Model.

For 2025, the following dates are the inflection points on the model plot:

- ✿ February 4, 21
- ✿ March 8, 25
- ✿ May 13, 26
- ✿ June 13
- ✿ July 7, 27
- ✿ August 13
- ✿ September 3, 11
- ✿ October 8, 27
- ✿ November 8, 22
- ✿ December 9, 23.

Lunar Declination Cycles

The Moon's orbit around the Earth can be described in terms of either synodic or sidereal cycles. The sidereal period of the Moon is 27.5 days (as viewed from a fixed reference like the Sun) and the synodic period is 29.53 days (as viewed from our vantage point here on Earth). This latter period lends itself to the expression *lunar month*.

During each synodic lunar cycle, the Moon can be seen to vary in its position above and below the lunar ecliptic; it will go from maximum declination to maximum declination.

Moon declination takes on an intriguing aspect when one considers that in 2020 two of the Moon declination minima events occurred on February 19 and March 18. The exact trend change turning point ahead of the COVID panic sell-off came at February 19. The panic lows came at March 23, mere days after the declination low.

W.D. Gann was reportedly a proponent of following lunar declination when trading Soybeans and Cotton. It is likely that he appreciated how the Moon's gravitational pull governs the ocean tides. With our bodies being substantially water, he likely postulated that the Moon was influencing the emotions of Soybean and Cotton traders.

Figure 5-10
Moon Declination and Soybeans

Figure 5-10 presents a chart of Soybeans with the Moon declination in the lower panel. The vertical lines overlaid on the chart illustrate the propensity for declination maxima, minima, and zero points to align to price swings. (Not all declination points have been overlaid on the chart.) A 4-hour chart with a Slow Stochastic would be the ideal way to study these price swings more closely.

Figure 5-10 helps one appreciate why a trader like W.D. Gann would have used lunar declination phenomenon to give himself an advantage in the Soybean market.

Figure 5-11 illustrates Moon declination and Gold futures. Maximum, minimum, and zero levels of lunar declination bear a strong correlation to swing pivots in price. The Moon, without doubt, affects human emotion and thereby price action on markets.

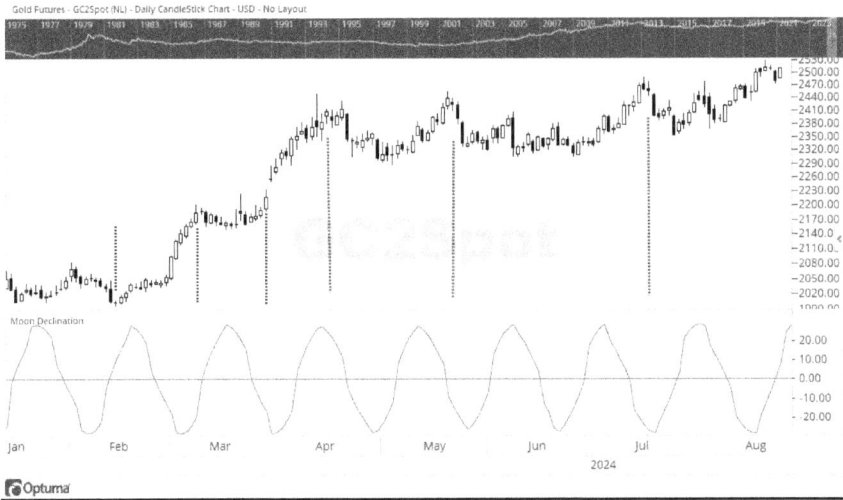

Figure 5-11
Moon Declination and Gold

Consider the favorite stocks you enjoy trading in and out of. Does Moon declination align to periodic price swing points? To assist you with some back-testing of your own, consider that in 2024:

Moon was at **maximum** declination: January 23, February 19, March 18, April 13, May 11, June 7, July 5, August 1, August 28, September 24, October 21, November 18, and December 16.

Moon was at **minimum** declination: January 10, February 6, March 5, April 1, April 28, May 25, June 22, July 19, August 16, September 12, October 9, November 5, December 3, and December 30.

Moon was at **zero** declination: January 3, 16 and 30, February 13, March 11, April 7, May 4, June 1 and 28, July 12 and 25, August 8 and 21, September 4 and 18, October 1, 16, and 29, November 11, and December 22.

For 2025,

- ✩ Moon will be at **maximum** declination: January 12, February 9, March 8, April 4, May 1, May 29, June 25, July 22, August 19, September 15, October 12, November 9, and December 6.
- ✩ Moon will be at **minimum** declination: January 27, February 23, March 22, April 19, May 16, May 25, June 12, July 9, August 6, September 2, September 29, October 27, November 23, and December 20.
- ✩ Moon will be at **zero** declination: January 6 and 19, February 2 and 15, March 1, 15, and 29, April 11 and 25, May 8 and 22, June 5 and 19, July 2, 16, and 29, August 12 and 25, September 8 and 22, October 6 and 19, November 3, 15, and 30, and December 13 and 27.

Planetary Declination Cycles

Individual planets experience declinations of up to about 25 degrees above and below the ecliptic plane. My introduction to planetary declination came several years ago with the discovery of a 25-year-old astrology book in a used bookshop.[3] The book suggested focusing on the planetary declination levels that were in place at the date a stock or commodity futures contract first started trading on an exchange (first trade date). It is possible that this approach was gleaned from the work of W.D. Gann.

In his 1927 book, *Tunnel Through the Air*, (4) Gann references days when the story's hero, Robert Gordon, was very certain trend changes would occur on his Major Motors stock. Gann hints strongly to watch for Mars and Venus to pass the same declination level as they were at on the first trade date (their natal declination levels). When I checked the Mars and Venus planetary declination at the Major Motors first trade date cited in the book and compared those figures to Robert Gordon's key dates, I found a correlation. Mr. Gann's book is more than just an interesting story. It is a resource of valuable information, carefully concealed in plain view.

Once you know the first trade date for an exchange, a stock or a commodity, historical declination data is readily available on the internet or from a software program such as *Solar Fire Gold*. Just remember–use heliocentric data when examining declination dates.

Remember also that not every occurrence of a planet passing through its natal declination will result in a trend change. Sometimes the trend that is in place will be so strong that it will not alter because of a declination event. This underscores the importance of using a technical chart indicator to help you gauge the trend.

Taking a cue from Gann's 1927 book, consider that the New York Stock Exchange (NYSE) traces its origins to May 17, 1792. At that date Venus was at -2 degrees declination and Mars was at -9 degrees of declination.

In 2023, Mars passed its natal declination level from September 5 to 21. The S&P 500 faded by 160 points as a result.

In 2023, Venus passed its natal declination level on three occasions, January 24 to February 1, May 21 to 26, and September 8-12. The late January transit triggered the start of a sell-off. The end of the May transit sparked a rally that lasted into early August. The September transit marked the start of a bearish decline.

In 2024, Venus passed its May 17, 1792 natal declination level on the following dates: January 1 to 5, April 19 to 25, August 11 to 17, and November 29 to December 5. Calendar year 2024 got off to a soft start. However, on January 5 the tenor of the S&P 500 became more robust as Venus passed its natal declination point. The month of April also proved to be soft. But on April 25, just as Venus passed its natal declination level, the S&P 500 shook off its doldrums and proceeded to power higher. The revisit of the natal Venus declination level in August added serious fuel to the fire as the S&P 500 surged higher after a dramatic drawdown.

In 2024, Mars passed its 1792 natal declination level May 12 to 23. The end of this declination revisit caused the S&P 500 to briefly weaken and lose 100 points.

For 2025,

- ☼ **Venus will pass its 1792 natal declination level: March 26 to 30, July 12 to 16, and November 7 to 10.**
- ☼ **Mars will pass its 1792 natal declination level: July 26-August 10.**

Chapter 7 will continue this look at natal declination in the context of commodity exchanges where futures contracts trade.

CHAPTER SIX
Lunar Cycles and Equity Markets

Lunations and the New York Stock Exchange (NYSE)

In our hyper-linked economy, events on the New York Stock Exchange can quickly reverberate across other global exchanges. It is for this reason that all of my Almanacs to date have focused on the New York Exchange.

No examination of the astrology of the New York Stock Exchange would be complete without a further mention of Louise McWhirter. After years of reading old papers and manuscripts, I still have no idea who Louise McWhirter was. What I *do* know is that Louise McWhirter focused not only on the 18.6-year cycle, but also on monthly lunation cycles. Planetary positions at the date of a New Moon and Moon passing key points of the New York Stock Exchange natal horoscope both define her analytical methodology. The one caveat to her technique, which did not exist in her day, is sudden, overt actions by the Federal Reserve.

In the aftermath of the COVID-19 panic selloff, massive amounts of fiat liquidity were pumped into the banking system to lift the economy and the equity markets. With the money spigots flowing, "buy the dip" became the resounding cry when markets expressed weakness. The Federal Reserve finally reined in its liquidity injections in early 2022 to quell inflation. Almost immediately, astrology in general - and the McWhirter method in particular - started to again correlate to market movements.

Lunation is the astrological term for a New Moon. At a lunation, the Sun and Moon are separated by 0-degrees and are together in the same sign of the zodiac. The correlation between the monthly lunation event and New York Stock Exchange price movements was first popularized in 1937 by McWhirter. In her book, *Theory of Stock Market Forecasting*, [1] she discussed how a lunation event exhibiting hard aspects to planets such as Mars, Jupiter, Saturn, Neptune, and Uranus was indicative of a lunar cycle during which the New York Stock Exchange would display notable volatility. In particular, she paid close attention to Mars and Neptune, the two planets that rule the New York Stock Exchange.

The concept of *planetary rulership* extends back to the 1800s when astrologers began denoting each zodiac sign as having a celestial body that ruled that sign. The planetary placements at the day and time the New York Stock Exchange was founded in 1792 were such that Mars and Neptune were the rulers of the 10th House of the zodiac. This was because the 10th House of the NYSE birth horoscope spanned the signs of Pisces and Aries. Neptune rules Pisces and Mars rules Aries. McWhirter said those times of a lunar month when the transiting Moon makes 0-degree aspects to the 1792 natal locations of Mars and Neptune should be watched carefully.

New York Stock Exchange – First Trade Chart

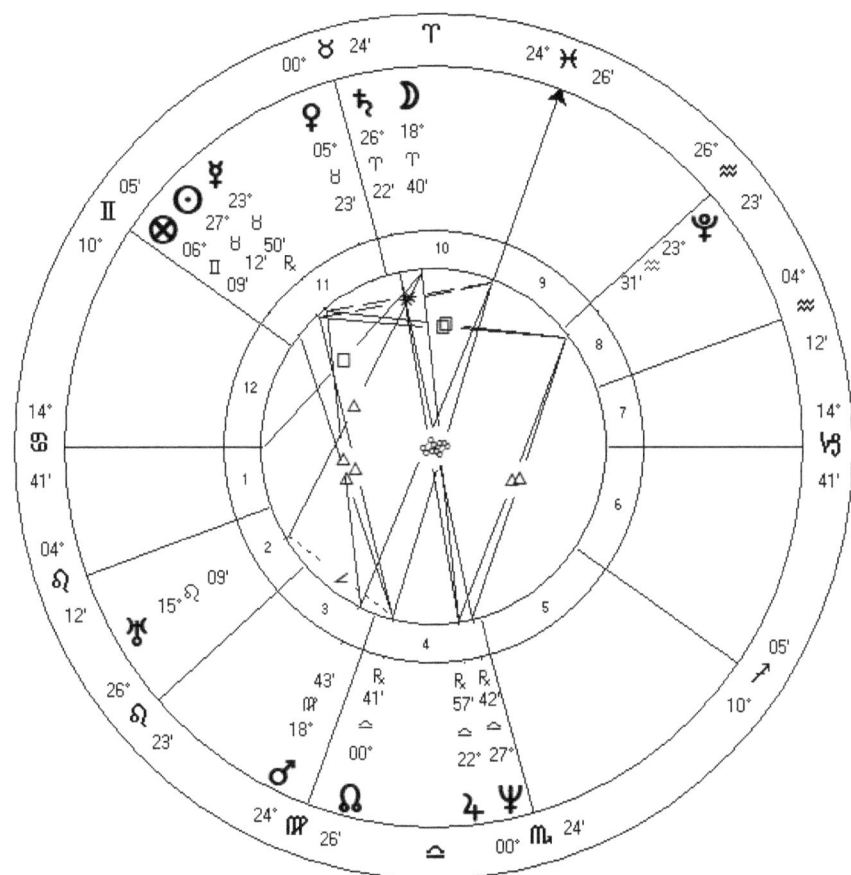

Figure 6-1
NYSE First Trade horoscope

The New York Stock Exchange officially opened for business on May 17, 1792 at 7:52 a.m.. As the horoscope in Figure 6-1 shows, the NYSE has its Ascendant (Asc) at 14-degrees of Cancer and its Mid-Heaven (MC) at 24-degrees of Pisces. The 14 of Cancer point appears numerous times in early American history. If I had to speculate, I would say that this degree point is important because it is where the star Sirius is located in the cosmos.

McWhirter further paid close attention to those times in the monthly lunar cycle when the transiting Moon passed by the NYSE natal Asc and MC locations at 14 Cancer and 24 Pisces respectively.

The McWhirter Methodology

When forecasting whether or not a coming month will be volatile or not for the NYSE, the McWhirter methodology starts with creating a horoscope chart for the New Moon date and positioning the Ascendant of the chart at 14-degrees Cancer (the Ascendant position on the 1792 natal chart of the New York Stock Exchange). Positioning the Ascendant is made easy with clicks of the mouse when using the *Solar Fire Gold* software program. Aspects to the lunation are then studied. If the lunation is at a 0, 90, or 120-degree aspect to 14 of Cancer, or 24 of Pisces, one can expect a volatile month ahead. Likewise for similar aspects to Mars, Neptune, Uranus, and Saturn. A lack of such aspects portends a less volatile period.

The McWhirter method hinges on the degree location of the Moon each day. Aspects of the transiting Moon to the natal Mars point at 18 Virgo, the natal Neptune point at 27 Libra, the natal Ascendant point at 14 Cancer, or the natal Mid-Heaven point at 24 Pisces all represent dates of potential short-term trend reversals and/or significant price volatility. In addition, dates when transiting Sun, Mars, and Venus pass these key points should be anticipated.

Although not expressly stated by McWhirter, it is also important to pay attention to those dates when Moon is at either maximum or minimum declination. As well, dates when Mercury is retrograde and dates when

Venus and Mars are at or near their maximum or minimum declination should also be considered carefully.

One must be alert at these aspects for the possibility of a trend change, the possibility of increased volatility within a trend, or even the possibility of a breakout from a chart consolidation pattern. Evidence of such trend changes will be found by applying chart technical indicators as discussed in Chapter Two.

February-March 2020: An Historical Example

The McWhirter method can be thoroughly appreciated by examining events around the 2020 COVID panic sell-off which started in late February:

A New Moon on February 23, 2020 came during Mercury retrograde

Within a day of the New Moon, the Moon transited past the NYSE natal Mid-Heaven (24 Pisces).

A day later, Moon made a hard 90-degree aspect to the natal Ascendant at 14 Cancer. Saturn was 90-degrees square the NYSE 1792 natal Saturn point and Jupiter was 120 degrees (trine) to the 1792 natal Mars point.

On February 27, Moon transited past the natal Moon. On March 1, Moon transited past the natal Sun location.

On March 4, Moon transited past the natal Ascendant point.

On March 9, Moon transited past the natal Mars location. On March 12, Moon transited past the natal Neptune location.

On March 24, the lunar cycle ended and a New Moon event materialized. The S&P 500 reached a low point and began to recover.

As a trader or investor, you can view the events of February-March 2020 through the lens of the Federal Reserve response to the selloff or you can view the events through the lens of the New Moons and aspects to key NYSE natal zodiac points.

What follows is a listing of the date for each lunar cycle in 2025 along with a list of times when Moon passes Mars, Neptune, the NYSE natal Mid-Heaven at 24 Pisces, and the NYSE natal Ascendant at 14 Cancer. In addition, dates of planetary retrograde, dates of declination maxima and minima, dates of planetary elongation, dates of aphelion, perihelion, and Moon VOC are included.

2025 Lunation Events – S&P 500

January 2025

Market action in January 2025 will be influenced by the New Moon cycle that commences on December 30, 2024 (Sun at 9 Capricorn) and runs to January 29, 2025 when Sun will be at 9 Aquarius.

Volatility appears to be a key theme for this lunar cycle. As this lunation gets underway, Venus will have crossed through its zero-degree declination level – an indicator of a possible trend change. In addition, Moon is at its declination minimum at this lunation which also supports the narrative for a trend change. Mid-month, Venus will be at its greatest easterly elongation – an indicator of a possible short term trend change. Later in the month, Mercury will be at Aphelion. This will be followed by Venus making her declination maximum – another indicator of trend volatility. Towards the end of this lunar cycle, Mars will start recording its declination maximum. Furthermore, this lunar cycle will be punctuated by three Moon Void of Couse (VOC) events.

Key dates during this lunar cycle are:

- ✿ January 5: Moon passes NYSE natal Mid-Heaven point
- ✿ January 6: Moon at zero-degrees declination
- ✿ January 7: Moon passes NYSE natal Moon point
- ✿ January 9: CPI data (USA) released
- ✿ January 9: Moon passes NYSE natal Sun point
- ✿ January 10: Venus at greatest easterly elongation
- ✿ January 12: Moon at maximum declination
- ✿ January 13: Moon passes NYSE natal Ascendant point
- ✿ January 15-16: Moon VOC
- ✿ January 17: S&P 500 index options last trading day
- ✿ January 17: Moon passes NYSE natal Mars point
- ✿ January 19: Moon at zero-degrees declination
- ✿ January 19: Mercury at Aphelion
- ✿ January 20-24: World Economic Forum meetings (Davos)
- ✿ January 21: Moon passes NYSE natal Neptune point
- ✿ January 23: Moon VOC
- ✿ January 25: Mars starts to record its declination maximum
- ✿ January 27: Moon at minimum declination
- ✿ January 27: Venus passes NYSE natal Mid-Heaven
- ✿ January 29: Federal Reserve interest rate decision
- ✿ January 29-30: Moon VOC

February 2025

Market action through February 2025 will be influenced by the New Moon cycle which commences on January 29, 2025 (Sun at 9 Aquarius) and runs until February 27 (Sun at 9 Pisces). The four key observations at this lunation are: Saturn is 120-degrees trine to the natal Ascendant point, the lunation is 120-degrees trine to Jupiter, Venus is conjunct to the natal Mid-Heaven, and Mars is widely within orb of being conjunct to the natal Ascendant. These placements should lend a favorable tone to the market for this lunar cycle.

Key dates during this lunar cycle are:

- ✡ February 1: Moon passes NYSE natal Mid-Heaven
- ✡ February 2: Moon at zero-degrees declination
- ✡ February 3: Moon passes NYSE natal Moon point
- ✡ February 3: Moon VOC
- ✡ February 5: Moon passes NYSE natal Sun point
- ✡ February 5: Moon VOC
- ✡ February 9: Moon at maximum declination
- ✡ February 9: Moon passes NYSE natal Ascendant point
- ✡ February 12: CPI data (USA) released
- ✡ February 14: Moon passes NYSE natal Mars point
- ✡ February 15: Moon at zero degrees declination
- ✡ February 17: Moon passes NYSE natal Neptune point
- ✡ February 19: Venus at Perihelion
- ✡ February 20: Moon VOC
- ✡ February 21: S&P 500 index options last trading day
- ✡ February 23: Moon at minimum declination
- ✡ February 24: Moon VOC

March 2025

Market action through March 2025 will be influenced by the New Moon cycle which commences early on February 27, 2025 and runs until March 29 (Sun at 9 Aries). This lunar cycle stands to deliver plenty of excitement with Mars situated 3 degrees from the natal Ascendant (14 Cancer) at the lunation. Moon is at zero-degrees declination at the lunation. Early in the month, Venus will turn retrograde – an almost sure sign of a short-term trend change. A couple days later, Mercury will be at Perihelion. This will be followed a few days later by Mercury at its greatest easterly elongation – a sign of trend volatility. Mid-month, Mercury retrograde will commence – another sign of increased volatility. In addition, Sun will transit past the NYSE natal Mid-Heaven point. Towards the end of the month, Venus will be at Inferior Conjunction and shortly afterwards will pass its 1792 natal declination level. This could add to any volatility on display. The month will be capped off with a sacred date from the Hebrew Calendar. All things considered, this lunar cycle could be a volatile time on the equity markets.

Key dates during this lunar cycle are:

- February 28: Moon passes NYSE natal Mid-Heaven point
- March 1: Moon at zero-degrees declination
- March 2: Moon passes NYSE natal Moon point
- March 2: Venus begins retrograde
- March 4: Mercury at Perihelion
- March 4: Mars completes its declination maximum
- March 5: Moon passes NYSE natal Sun point
- March 7: Moon VOC
- March 8: Moon at declination maximum
- March 8: Mercury at greatest easterly elongation
- March 11: Moon VOC
- March 12: CPI data (USA) released
- March 13: Moon passes NYSE natal Mars point
- March 14: Moon VOC
- March 14: Sun passes NYSE natal Mid-Heaven
- March 15: Moon at zero degrees declination
- March 15: Mercury begins retrograde
- March 17: Moon passes NYSE natal Neptune point
- March 19: Federal Reserve interest rate decision

- ✿ March 21: S&P 500 index options last trading day
- ✿ March 21: Triple Witching Day
- ✿ March 22: Moon at declination minimum
- ✿ March 23: Venus at Inferior Conjunction
- ✿ March 24: Moon VOC
- ✿ March 25-30: Venus passes its natal declination level
- ✿ March 26: Moon VOC
- ✿ March 28: Moon passes NYSE natal Mid-Heaven point
- ✿ March 30: 1st day of Nissan on Hebrew Calendar

April 2025

Market action through April 2025 will be influenced by the lunation cycle that runs from March 29 through April 27, 2025 (Sun at 7 Taurus). The lunation is within orb of being conjunct to the NYSE natal Moon point. The lunation is also within 5-degrees of being square the NYSE natal Ascendant. This is all suggestive of added volatility. Furthermore, Saturn is parked right at the NYSE natal Mid-Heaven point. However, it is sextile (60-degrees) to Uranus, so its full force may not be felt. As noted in an earlier chapter, Professor Weston's work calls for a market maxima point in April 2025. These placements seem to support Weston's hypothesis. Mercury and Venus both completing their retrogrades in this lunar cycle also seem to tie to Weston's market maxima theme.

Key dates during this lunar cycle are:

- ✿ March 29: Moon passes NYSE natal Moon point
- ✿ April 1: Moon passes NYSE natal Sun point
- ✿ April 1: Venus becomes visible as the Morning Star
- ✿ April 4: Moon at declination maximum
- ✿ April 4: Moon passes NYSE natal Ascendant

☼ April 7: Mercury retrograde complete
☼ April 7: Sun passes NYSE natal Moon
☼ April 7: Moon VOC
☼ April 9: CPI data (USA) released
☼ April 9: April 11: Moon at zero-degrees declination
☼ April 9: Moon passes NYSE natal Mars point
☼ April 12: Venus retrograde complete
☼ April 13: Moon passes NYSE natal Neptune point
☼ April 13: Venus turns Direct at the NYSE natal Mid-Heaven
☼ April 17: S&P 500 index options last trading day
☼ April 19: Moon at declination minimum
☼ April 21: Mercury at greatest westerly elongation
☼ April 22: Moon VOC
☼ April 24: Moon passes NYSE natal Mid-Heaven point
☼ April 25: Moon at zero-degrees declination
☼ April 26: Moon VOC.

May 2025

Market action during May will be influenced by the lunation cycle that runs from April 27 (Sun at 7 Taurus) to May 27 (Sun at 6 Gemini). The lunation sits atop the NYSE natal Venus point. The lunation is also a hard 90-degrees square to Mars. These placements imply added volatility. Midway through this lunar cycle, Venus will start to record her declination minimum – a further indicator of increased volatility.

Key dates during this lunar cycle are:

☼ April 29: Moon passes NYSE natal Sun point
☼ May 1: Moon at declination maximum
☼ May 2: Moon passes NYSE natal Ascendant
☼ May 5: Moon VOC
☼ May 7: Federal Reserve interest rate decision

- ✿ May 7: Moon passes NYSE natal Mars point
- ✿ May 8: Moon at zero degrees declination
- ✿ May 10: Moon passes NYSE natal Neptune point
- ✿ May 12: Venus starts to make her declination minimum
- ✿ May 14: Sun begins its transit past Pleiades point
- ✿ May 14: CPI data (USA) released
- ✿ May 16: Moon at declination minimum
- ✿ May 16: S&P 500 index options last trading day
- ✿ May 18: Sun begins its transit past Pleiades point
- ✿ May 18: Sun passes NYSE natal Sun point
- ✿ May 22: Moon at zero degrees declination
- ✿ May 22: Moon passes NYSE natal Mid-Heaven point
- ✿ May 22: Sun completes its transit past Pleiades point
- ✿ May 23: Moon passes NYSE natal Moon point
- ✿ May 24: Venus passes NYSE natal Moon point
- ✿ May 25: Moon at declination minimum
- ✿ May 26: Moon passes NYSE natal Sun point
- ✿ May 26: Moon VOC

June 2025

Market action through June 2025 will be influenced by the New Moon cycle which commences on May 27 (Sun at 6 Gemini) and runs until June 25, 2025 (Sun at 4 Cancer). To start the lunar cycle off, Venus will record her greatest westerly elongation and shortly afterward her declination minima. Mid-way through the cycle, Venus will pass the NYSE natal Venus point. As the cycle nears completion, Sun and Jupiter will make their annual conjunction – generally a trend changing event.

Key dates during this lunar cycle are:

- ✿ May 28: Moon VOC
- ✿ May 29: Moon passes NYSE natal Ascendant

- ✿ May 30: Moon VOC
- ✿ June 1: Venus at greatest westerly elongation
- ✿ June 2: Venus completes her declination minima
- ✿ June 3: Moon passes NYSE natal Mars point
- ✿ June 5: Moon at zero-degrees declination
- ✿ June 6: Moon passes NYSE natal Neptune point
- ✿ June 9: Moon VOC
- ✿ June 11: CPI data (USA) released
- ✿ June 11: Venus passes NYSE natal Venus point
- ✿ June 12: Moon at declination minimum
- ✿ June 12: Moon VOC
- ✿ June 12: Venus at Aphelion
- ✿ June 13: Moon VOC
- ✿ June 18: Federal Reserve interest rate decision
- ✿ June 18: Moon passes NYSE natal Mid-Heaven point
- ✿ June 19: Moon at zero-degrees declination
- ✿ June 20: S&P 500 index options last trading day
- ✿ June 20: Triple Witching Day
- ✿ June 20: Moon passes NYSE natal Moon point
- ✿ June 22: Moon passes NYSE natal Sun point
- ✿ June 22: Sun and Jupiter make a conjunction
- ✿ June 23-24: Moon VOC
- ✿ June 25: Moon at declination maximum

July 2025

Market action through July 2025 will be influenced by the New Moon cycle that commences on June 25, 2025 (Sun at 4 Cancer) and runs until July 24 (Sun at 2 Leo). The lunation is widely (10 degrees) within orb of the NYSE natal ascendant point. This could signal a period of volatile behavior. Adding to any theme of volatility will be Mercury at Aphelion followed by Mercury turning retrograde. In addition, Venus will pass the Pleiades point at the same time as the 9th of Tammuz sacred date.

Acting to regulate matters are Saturn and Uranus, still at a 60-degree sextile angle to one another.

Key dates during this lunar cycle are:

- ✿ June 26: Moon passes NYSE natal Ascendant
- ✿ June 29: Venus begins its transit past Pleiades point
- ✿ June 30: Moon passes NYSE natal Mars point
- ✿ July 1: Moon VOC
- ✿ July 2: Moon at zero-degrees declination
- ✿ July 4: Mercury at greatest easterly elongation
- ✿ July 4: Moon passes NYSE natal Neptune point
- ✿ July 5: 9th day of Tammuz on Hebrew calendar
- ✿ July 6: Venus completes its transit past the Pleiades point
- ✿ July 6: Sun passes NYSE natal Ascendant
- ✿ July 8: Moon VOC
- ✿ July 9: Moon at declination minimum
- ✿ July 10: CPI data (USA) released
- ✿ July 12: Mars starts transit past the NYSE natal Mars point
- ✿ July 13-18: Venus passes its 1792 natal declination level
- ✿ July 14: Mercury at Aphelion
- ✿ July 14-25: Mars passes the NYSE natal Mars point
- ✿ July 15: Moon passes NYSE natal Mid-Heaven point
- ✿ July 15: Moon VOC
- ✿ July 16: Moon at zero degrees declination
- ✿ July 17: Moon passes NYSE natal Moon
- ✿ July 18: Mercury begins retrograde
- ✿ July 18: S&P 500 index options last trading day
- ✿ July 20: Moon passes NYSE natal Sun point
- ✿ July 22: Moon at declination maximum
- ✿ July 23: Moon passes NYSE natal Ascendant

August 2025

Market action through August 2025 will be influenced by the New Moon cycle that commences on July 24 (Sun at 2 Leo) and runs until August 23 (Sun at zero degrees Virgo). The lunation itself is not at any malefic (harmful) aspects to other planets. However, expansive Jupiter is situated within 4-degrees of the NYSE natal Ascendant point. This is suggestive of bullish activity. In addition, most of this lunar cycle will have Sun in the sign of Leo. Sun is the ruler of this sign and is therefore exalted. Mercury being retrograde during the first part of this lunar cycle might provide some drama. Venus passing the NYSE natal Ascendant point could also enliven the party, especially with Jupiter exact at 14 of Cancer on August 12th. Note also the number of Moon VOC events which also stand to add to volatility.

Key dates during this lunar cycle are:

- ✿ July 24: Moon VOC
- ✿ July 27: Mars completes transit past NYSE natal Mars
- ✿ July 28: Moon passes NYSE natal Mars point
- ✿ July 28: Jupiter begins its transit past NYSE natal Ascendant
- ✿ July 29: Moon at zero-degrees declination
- ✿ July 30: Federal Reserve interest rate decision
- ✿ July 31: Moon passes NYSE natal Neptune point
- ✿ July 31: Moon VOC
- ✿ August 3: 9th day of Av on Hebrew calendar
- ✿ August 5: Moon VOC
- ✿ August 6: Moon at declination minimum
- ✿ August 7: Moon VOC
- ✿ August 9-15: Venus passes NYSE natal Ascendant point
- ✿ August 10: Mercury completes retrograde
- ✿ August 11: Moon passes NYSE natal Mid-Heaven point
- ✿ August 11: Moon VOC

- ☿ August 12: Moon at zero-degrees declination
- ☿ August 12: Jupiter and Venus at 14 degrees Cancer
- ☿ August 13: CPI data (USA) released
- ☿ August 13: Moon passes NYSE natal Moon
- ☿ August 15: S&P 500 index options last trading day
- ☿ August 16: Moon passes NYSE natal Sun point
- ☿ August 18: Moon VOC
- ☿ August 19: Moon at declination maximum
- ☿ August 19: Moon passes NYSE natal Ascendant
- ☿ August 19: Mercury at greatest westerly elongation
- ☿ August 20: Moon VOC
- ☿ August 22: Moon VOC

September 2025

Market action through September 2025 will be influenced by the New Moon cycle that commences on August 23 (Sun at 0 Virgo) and runs until September 21 (Sun at 29 Virgo). Jupiter is still within 2 degrees of the NYSE natal Ascendant point at this lunation. This is suggestive of expansive action during this lunar cycle. However, the lunation is 90-degrees square to Uranus which could cast something of a volatile shadow on the NYSE. In addition, Venus recording her declination maxima during this cycle will add to any volatility as will Sun passing the NYSE natal Mars point and Mars passing the NYSE natal Neptune point.

Key dates during this lunar cycle are:

- ☿ August 24: Moon passes NYSE natal Mars point
- ☿ August 25: Moon at zero-degrees declination
- ☿ August 27: Moon passes NYSE natal Neptune point
- ☿ August 27: Moon VOC

- ✷ September 2: Moon at declination minimum
- ✷ September 2-19: Venus making declination maxima
- ✷ September 6: Sun begins transit of NYSE natal Mars
- ✷ September 8: Moon at zero-degrees declination
- ✷ September 8: Moon passes NYSE natal Mid-Heaven
- ✷ September 8: Jupiter completes transit of natal Ascendant
- ✷ September 9: Moon passes NYSE natal Moon point
- ✷ September 10: Moon VOC
- ✷ September 11: CPI data (USA) released
- ✷ September 11: Mars begins transit of NYSE natal Neptune
- ✷ September 11: Sun passes NYSE natal Mars
- ✷ September 12: Moon passes NYSE natal Sun point
- ✷ September 15: Moon at declination maximum
- ✷ September 15: Moon passes NYSE natal Ascendant
- ✷ September 17: Federal Reserve interest rate decision
- ✷ September 17: Sun completes natal Mars transit
- ✷ September 18: Mars passes NYSE natal Neptune
- ✷ September 19: S&P 500 index options last trading day
- ✷ September 19: Triple Witching Day
- ✷ September 19: Moon passes NYSE natal Mars

October 2025

Market action during October will be influenced by the New Moon cycle that commences on September 21 (Sun at 29 Virgo) and runs until October 21 (Sun at 27 Libra). This lunar cycle contains three sacred holiday dates from the Hebrew calendar. Any of which could trigger added volatility. The lunation being 180 degrees opposite to Saturn is supportive of added volatility for this lunar cycle. Mars being conjunct to the NYSE natal Neptune point will add to the volatility, as will the four Moon VOC events.

Key dates during this lunar cycle are:

- ✡ September 22: Mars completes passage of NYSE natal Neptune
- ✡ September 22: Moon at zero-degrees declination
- ✡ September 23: 1st day of Tishrei on Hebrew calendar
- ✡ September 23: Moon VOC
- ✡ September 23: Moon passes NYSE natal Neptune point
- ✡ September 26: Moon VOC
- ✡ September 29: Moon at declination minimum
- ✡ October 1: Moon VOC
- ✡ October 2: 10th day of Tishrei on Hebrew calendar
- ✡ October 2: Venus at Perihelion
- ✡ October 5: Moon passes NYSE natal Mid-Heaven
- ✡ October 6: Moon at zero-degrees declination
- ✡ October 7: Moon passes NYSE natal Moon
- ✡ October 8: CPI data (USA) released
- ✡ October 9: Moon passes NYSE natal Sun
- ✡ October 12: Moon at declination maximum
- ✡ October 12: Moon passes NYSE natal Ascendant
- ✡ October 13-15: Shemini Atzeret on Hebrew calendar
- ✡ October 16: Sun starts transit of NYSE natal Neptune
- ✡ October 16: Moon VOC
- ✡ October 17: S&P 500 index options last trading day
- ✡ October 17: Moon passes NYSE natal Mars
- ✡ October 19: Moon at zero-degrees declination

November 2025

Market action during November 2025 will be influenced by the New Moon cycle which commences on October 21 (Sun at 27 Libra) and runs until November 20 (Sun at 28 Scorpio). The lunation is conjunct to the NYSE natal Neptune point which could provide for increased volatility.

Mars starting to make its declination minimum along with Mercury turning retrograde should enliven the volatility of this lunar cycle.

Key dates during this lunar cycle are:

- ✿ October 21: Moon VOC
- ✿ October 25: Sun completes natal Neptune transit
- ✿ October 27: Moon at declination minimum
- ✿ October 29: Mercury at greatest easterly elongation
- ✿ October 29: Federal Reserve interest rate decision
- ✿ November 2: Moon passes NYSE natal Mid-Heaven
- ✿ November 2-8: Venus passes NYSE natal Neptune
- ✿ November 3: Moon at zero degrees declination
- ✿ November 3: Moon at NYSE natal Moon
- ✿ November 4: Moon VOC
- ✿ November 4-9: Venus passes its 1792 natal declination level
- ✿ November 6: Moon passes NYSE natal Sun
- ✿ November 9: Moon at declination maximum
- ✿ November 9: Moon passes NYSE natal Ascendant
- ✿ November 10: Moon VOC
- ✿ November 11: Mercury begins retrograde
- ✿ November 12: CPI data (USA) released
- ✿ November 12: Moon VOC
- ✿ November 14: Moon passes NYSE natal Mars
- ✿ November 17: Moon passes NYSE natal Neptune
- ✿ November 17: Moon VOC

December 2025

Market action during December 2025 will be influenced by the New Moon cycle that commences on November 20 (Sun at 28 Scorpio) and runs until December 19 (Sun at 28 Sagittarius). The lunation is 120-degrees trine to the NYSE natal Mid-Heaven point which could be a trigger for increased volatility – perhaps in a positive way, with Mercury finishing retrograde early in the cycle. The lunation is also 120-degrees trine to Jupiter which will add to a positive tone. The cycle starting off with Mars approaching its declination maximum will also be a contributing factor.

Key dates during this lunar cycle are:

- ✿ November 20: Mars starts making declination minimum
- ✿ November 21: S&P 500 index options last trading day
- ✿ November 23: Moon at declination minimum
- ✿ November 23: Mercury at Perihelion
- ✿ November 27: Moon VOC
- ✿ November 29: Mercury finishes retrograde
- ✿ November 29: Moon passes NYSE natal Mid-Heaven
- ✿ November 30: Moon at zero-degrees declination
- ✿ December 1: Moon passes NYSE natal Moon
- ✿ December 1: Moon VOC
- ✿ December 3: Moon passes NYSE natal Sun
- ✿ December 3: Moon VOC
- ✿ December 5: Moon VOC
- ✿ December 6: Moon at declination maximum
- ✿ December 7: Mercury at greatest westerly elongation
- ✿ December 7: Moon passes NYSE natal Ascendant
- ✿ December 10: Federal Reserve interest rate decision
- ✿ December 10: CPI data (USA) released
- ✿ December 11: Moon passes NYSE natal Mars
- ✿ December 12: Moon VOC
- ✿ December 13: Moon at zero-degrees declination
- ✿ December 14: Moon passes NYSE natal Neptune
- ✿ December 19: S&P 500 index options last trading day
- ✿ December 19: Triple Witching Day
- ✿ December 20: Moon at declination minimum

Market action for the remainder of December 2025 will be influenced by the New Moon cycle that starts on December 19 (Sun at 28 Sagittarius) and runs into January 2026. The lunation will be within 4-degrees of being at a hard 90-degrees square to the NYSE natal Mid-Heaven.

- ☼ December 19: Venus starts to record her declination minimum
- ☼ December 26: Moon passes NYSE natal Mid-Heaven
- ☼ December 28: Moon passes NYSE natal Moon
- ☼ December 31: Moon passes NYSE natal Sun

CHAPTER SEVEN
Planetary Events and Commodities

W.D. Gann was a proponent of following planetary aspects to the natal planetary positions of the exchange that a commodity future traded on.

This chapter presents the natal horoscopes of the various exchanges in Chicago and New York that started trading commodity futures contracts in the mid-1800s. In addition, the natal horoscope wheels are presented for the various commodities.

Traders and investors should pay attention to planetary transits of key points in the exchange's natal horoscopes as well as to planetary transits of key points in an individual commodity's natal horoscope.

The Commodity Exchange (COMEX)

The Commodity Exchange was started July 5, 1933 with the merger of the National Metal Exchange, the Rubber Exchange, the Raw Silk Exchange, and the Raw Hide Exchange. This exchange eventually came to be known as COMEX.

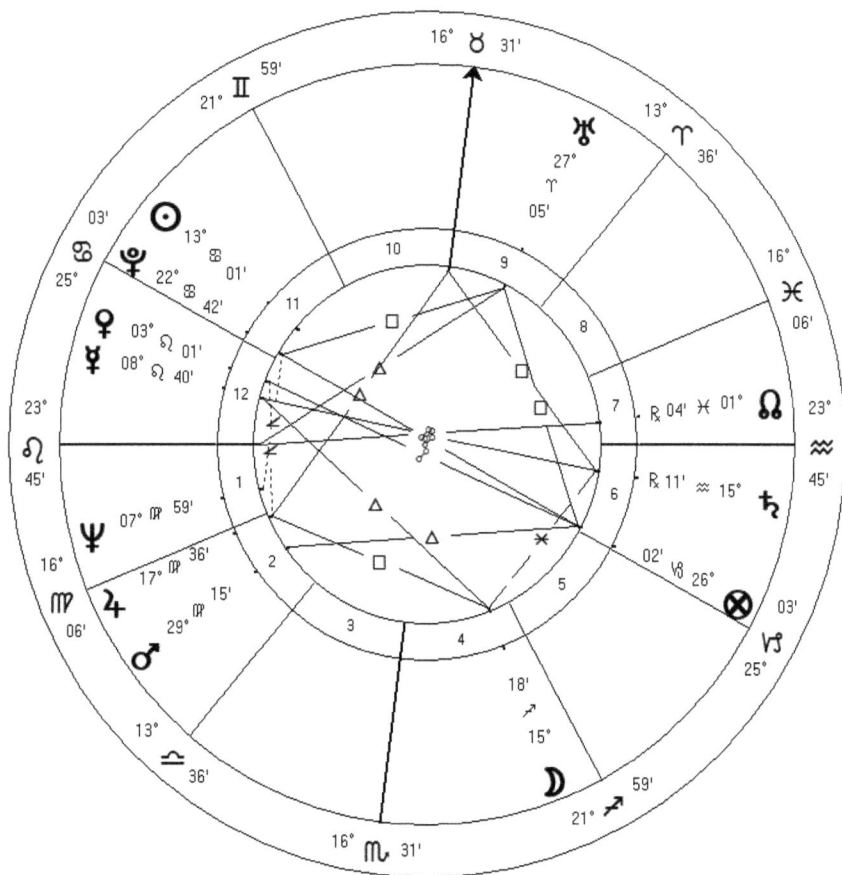

Figure 7-1
1933 COMEX Natal Horoscope

On July 5, 1933, the Sun was at 13 of Cancer. This is very nearly the same degree point as the Ascendant was at on May 17, 1792 when the NYSE was founded. The choice of July 5, 1933 was not a random selection. Moreover, on July 5, 1933, Neptune, Mars and Jupiter are all in the sign of Virgo - which throughout history has been connected with the ancient Egyptian female goddess Isis. This is further evidence that the choice of July 5 was not an accident. A few days later and Sun would have been past 13 of Cancer and Mars would have been out of the sign of Virgo.

Figure 7-1 illustrates the planetary placements at July 5, 1933. Assuming a 9:00 a.m. start time, notice how Mid-Heaven (16 Taurus), Jupiter (17 Virgo), Moon (15 Sagittarius), and Saturn (15 Aquarius) trace out a 4-sided parallelogram.

The following 2025 planetary transits of the COMEX 1933 natal chart should be watched carefully:

Natal Sun Transits (13 Cancer)
- ☼ Sun will pass the 1933 natal Sun June 30 to July 9
- ☼ Jupiter will pass the 1933 natal Sun July 24 to August 4
- ☼ Venus will pass the 1933 natal Sun August 8 to 14

Natal Ascendant Transits (23 Leo)
- ☼ Mars passes the natal Ascendant May 29 to June 10
- ☼ Sun will pass the natal Ascendant August 10 to 20
- ☼ Venus passes the natal Ascendant September 10 to 16

Natal Jupiter Transits (17 Virgo)
- ☼ Mars will pass natal Jupiter July 11 to 22
- ☼ Sun will pass natal Jupiter September 5 to 13
- ☼ Venus will pass natal Jupiter October 1 to 6

Natal Saturn Transits (15 Aquarius)

✪ Sun passes natal Saturn January 30 to February 7

Natal Mid-Heaven Transits (16 Taurus)

✪ Sun will pass the natal Mid-Heaven May 1 to 10
✪ Venus will pass the natal Mid-Heaven June 19 to 25

Natal Moon Transits (15 Sagittarius)

✪ Mars passes natal Moon November 21 to 29
✪ Sun will pass natal Moon December 3 to 11
✪ Venus passes natal Moon December 9 to 16

Natal Venus Transits (3 Leo)

✪ Mars passes natal Venus April 18 to May 2

Natal Mars Transits (29 Virgo)

✪ Mars passes natal Mars August 1 to 10
✪ Sun passes natal Mars September 18 to 27
✪ Venus passes natal Mars October 10 to 16.

Gold

Investors who follow daily Gold prices may not realize that working behind the scenes to define the daily price of Gold is an archaic methodology called the *London Gold Fix*. This archaic price-setting method dates to 1919.

The 1919 Gold Fix

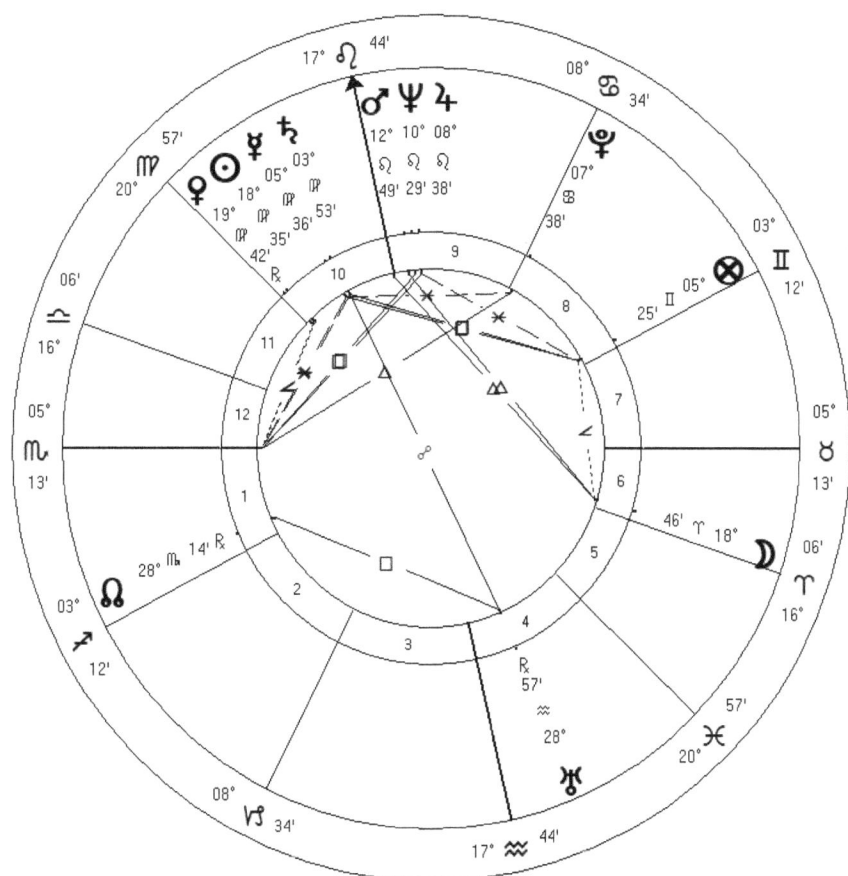

Figure 7-2
1919 London Gold Fix Horoscope

The London Gold Fix occurs at 10:30 a.m. and 3:00 p.m. local time each business day in London. Participants in the daily fixes are: Barclay's, HSBC, Scotia Mocatta (a division of Scotia Bank of Canada), and Societe Generale. These twice-daily collaborations (some would say collusions) provide a benchmark price that is then used around the globe to settle and mark-to-market the value of all the various Gold-related derivative contracts in existence.

The history of the Gold Fix dates back over one hundred years. On September 12th, 1919, the Bank of England made arrangements with N.M. Rothschild & Sons for the formation of a Gold-market in which there would be one official price for Gold bullion quoted on any one day. At 11:00 a.m., the first Gold fixing took place with the five principal Gold-bullion traders and refiners of the day present. These traders and refiners were: N.M. Rothschild & Sons, Mocatta & Goldsmid, Pixley & Abell, Samuel Montagu & Co., and Sharps Wilkins.

The horoscope in Figure 7-2 depicts planetary positions at the 1919 Gold Fix creation date. The Ascendant (5 Scorpio), Sun (18 Virgo), Mid-Heaven (17 Leo), Saturn (3 Virgo), Mars (12 Leo), Jupiter (8 Leo), Moon (18 Aries), and Venus (19 Virgo) are points to focus on. Notice that there are four planets in the sign of Virgo; a reference to Isis. Moreover, Sun's position in Virgo is only one degree off from Jupiter's position in Virgo in the 1933 COMEX natal horoscope.

Was the 1933 COMEX start date picked for this reason?

In addition to following transits of key points in the COMEX 1933 natal horoscope, traders and investors may wish to also follow transits of key points in the 1919 Gold Fix natal horoscope.

For 2025, the following are dates to watch:

Natal Sun/Natal Venus Transits (18-19 Virgo)
- Mars will pass this natal point July 13 to 25
- Sun will pass this natal point September 6 to 15
- Venus will pass this natal point October 1 to 8

Natal Ascendant Transits (5 Scorpio)
- Mars passes the natal Ascendant Sept 24 to October 5
- Sun will pass the natal Ascendant Oct 25 to Nov 1
- Venus passes the natal Ascendant November 8 to 14

Natal Mid-Heaven/Natal Mars Transits (12-17 Leo)
- Mars will pass this natal point May 16 to 31
- Sun will pass this natal point August 1 to 13
- Venus will pass this natal point September 2 to 11
- Natal Moon Transits (18 Aries)
- Sun will pass natal Moon April 3 to 12
- Venus will pass natal Moon May 21 to 28

Natal Jupiter Transits (8 Leo)
- Mars will pass natal Jupiter April 29 to May 2
- Sun will pass natal Jupiter July 27 to August 4
- Venus will pass natal Jupiter August 29 to September 4

Natal Saturn Transits (3 Virgo)
- Mars will pass natal Saturn June 17 to 28
- Sun will pass natal Saturn August 21 to 30
- Venus will pass natal Saturn September 19 to 25.

1974 Gold Futures

The third horoscope that Gold investors should watch is that of the Gold futures contract. In 1971, President Nixon eliminated the convertibility of Gold into U.S. Dollars. A market then emerged for trading Gold futures contracts which made their debut on COMEX on December 31, 1974. Figure 7-3 illustrates the planetary positions in 1974 at the first trade date of Gold futures.

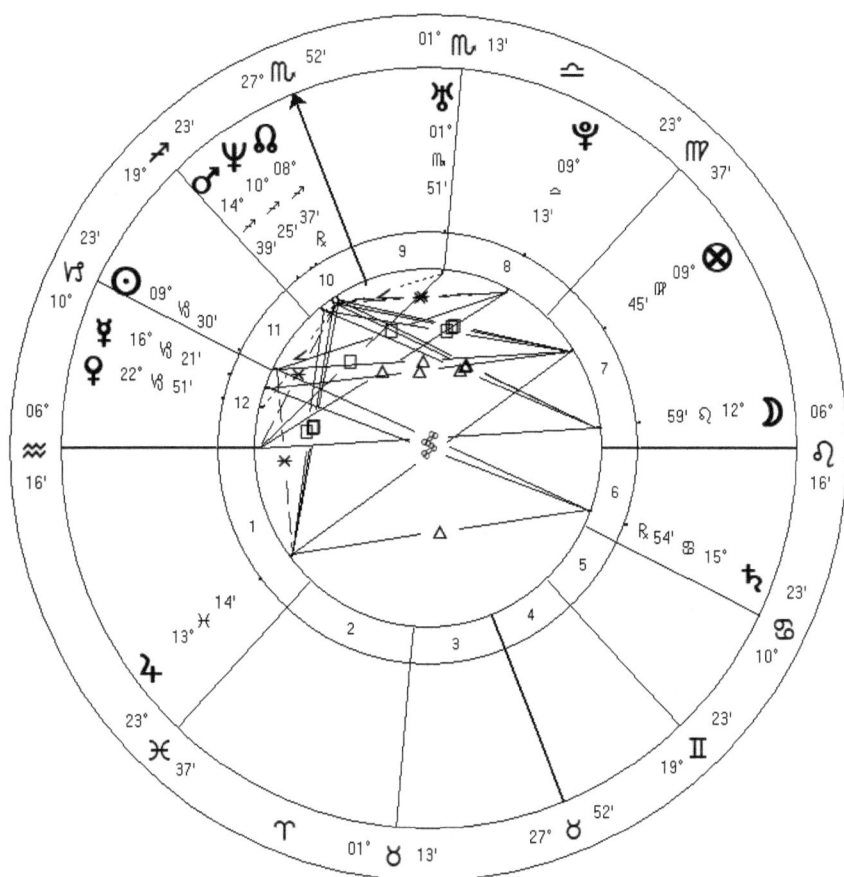

Figure 7-3
Gold futures 1974 First Trade Horoscope

If you are wondering why the COMEX administrators would launch a new futures contract on December 31, a time when most staff would be off for Christmas holidays, you are not alone in your thoughts. To me, it appears that astrology was very much used when determining important first trade dates.

The horoscope in Figure 7-3 illustrates planetary positions on December 31, 1974. Note the saw-tooth pattern with Saturn (15 Cancer), Moon (12 Leo), Mars (14 Sagittarius), and Jupiter (13 Pisces). In addition, the Ascendant is at 6 Aquarius and the Mid-Heaven is at 27 Scorpio.

In 2025, transits past these points will occur:

Natal Mars Transits (14 Sagittarius)
- ✿ Mars will pass natal Mars Nov 20 to 28
- ✿ Sun will pass natal Mars December 1 to 9
- ✿ Venus will pass natal Mars December 9 to 15

Natal Jupiter Transits (13 Pisces)
- ✿ Venus will pass natal Jupiter point January 12 to 20
- ✿ Saturn will complete its transit of natal Jupiter at this time too
- ✿ Sun passes natal Jupiter February 27 to March 8

Natal Saturn Transits (15 Cancer)
- ✿ Mars nears the 1974 natal Saturn point February 23 to March 9
- ✿ Sun will pass the 1974 natal Saturn point July 3 to 11
- ✿ Jupiter will pass the 1974 natal Saturn point Aug 4 to Sept 12
- ✿ Venus will pass the 1974 natal Saturn point August 9 to 16

Natal Moon Transits (12 Leo)
- ✿ Mars will pass natal Moon point May 6 to 21
- ✿ Sun will pass natal Moon point July 31 to August 9
- ✿ Venus will pass natal Moon point September 1 to 8

Natal Mid-Heaven Transits (27 Scorpio)

- ✡ Mars will pass the natal Mid-Heaven Oct 27 to Nov 5
- ✡ Sun will pass the natal Mid-Heaven November 15 to 23
- ✡ Venus will pass the natal Mid-Heaven Nov 25 to Dec 1

Natal Ascendant Transits (6 Aquarius)

- ✡ Sun will pass the 1974 natal Ascendant January 22 to 29

Natal Venus Transits (22 Capricorn)

- ✡ Sun will pass the natal Venus point January 9 to 16.

Moon Transits

Using the geocentric Moon data in Appendix A, take note of the dates when Moon transits past the key points just mentioned for COMEX, Gold Fix, and 1974 Gold futures. Watch for increased volatility and possibly even short-term trend changes on these dates.

Declination

On July 5, 1933, when COMEX began trading operations, Mars was at minus 13.5-degrees declination and Venus was at plus 13.5-degrees declination. Two planets being at the same declination level (but opposite in position relative to the ecliptic) is termed a *contra-parallel event*. No doubt this cosmic event contributed to the choice of July 5 as the start date for COMEX. Furthermore, Moon was at its declination minimum at July 5, 1933.

For 2025:

- ✡ **Venus will be at plus 13.5-degrees declination March 2 to 8, August 5 to 12, and October 11 to 17**
- ✡ **Mars will be at minus 13.5-degrees declination August 15 to September 2**

☼ **Moon will be at declination minimum: January 27, February 23, March 22, April 19, May 16, May 25, June 12, July 9, August 6, September 2, September 29, October 27, November 23, and December 20.**

On December 31, 1974 when Gold futures started trading, Mars was at minus 20-degrees declination and Venus was at minus 20-degrees declination. Two planets at the same declination (and on the same side of the ecliptic) is termed a *parallel event*. In my opinion, these two planets both being at the same declination level further explains the choice of the unusual date of December 31 as the first trade date.

In 2025,
   ☼ **Venus will be at minus 20-degrees declination April 26 to May 4, and December 8 to 15**
   ☼ **Mars will be at minus 20-degrees declination September 30 to October 24.**

Mercury Retrograde

A valuable tool for Gold traders to consider is Mercury retrograde events. Watch for technical chart trend indicators to suggest a short-term trend change at a Mercury retrograde event. The retrograde event in April 2024 aligned to an interim topping pattern on the Gold price chart. The end of a retrograde event in late August 2024 seems to have aligned to another interim topping pattern.

   For 2025, Mercury will be:
   ☼ **retrograde from March 15 to April 6**
   ☼ **retrograde from July 18 to August 10**
   ☼ **retrograde from November 9 to November 28.**

Venus Retrograde

Another valuable tool for Gold traders to consider is Venus retrograde events. Watch for technical chart trend indicators to suggest a short-term trend change at a Venus retrograde event.

☼ **For 2025, Venus will be retrograde March 2 to April 12.**

Mars Retrograde

Lastly, Mars retrograde events should be given attention. Mars retrograde events going back to 2018 have all aligned to significant price inflection points on the Gold price chart.

☼ **For 2025, Mars will be retrograde January 1 through February 23.**

Silver

Silver futures started trading on COMEX on July 5, 1933 – the very date that COMEX officially became operational. Figure 7-4 shows the First Trade horoscope for Silver futures in geocentric format. The first trade date is the same as the start date for COMEX, so the Silver natal chart is identical to the COMEX natal chart

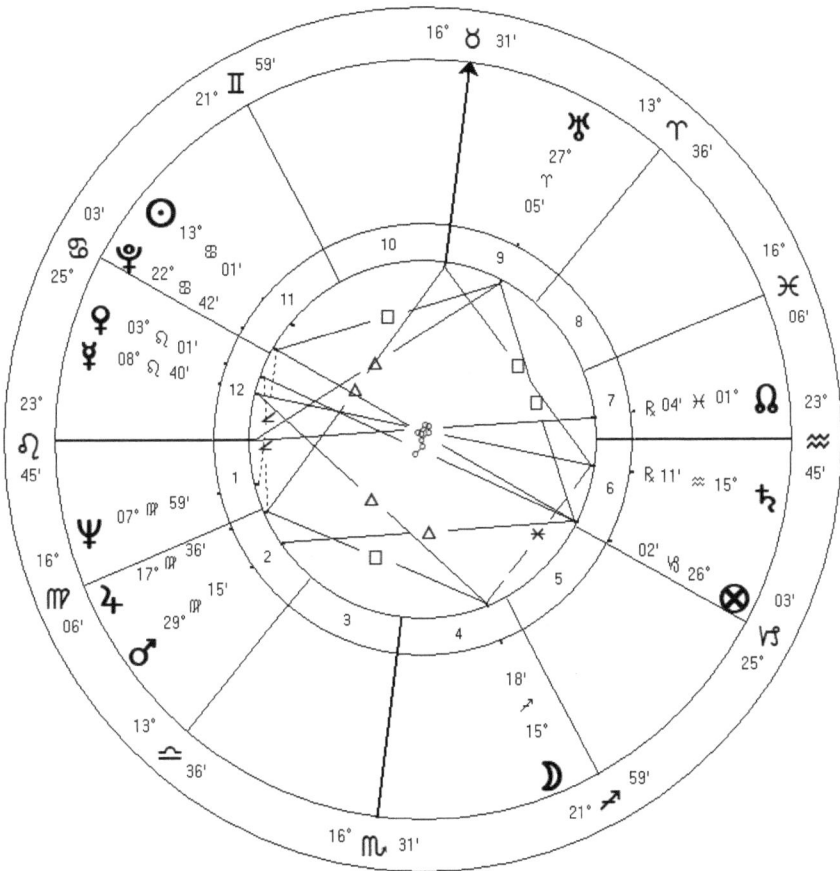

Figure 7-4
Silver futures First Trade Horoscope

For 2025, traders and investors who follow Silver futures, silver mining companies or silver miner ETFs may wish to focus on the following transits:

Natal Sun Transits (13 Cancer)
✿ Sun will pass the 1933 natal Sun June 30 to July 9
✿ Jupiter will pass the 1933 natal Sun July 24 to August 4
✿ Venus will pass the 1933 natal Sun August 8 to 14

Natal Ascendant Transits (23 Leo)
✿ Mars will pass the natal Ascendant May 29 to June 10
✿ Sun will pass the natal Ascendant August 10 to 20
✿ Venus passes the natal Ascendant September 10 to 16

Natal Jupiter Transits (17 Virgo)
✿ Mars will pass natal Jupiter July 11 to 22
✿ Sun will pass natal Jupiter September 5 to 13
✿ Venus will pass natal Jupiter October 1 to 6

Natal Saturn Transits (15 Aquarius)
✿ Sun passes natal Saturn January 30 to February 7

Natal Mid-Heaven Transits (16 Taurus)
✿ Sun will pass the natal Mid-Heaven May 1 to 10
✿ Venus will pass the natal Mid-Heaven June 19 to 25

Natal Moon Transits (15 Sagittarius)
✿ Mars will pass the 1933 natal Moon November 21 to 29
✿ Sun will pass the 1933 natal Moon December 3 to 11
✿ Venus passes the 1933 natal Moon December 9 to 16

Natal Venus Transits (3 Leo)
✿ Mars passes natal Venus April 18 to May 2

Natal Mars Transits (29 Virgo)
- ☼ Mars passes natal Mars August 1 to 10
- ☼ Sun passes natal Mars September 18 to 27
- ☼ Venus passes natal Mars October 10 to 16.

Moon Transits

Using the geocentric Moon data in Appendix A, take note of the dates when Moon transits past the key points just mentioned for Silver futures. Watch for increased volatility and possibly even short-term trend changes on these dates.

Declination

On July 5, 1933 when COMEX was started and Silver futures started trading, Mars was at minus 13.5-degrees declination and Venus was at plus 13.5-degrees declination. Moon was at its declination minimum.

For 2025:
- ☼ **Venus will be at plus 13.5-degrees declination March 2-8, August 5-12, and October 11-17**
- ☼ **Mars will be at minus 13.5-degrees declination August 15-September 2**
- ☼ **Moon will be at declination minimum: January 27, February 23, March 22, April 19, May 16, May 25, June 12, July 9, August 6, September 2, September 29, October 27, November 23, and December 20.**

Mercury Retrograde

A valuable tool for Silver traders to consider is Mercury retrograde events. Watch for technical chart trend indicators to suggest a short-term trend change at a Mercury retrograde event.

For 2025, Mercury will be:
- ☼ **retrograde from March 15 to April 6**
- ☼ **retrograde from July 18 to August 10**
- ☼ **retrograde from November 9 to November 28.**

Venus Retrograde

Another valuable tool for Silver traders to consider is Venus retrograde events. Watch for technical chart trend indicators to suggest a short-term trend change at a Venus retrograde event. The conclusion of the Venus retrograde event in 2023 marked the start of a $3 per ounce drawdown on Silver prices.

- ☼ **For 2025, Venus will be retrograde March 2 to April 12.**

Mars Retrograde

Lastly, Mars retrograde events should be given attention. The conclusion of the Mars retrograde event in late 2022 marked the start of a $4 per ounce drawdown on Silver prices.

- ☼ **For 2025, Mars will be retrograde January 1 to February 23.**

Copper

The first trade date for Copper futures was July 29, 1988. Figure 7-5 illustrates the first trade horoscope. A first trade time of 9:00 a.m. (New York time) is assumed.

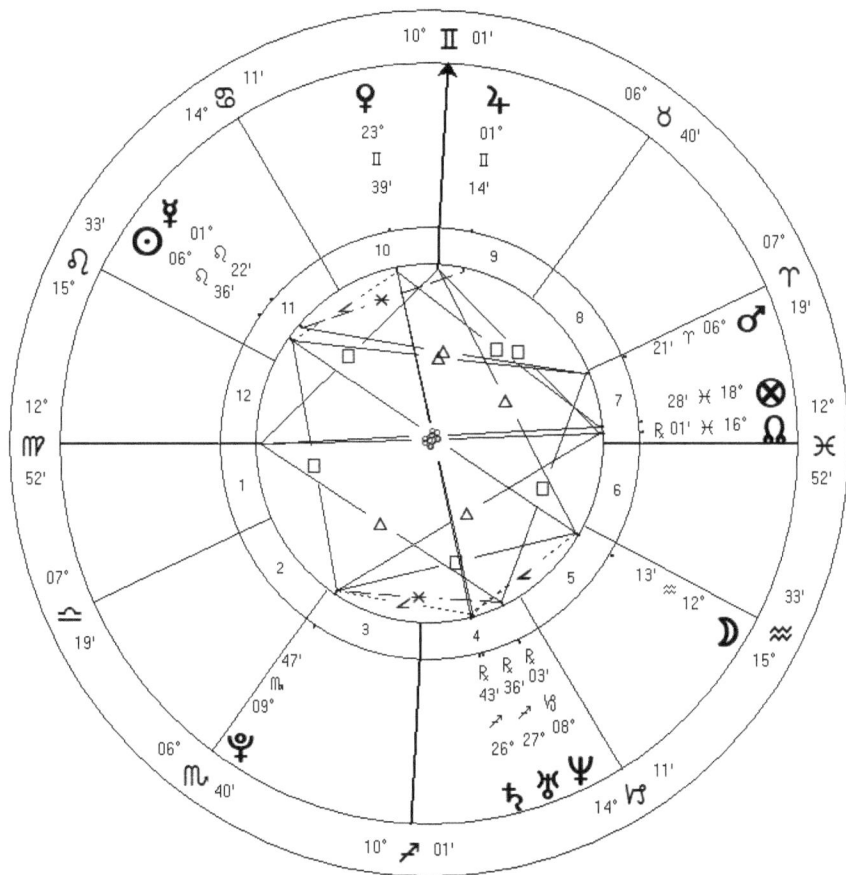

Figure 7-5
Copper futures First Trade Horoscope

Notice how the Ascendant is in the sign of Virgo – a reference to the goddess Isis. Sun is conjunct to the 1933 COMEX natal Venus point. Moreover, Pluto, Neptune, Mars, and Sun trace out a perfect 4-sided parallelogram shape with corner points Sun (6 Leo), Mars (6 Aries), Pluto (9 Scorpio), and Neptune (8 Capricorn). In addition to the parallelogram shape, two other points of interest are the Ascendant (12 Virgo) and the Mid-Heaven (10 Gemini).

In addition to transits past the 1933 COMEX natal horoscope points, consider the following 2025 transits past the 1988 Copper futures natal points:

Natal Sun Transits (6 Leo)
- ✷ Mars will pass the natal Sun April 26 to May 9
- ✷ Sun will pass the natal Sun from July 24 to August 2

Natal Mars Transits (6 Aries)
- ✷ Venus will pass natal Mars February 8 to 20
- ✷ Sun will pass natal Mars March 22 to 30
- ✷ Venus will pass natal Mars May 4 to 15

Natal Pluto Transits (9 Scorpio)
- ✷ Mars will pass natal Pluto October 1 to 10
- ✷ Sun will pass natal Pluto October 28 to Nov 6

Natal Neptune Transits (8 Capricorn)
- ✷ Sun will pass natal Neptune December 25 to 31
- ✷ Mars will pass natal Neptune December 20 to 31

Natal Mid-Heaven Transits (10 Gemini)
- ✷ Jupiter will be retrograde January 1 to February 3 and in close proximity to the natal Mid-Heaven point

- ☼ Jupiter will turn Direct again on February 3 and up to March 90 will be in close proximity to the natal Mid-Heaven point
- ☼ Sun will pass the natal Mid-Heaven May 26 to June 5
- ☼ Venus will pass the natal Mid-Heaven July 10 to 17

Natal Ascendant Transits (12 Virgo)
- ☼ Sun passes the natal Ascendant August 31 to Sept 8
- ☼ Mars will pass the natal Ascendent July 3 to 15
- ☼ Venus passes the natal Ascendent Sept 26 to October 2

Natal Venus Transits (23 Gemini)
- ☼ Sun will pass natal Venus June 9 to 18
- ☼ Venus will pass natal Venus July 22 to 28

Natal Moon Transits (12 Aquarius)
- ☼ Sun passes the natal Moon January 27 to February 4.

Moon Transits

Using the geocentric Moon data in Appendix A, take note of the dates when Moon transits past the key 1988 points mentioned for Copper futures and for COMEX. Watch for increased volatility and possibly even short-term trend changes on these dates.

Declination

In addition to the natal declination of Mars and Venus at the 1933 founding of COMEX, one must also be cognizant that at the 1988 first trade date for Copper futures, Mars was at minus 14-degrees of declination and Venus was at minus 13-degrees of declination. A first trade date where the declinations of these two planets are parallel (within a degree of each other) is more than just a little intriguing. On July 29, 1988 Moon had just finished its declination minimum. Moreover, at the 1933 COMEX founding, these same declination levels were noted. The choice of July 29, 1988 as a first trade date for Copper futures was no accident.

For 2025:
- ☼ **Mars will be at its 1988 natal declination level August 24 to September 7**
- ☼ **Venus will be at its 1988 natal declination point April 12 to 18, June 22 to 30, and November 23 to 28.**
- ☼ **Venus will be at plus 13.5-degrees declination February 28 to March 6, August 5 to 12, and October 11 to 16**
- ☼ **Mars will be at minus 13.5-degrees declination August 15 to September 2**
- ☼ **Moon will be at declination minimum: Moon will be at minimum declination: January 27, February 23, March 22, April 19, May 16, May 25, June 12, July 9, August 6, September 2, September 29, October 27, November 23, and December 20.**

Mercury Retrograde

Back testing has shown a strong correlation between Mercury retrograde events and swing pivot points on Copper futures price charts. This was again observed in 2024 when Copper futures embarked on a sizeable rally just as retrograde was ending in early April. At the retrograde event in August, Copper price recorded a swing low.

For 2025, Mercury will be:
- ☼ **retrograde from March 15 to April 6**
- ☼ **retrograde from July 18 to August 10**
- ☼ **retrograde from November 9 to November 28.**

Venus Retrograde

For a reason yet to be determined, Venus retrograde events do not seem to impact Copper price trends.

Mars Retrograde

However, Mars retrograde events should be given attention. A look back at several years of Copper price action shows that Mars retrograde events have a good alignment to short, sharp price swings.

☼ **For 2025, Mars will be retrograde January 1 through February 23**

Platinum

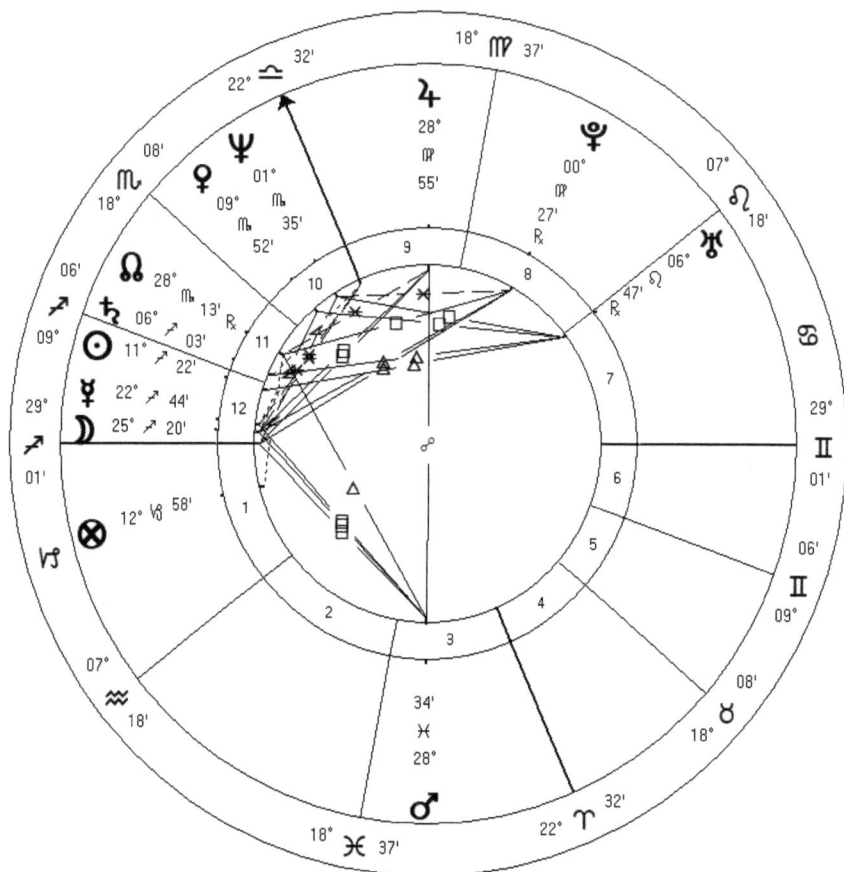

Figure 7-6
Platinum First Trade Horoscope

Platinum futures started trading on COMEX in New York on December 3, 1956. Assuming an 8:30 a.m. first-trade transaction, note the triangle pattern that emerges with apex points Mars, Jupiter, and Moon. Moon is conjunct to the Ascendant, Mars is 180-degrees opposite to the 1933 COMEX natal Mars location, and Jupiter at 28 Virgo is conjunct to the 1933 COMEX natal Mars location. Clearly, the choice of December 3 in 1956 was not a random selection.

In addition to transits past the 1933 COMEX natal horoscope points, consider the following 2025 transits past the 1956 natal Platinum points:

Natal Sun Transits (11 Sagittarius)
✧ Mars will pass the 1956 natal Sun November 14 to 23
✧ Sun passes the natal Sun November 28 to December 6
✧ Venus will pass the 1956 natal Sun December 6 to 13

Natal Mars Transits (28 Pisces)
✧ Venus will pass the 1956 Mars January 29 to February 6
✧ Sun will pass the 1956 Mars point March 13 to 22
✧ Venus will pass the 1956 Mars April 13 to May 4

Natal Jupiter Transits (28 Virgo)
✧ Mars will pass natal Jupiter July 29 to August 10
✧ Sun will pass natal Jupiter September 16 to 24

Natal Mid-Heaven Transits (22 Libra)
✧ Mars passes natal Mid-Heaven September 6 to 14
✧ Sun will pass the natal Mid-Heaven October 11 to 19
✧ Venus will pass the natal Mid-Heaven October 28 to November 3

Natal Ascendant/natal Moon Transits (25-29 Sagittarius)
✧ Mars will pass this natal point December 4 to 19
✧ Sun will pass this natal point December 12 to 23
✧ Venus will pass this natal point December 17 to 25.

Moon Transits

Using the geocentric Moon data in Appendix A, take note of the dates when Moon transits past the key points mentioned for Platinum futures and for COMEX. Watch for increased volatility and possibly even short-term trend changes on these dates.

Declination

At the 1956 first trade date, Mars was at plus 14-degrees declination. This is the contra-parallel value to the declination of Mars at the 1933 COMEX start date. In 1956, Venus was at plus 4-degrees declination at the Platinum first trade date. Moon was at its declination minimum.

> **For 2025:**
> ✿ **Mars will be at 14-degrees declination May 31 to June 16**
> ✿ **Venus will be at 4-degrees declination February 6 to 10, March 31 to April 10, May 17 to 28, and October 3 to 10**
> ✿ **Venus will be at the COMEX natal declination of plus 13.5- degrees February 28 to March 6, August 5 to 12, and October 11 to 16**
> ✿ **Mars will be at the COMEX natal declination of minus 13.5-degrees August 15-September 2**
> ✿ **Moon will be at declination minimum: January 27, February 23, March 22, April 19, May 16, May 25, June 12, July 9, August 6, September 2, September 29, October 27, November 23, and December 20.**

Mercury Retrograde

Back testing has shown a strong correlation between Mercury retrograde events and swing pivot points on Platinum futures price charts. This was again observed in 2024 when Platinum futures embarked on a sizeable rally just as retrograde was ending in early April. At the retrograde event in August, Platinum price recorded a swing low.

For 2025, Mercury will be:
☼ **retrograde from March 15 to April 6**
☼ **retrograde from July 18 to August 10**
☼ **retrograde from November 9 to November 28.**

Venus Retrograde

Another valuable tool for Platinum traders to consider is Venus retrograde events. Watch for technical chart trend indicators to suggest a short-term trend change at a Venus retrograde event. The Venus retrograde event in August 2023 gave way to a $100 per ounce rally in Platinum prices.

☼ **For 2025, Venus will be retrograde March 2 through April 12.**

Mars Retrograde

Mars retrograde events should also be given attention. The end of a Mars retrograde event in early 2023 gave rise to a $200 per ounce drawdown in Platinum price.

☼ **For 2025, Mars will be retrograde January 1 to February 23.**

Palladium

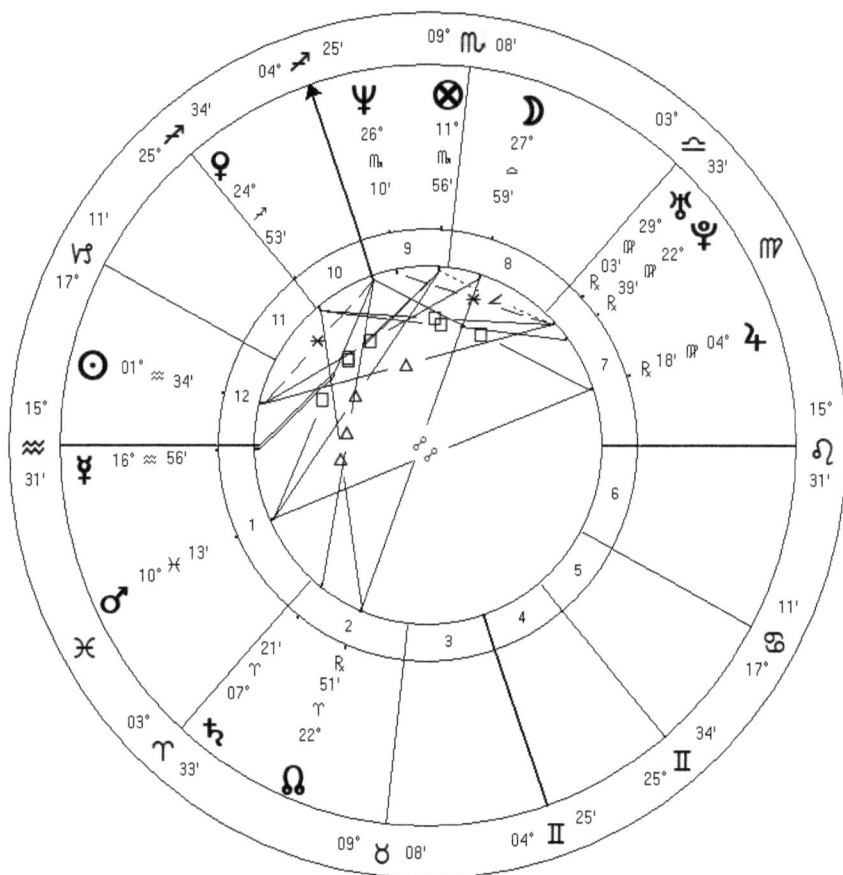

Figure 7-7
Palladium First Trade Horoscope

Palladium futures started trading in New York on January 22, 1968.

Assuming an 8:00 a.m. first trade time, notice the triangle pattern that emerges with corner points Jupiter, Mars, and Mid-Heaven. Jupiter, Pluto, and Uranus in the sign of Virgo all pay homage to the goddess Isis.

In addition to transits past the 1933 COMEX natal horoscope points, consider the following 2025 transits past the 1968 Palladium natal points:

Natal Sun Transits (1 Aquarius)
✪ Sun will pass the 1968 natal Sun January 16 to 25
✪ Natal Mars Transits (10 Pisces)
✪ Venus will pass natal Mars January 9 to 17
✪ Sun will pass natal Mars February 24 to March 4

Natal Jupiter Transits (4 Virgo)
✪ Mars will pass natal Jupiter point June 17 to 30
✪ Sun will pass natal Jupiter point August 21 to 31

Natal Mid-Heaven Transits (4 Sagittarius)
✪ Mars will pass natal Mid-Heaven November 5 to 14
✪ Sun will pass natal Mid-Heaven November 21 to 30
✪ Venus will pass the natal Mid-Heaven December 1 to 6
✪ Natal Ascendant Transits (15 Aquarius)
✪ Sun will pass the natal Ascendant January 29 to February 7

Natal Moon Transits (27 Libra)
✪ Mars passes natal Moon September 13 to 22
✪ Sun will pass natal Moon October 16 to 24
✪ Venus passes natal Moon November 1 to 8

Natal Venus Transits (24 Sagittarius)
✪ Mars will pass natal Venus December 1 to 11
✪ Sun will pass natal Venus December 11 to 19
✪ Venus will pass natal Venus December 17 to 22.

Moon Transits

Using the geocentric Moon data in Appendix A, take note of the dates when Moon transits past the key points mentioned for Palladium futures and for COMEX. Watch for increased volatility and possibly even short-term trend changes on these dates.

Declination

On January 22, 1968, Venus was at minus 9-degrees declination and Mars was at plus 1-degree of declination. Moon had just passed the zero degree declination point.

For 2025:
- ☼ **Mars will be at plus 1-degree declination June 3 to 19**
- ☼ **Venus will be at minus 9-degrees declination April 6 to 12, June 30 to July 5, and November 16 to 20**
- ☼ **Venus will be at the COMEX natal declination of plus 13.5-degrees February 28 to March 6, August 5 to 12, and October 11 to 16**
- ☼ **Mars will be at the COMEX natal declination of minus 13.5-degrees August 15 to September 2.**
- ☼ **Moon will be at zero degrees of declination: January 6 and 19, February 2 and 15, March 1, 15, and 29, April 11 and 25, May 8 and 22, June 5 and 19, July 2, 16, and 29, August 12 and 25, September 8 and 22, October 6 and 19, November 3, 15, and 30, and December 13 and 27.**

Mercury Retrograde

Back testing has shown a strong correlation between Mercury retrograde events and swing pivot points on Palladium futures price charts.

For 2025, Mercury will be:
- ☼ **retrograde from March 15 to April 6**
- ☼ **retrograde from July 18 to August 10**
- ☼ **retrograde from November 9 to November 28.**

Venus Retrograde

Venus retrograde events on the Palladium price chart sometimes align to price inflection points, but not consistently. Nevertheless, one should watch for technical chart trend indicators to suggest a short-term trend change at a Venus retrograde event.

- ☼ **For 2025, Venus will be retrograde March 2 to April 12.**

Mars Retrograde

Mars retrograde events on the Palladium price chart sometimes align to price trend reversals, but not consistently.

- ☼ **For 2025, Mars will be retrograde January 1 through February 23.**

Chicago Mercantile Exchange

The Chicago Mercantile Exchange traces its roots to January 5, 1898 when the Chicago Butter and Egg Board was founded. On December 1, 1919 the Board changed its name to the Chicago Mercantile Exchange when it received its clearing-house license.

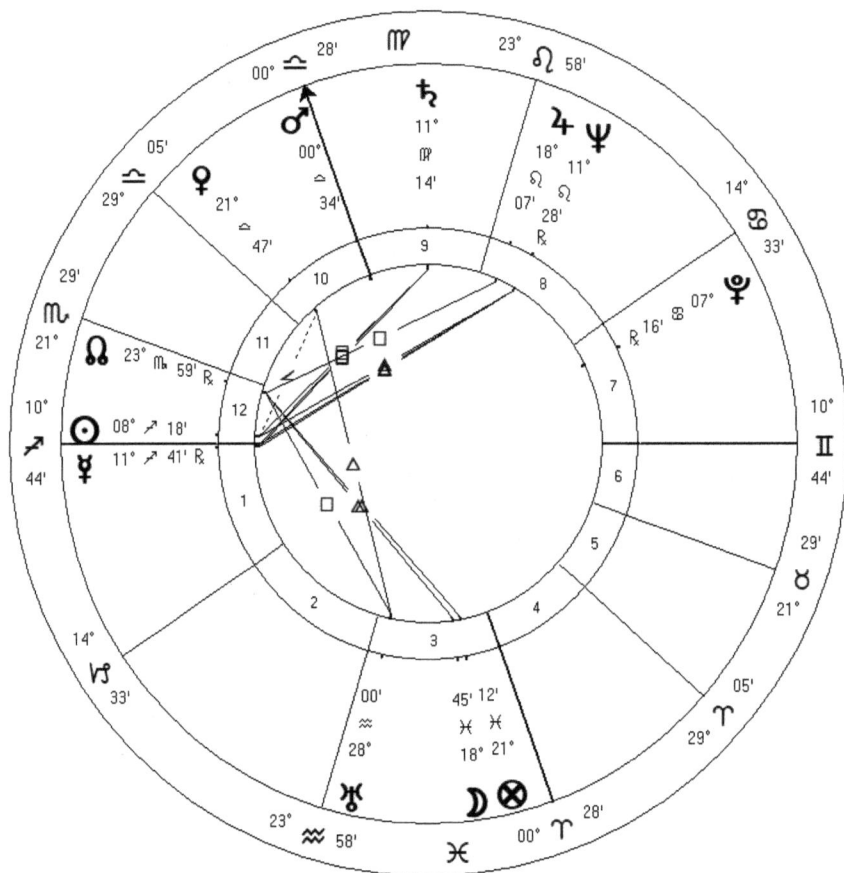

Figure 7-8
1919 Chicago Mercantile Exchange Founding

The horoscope wheel in Figure 7-8 shows the planetary positions at the December 1919 date. Assuming a 7:15 a.m. first trade time, Sun and Mercury are at the Ascendant and Mars is at the Mid-Heaven. The choice of this date was not a random occurrence.

The array of contracts trading on the Chicago Mercantile Exchange eventually grew to include Currencies, Meats, and Lumber. Today, the Mercantile Exchange is part of the holdings of the CME Group. Currency, Cattle, and Hogs, all trade on this exchange..

For 2025, the following transit dates of key points in the 1919 Chicago Mercantile Exchange horoscope should be watched:

Natal Sun/Ascendant Transits (8-10 Sagittarius)
✧ Mars will pass this natal point November 11 to 22
✧ Sun will pass this natal point November 26 to December 4
✧ Venus will pass this natal point December 4 to 11

Natal Jupiter Transits (18 Leo)
✧ Mars will pass natal Jupiter May 21 to June 3
✧ Sun will pass natal Jupiter August 6 to 14

Natal Saturn Transits (11 Virgo)
✧ Mars will pass the 1919 natal Saturn July 1 to 11
✧ Sun passes the 1919 natal Saturn August 30 to September 6

Natal Mid-Heaven/Natal Mars Transits (0 Libra)
✧ Mars will pass this 1919 natal point August 1 to 12
✧ Sun will pass this 1919 natal point September 18 to 26
✧ Venus will pass this 1919 natal point October 11 to 16

Natal Moon Transits (18 Pisces)
✧ Venus will pass the 1919 natal Moon January 17 to 24
✧ Sun passes the 1919 natal Moon March 4 to 12.

Declination

On December 1, 1919 at the start of the Chicago Mercantile Exchange, Mars was at plus 14-degrees of declination and Venus was at plus 23-degrees of declination. Moon was at zero degrees declination.

For 2025,
- ☼ **Mars will be at plus 14-degrees of declination March 17 to February 14**
- ☼ **Venus will be at plus 23-degrees of declination from January 11 to February 14 and again from August 24 to September 27**
- ☼ **Moon will be at zero degrees declination: January 6 and 19, February 2 and 15, March 1, 15, and 29, April 11 and 25, May 8 and 22, June 5 and 19, July 2, 16, and 29, August 12 and 25, September 8 and 22, October 6 and 19, November 3, 15, and 30, and December 13 and 27.**

Canadian Dollar and British Pound

These two currency futures started trading on May 16th, 1972 on the Chicago Mercantile Exchange. The horoscope in Figure 7-9 illustrates planetary placements at this date. Assuming an 8:00 a.m. trade start time, Venus and Mars are at the Ascendant point and are 90-degrees square to the Chicago Mercantile 1919 natal Mars point. Moreover, Sun, Node, and Pluto form a triangular pattern. The selection of May 16, 1972 as a first trade date was not just a random selection.

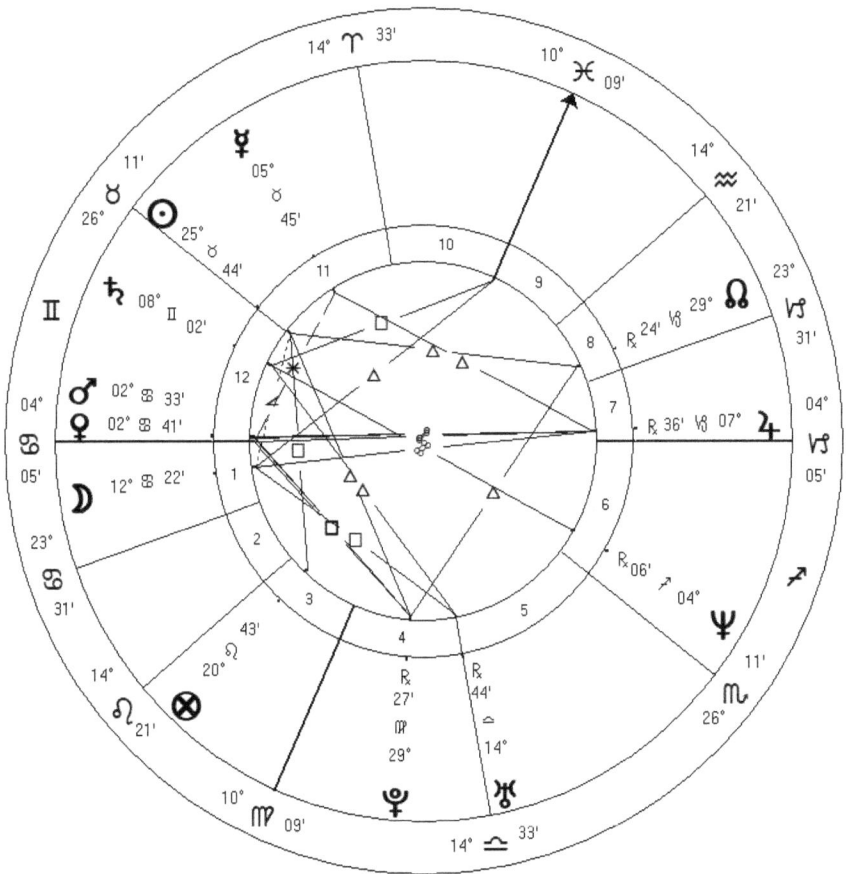

Figure 7-9
British Pound, and Canadian Dollar First Trade Horoscope

In addition to the transit dates past the Chicago Mercantile 1919 natal planetary locations, transits of the 1972 natal locations must be watched also.

For 2025:

Natal Node Transits (24 Capricorn)
☼ Sun passes the natal Node position January 15 to 24

Natal Sun Transits (25 Taurus)
☼ Sun will pass the 1972 natal Sun May 11 to 20

Natal Ascendant/Mars/Venus Transits (2-4 Cancer)
☼ Jupiter will pass this 1972 natal point June 6 to July 6
☼ Sun will pass this 1972 natal point June 19 to June 29

Natal Jupiter Transits (7 Capricorn)
☼ Mars will pass natal Jupiter December 20 to 28
☼ Sun will pass natal Jupiter December 24 to 31
☼ Venus will pass natal Jupiter December 27 to 31

Mid-Heaven Transits (10 Pisces)
☼ Venus will pass the 1972 Mid-Heaven January 9 to 17
☼ Sun will pass the 1972 Mid-Heaven February 24 to March 4

Natal Moon Transits (12 Cancer)
☼ Sun will pass natal Moon June 28 to July 7
☼ Jupiter will pass natal Moon July 27 to August 12
☼ Venus will pass natal Moon August 8 to 13

Natal Pluto Transits
☼ Mars passes natal Pluto August 1 to 11
☼ Sun passes natal Pluto September 17 to 25
☼ Venus passes natal Pluto October 10 to 16.

Moon Transits

Using the geocentric Moon data in Appendix A, take note of the dates when Moon transits past the key points mentioned for the Chicago Mercantile Exchange and for the Canadian Dollar/British Pound futures. Watch for increased volatility and possibly even short-term trend changes on these dates.

Declination

In addition to the natal declination of Mars and Venus at the 1919 start date of the Chicago Mercantile, one must also be cognizant that at the 1972 first trade date for these currencies, Mars was at plus 22-degrees declination, and Venus was at minus 11-degrees declination. Moon was at its declination maxima.

For 2025:
- ☿ **Mars will be at plus 22 degrees declination January 1 to February 5**
- ☿ **Venus will be at minus 11 degrees declination April 9 to 14, June 26 to July 2, and November 21 to 25**
- ☿ **Moon will be at maximum declination: January 12, February 9, March 8, April 4, May 1, May 29, June 25, July 22, August 19, September 15, October 12, November 9, and December 6.**

Mercury Retrograde

Currency traders should pay close attention to Mercury retrograde events as they show a good alignment to trend changes on the British pound, and Canadian dollar.

For 2025, Mercury will be:
- ☼ **retrograde from March 15 to April 6**
- ☼ **retrograde from July 18 to August 10**
- ☼ **retrograde from November 9 to November 28.**

Venus Retrograde

Venus retrograde events on the Canadian Dollar and British Pound price charts tend to align with sharp pivot swings. These retrograde events should be anticipated by currency traders.

- ☼ **For 2025, Venus will be retrograde March 2 to April 12.**

Mars Retrograde

Mars retrograde events on the Canadian Dollar and British Pound price charts also tend to align with sharp pivot swings. Currency traders should anticipate these events.

- ☼ **For 2025, Mars will be retrograde January 1 to February 23.**

Euro Currency

The Euro became the official currency for the European Union on January 1, 2002 when Euro bank notes became freely and widely circulated. However, futures contracts started trading on the Chicago Mercantile Exchange on January 4, 1999. The horoscope wheel in Figure 7-10 shows planetary placements at this date, assuming a 7:30 a.m. first trade time.

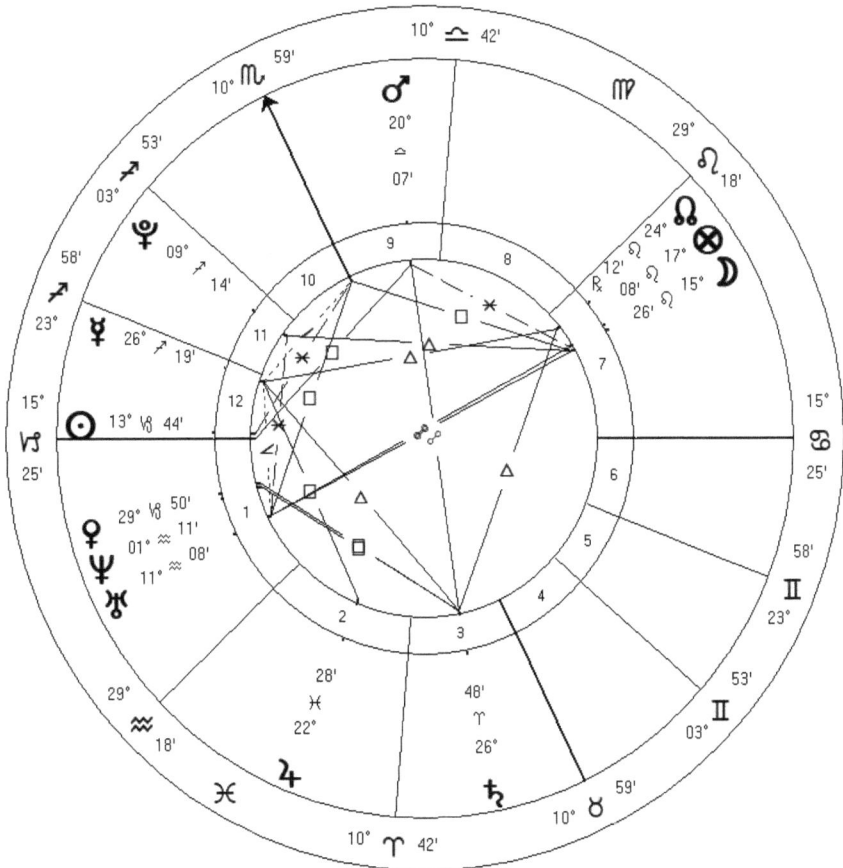

Figure 7-10
Euro Currency First Trade Horoscope

It is more than just a little curious that the 1919 Chicago Mercantile natal Jupiter is conjunct the 1999 Euro currency futures natal Moon. The 1919 Chicago Mercantile natal Moon is conjunct the 1999 Euro currency futures natal Jupiter. The 1919 Chicago Mercantile natal Venus is conjunct the 1999 Euro currency futures natal Mars. In addition, Node, Mercury, and Saturn trace out a triangular shape within the horoscope wheel. The choice of January 4, 1999 as a first trade date for this futures contract was not a random selection.

In addition to the transit dates past the Chicago Mercantile 1919 natal planetary locations, transits of the 1999 Euro natal locations must also be watched.

For 2025:

Natal Sun/Ascendant Transits (13-15 Capricorn)
- ✪ Sun will pass this 1999 natal point January 1 to 7
- ✪ Mars will pass this 1999 natal point December 27 to 31

Natal Jupiter Transits (22 Pisces)
- ✪ Venus will pass the 1999 natal Jupiter January 22 to 28
- ✪ Saturn will pass the 1999 natal Jupiter February 8 to April 8
- ✪ Sun will pass the 1999 natal Jupiter March 8 to 16

Natal Saturn Transits (26 Aries)
- ✪ Sun will pass the 1999 natal Saturn point April 12 to 20
- ✪ Venus passes the 1999 natal Saturn point May 30 to June 5

Mid-Heaven Transits (10 Scorpio)
- ✪ Mars will pass the 1999 Mid-Heaven October 1 to 12
- ✪ Sun will pass the 1999 Mid-Heaven October 29 to Nov 6
- ✪ Venus will pass the 1999 Mid-Heaven November 11 to 18

Natal Moon Transits (15 Leo)
- ✿ Mars will pass the 1999 natal Moon May 12 to 28
- ✿ Sun will pass the 1999 natal Moon August 3 to 11

Natal Mars Transits (20 Libra)
- ✿ Mars will pass the 1999 natal Mars point September 1 to 14

Natal Node Transits (24 Leo)
- ✿ Mars will pass the natal Node point June 2 to 12
- ✿ Sun will pass the natal Node point August 12 to 21

Natal Mercury (26 Sagittarius)
- ✿ Mars will pass natal Mercury December 6 to 14
- ✿ Sun will pass natal Mercury December 14 to 21
- ✿ Venus will pass natal Venus December 19 to 24.

Moon Transits

Using the geocentric Moon data in Appendix A, take note of the dates when Moon transits past the key points mentioned for the Chicago Mercantile Exchange and for the Euro currency futures. Watch for increased volatility and possibly even short-term trend changes on these dates.

Declination

In addition to the natal declination of Mars and Venus at the 1919 start date of the Chicago Mercantile, one must also be cognizant that at the 1999 first trade date for these currencies, Mars was at plus 7-degrees declination, and Venus was at minus 17-degrees declination. Moon was at its declination maxima.

For 2025:

☼ **Mars will be at plus 7-degrees declination April 28 to May 14**

☼ **Venus will be at minus 17 degrees declination April 20 to 24, June 15 to 22, and December 1 to 6**

☼ **Venus will be at the Chicago Mercantile 1919 natal declination of plus 23 degrees January 11 to February 14, and August 24 to September 27**

☼ **Mars will be at the Chicago Mercantile 1919 natal declination of plus 14-degrees March 17 to February 14**

☼ **Moon will be at maximum declination: January 12, February 9, March 8, April 4, May 1, May 29, June 25, July 22, August 19, September 15, October 12, November 9, and December 6.**

Mercury Retrograde

Currency traders should pay close attention to Mercury retrograde events as they show a very good alignment to trend changes on the Euro currency futures.

For 2025, Mercury will be:

☼ **retrograde from March 15 to April 6**

☼ **retrograde from July 18 to August 10**

☼ **retrograde from November 9 to November 28.**

Venus Retrograde

Venus retrograde events on the Euro currency futures price chart tend to align with significant trend changes. These retrograde events should be anticipated by currency traders.

☼ **For 2025, Venus will be retrograde March 2 to April 12.**

Mars Retrograde

Mars retrograde events on the Euro currency futures price chart also tend to align with trend changes, although not as consistently as Mercury and Venus retrograde events. Currency traders should nevertheless anticipate these events.

☼ **For 2025, Mars will be retrograde January 1 to February 23.**

Australian Dollar

Australian dollar futures started trading on the Chicago Mercantile Exchange on January 13, 1987. Assuming a first trade time of 8:55 a.m., the planetary positions show the Mid-Heaven point identical to the Chicago Mercantile 1919 natal Ascendant point.

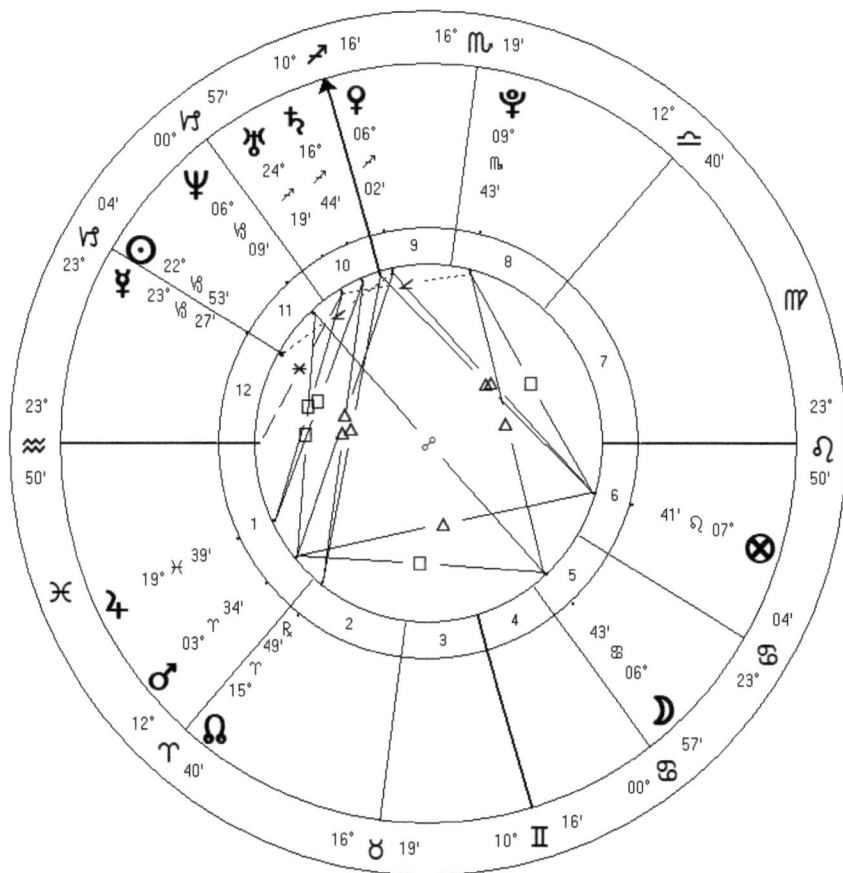

Figure 7-11
Australian Dollar First Trade Horoscope

In addition to the transit dates past the Chicago Mercantile 1919 natal planetary locations, transits of the 1987 Australian Dollar natal locations must be watched also.

For 2025:

Natal Sun Transits (22 Capricorn)
☼ Sun will pass the natal Sun point January 8 to 16

Natal Ascendant Transits (23 Aquarius)
☼ Sun will pass the natal Ascendant point February 7 to 15

Natal Mars Transits (3 Aries)
☼ Venus will pass natal Mars February 3 to 15
☼ Sun will pass natal Mars March 19 to 27

Natal Jupiter Transits (19 Pisces)
☼ Venus will pass natal Jupiter January 19 to 24
☼ Saturn will pass natal Jupiter January 28 to March 14
☼ Sun will pass natal Jupiter March 5 to 13

Mid-Heaven Transits (10 Sagittarius)
☼ Mars will pass the natal Mid-Heaven November 13-24
☼ Sun will pass the natal Mid-Heaven Nov 28 to December 6

Natal Moon Transits (6 Cancer)
☼ Sun will pass the natal Moon June 23 to July 1
☼ Jupiter will pass the natal Moon July 1 to 21
☼ Venus will pass the natal Moon August 2 to 8.

Moon Transits

Using the geocentric Moon data in Appendix A, take note of the dates when Moon transits past the key points mentioned for the Chicago Mercantile Exchange and for the Australian Dollar futures. Watch for increased volatility and possibly even short-term trend changes on these dates.

Declination

In addition to the natal declination of Mars and Venus at the 1919 start date of the Chicago Mercantile, one must also be cognizant that at the 1987 first trade date for this currency futures contract, Mars was at plus 15 degrees declination, and Venus was at plus 12-degrees declination. Moon was at its declination maxima.

For 2025:
- ☼ **Mars will be at plus 15-degrees declination March 9 to 28**
- ☼ **Venus will be at plus 12-degrees declination March 3 to 10, August 3-9, and October 14-19**
- ☼ **Moon will be at maximum declination: January 12, February 9, March 8, April 4, May 1, May 29, June 25, July 22, August 19, September 15, October 12, November 9, and December 6**
- ☼ **Venus will be at the Chicago Mercantile 1919 natal declination of plus 23-degrees January 11 to February 14, and August 24 to September 27**
- ☼ **Mars will be at the Chicago Mercantile 1919 natal declination of plus 14-degrees March 17 to February 14.**

Mercury Retrograde

Currency traders should pay close attention to Mercury retrograde events as they can bear a good alignment to trend changes on the Australian Dollar.

For 2025, Mercury will be:
- ☼ **retrograde from March 15 to April 6**
- ☼ **retrograde from July 18 to August 10**
- ☼ **retrograde from November 9 to November 28.**

Venus Retrograde

Venus retrograde events on the Australian Dollar futures price chart occasionally align with significant trend changes. It might be worthwhile for currency traders to watch for these retrograde events.

☼ **For 2025, Venus will be retrograde March 2 to April 12.**

Mars Retrograde

Mars retrograde events on the Australian Dollar futures price chart also tend to align with trend changes, although not as consistently as Mercury retrograde events. Currency traders should nevertheless anticipate these events.

☼ **For 2025, Mars will be retrograde January 1 to February 23.**

Feeder Cattle

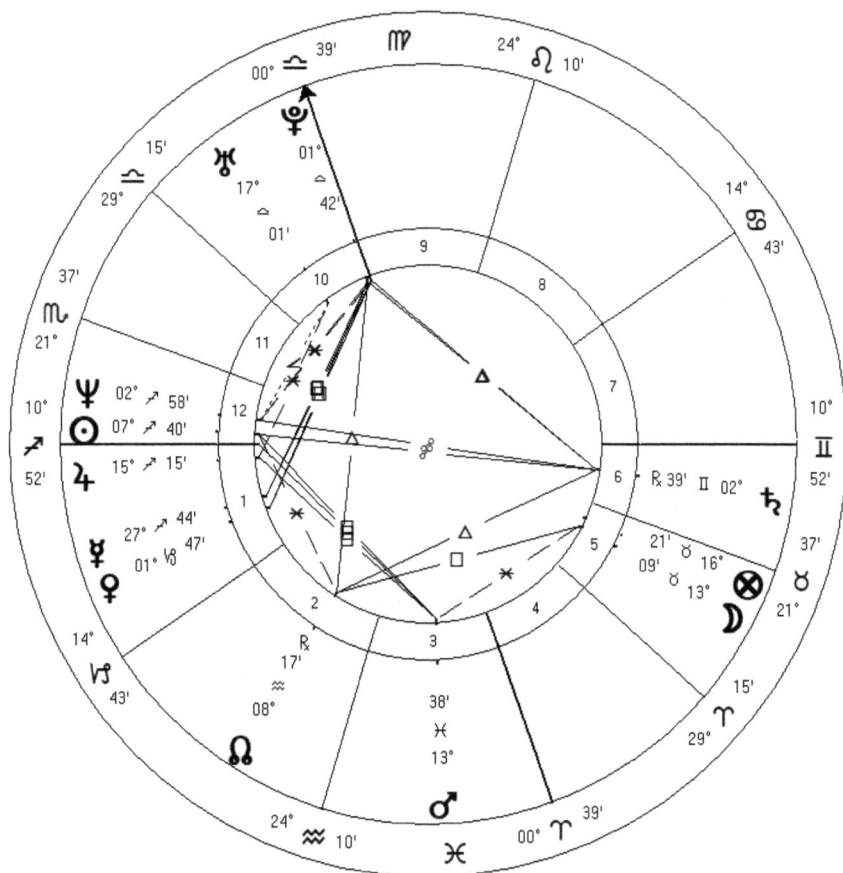

Figure 7-12
Feeder Cattle First Trade Horoscope

Feeder Cattle futures started trading on the Chicago Mercantile Exchange on November 30, 1971. The horoscope in Figure 7-12 shows planetary placements at the first trade date.

Assuming a first-transaction time of 7:18 a.m., the Ascendant is at 10 Sagittarius, the same location as the Ascendant in the 1919 Chicago Mercantile natal chart. Sun is situated at the Ascendant. Note also how Node, Saturn, and Mid-Heaven trace out a triangle pattern in the horoscope wheel. The choice of this first trade date was carefully thought out. It was not a random selection.

In addition to the planetary transits of key points in the 1919 Chicago Mercantile natal horoscope, one must watch transits past key points in the 1971 Feeder Cattle natal horoscope.

For 2025:

Natal Node Transits (8 Aquarius)
☼ Sun passes the natal Node January 23 to 31

Natal Mars Transits (13 Pisces)
☼ Venus will pass the natal Mars point January 13 to 19
☼ Sun will pass the natal Mars point February 27 to March 6

Natal Saturn Transits (2 Gemini)
☼ Sun passes natal Saturn May 17 to 26
☼ Venus passes natal Saturn July 2 to 9

Natal Moon Transits (13 Taurus)
☼ Sun will pass the natal Moon point April 29 to May 7

Mid-Heaven Transits (0 Libra)
☼ Mars will pass the natal Mid-Heaven August 1 to 12
☼ Sun will pass the natal Mid-Heaven September 18 to 27
☼ Venus will pass the natal Mid-Heaven October 11 to 17

Natal Ascendant/Natal Sun Transits (7-10 Sagittarius)
☼ Mars will pass this natal point November 8 to 23
☼ Sun will pass this natal point November 25 to December 6
☼ Venus will pass this natal point December 4 to 11.

Moon Transits

Using the geocentric Moon data in Appendix A, take note of the dates when Moon transits past the key points mentioned for the Chicago Mercantile Exchange and for Feeder Cattle futures. Watch for increased volatility and possibly even short-term trend changes on these dates.

Declination

At the first trade date for Feeder Cattle futures, Venus was at minus 21-degrees declination. Mars was at plus 9-degrees declination.

For 2025:
- ☼ **Venus will be at minus 21-degrees declination April 29 to May 10, June 3 to 11, and December 10 to 21**
- ☼ **Mars will be plus 9-degrees declination April 21 to May 3**
- ☼ **Venus will be at the Chicago Mercantile 1919 natal declination of plus 23-degrees January 11 to February 14, and August 24 to September 27**
- ☼ **Mars will be at the Chicago Mercantile 1919 natal declination of plus-14 degrees March 17 to February 14.**

Mercury Retrograde

Futures and options traders should pay attention to Mercury retrograde events as they often align to tradeable price moves on Feeder Cattle futures.

For 2025, Mercury will be:
- ☼ **retrograde from March 15 to April 6**
- ☼ **retrograde from July 18 to August 10**
- ☼ **retrograde from November 9 to November 28.**

Venus Retrograde

Looking at past price data of Feeder Cattle futures going back many years, I would say that Venus retrograde events tend to have a better correlation than Mercury retrograde events to significant trend changes. It is definitely worthwhile for futures and options traders to watch for these retrograde events.

☼ **For 2025, Venus will be retrograde March 2 to April 12.**

Mars Retrograde

Mars retrograde events definitely align with trend changes on Feeder Cattle futures prices. Futures and options traders must anticipate these retrograde events.

☼ **For 2025, Mars will be retrograde January 1 to February 23.**

Live Cattle

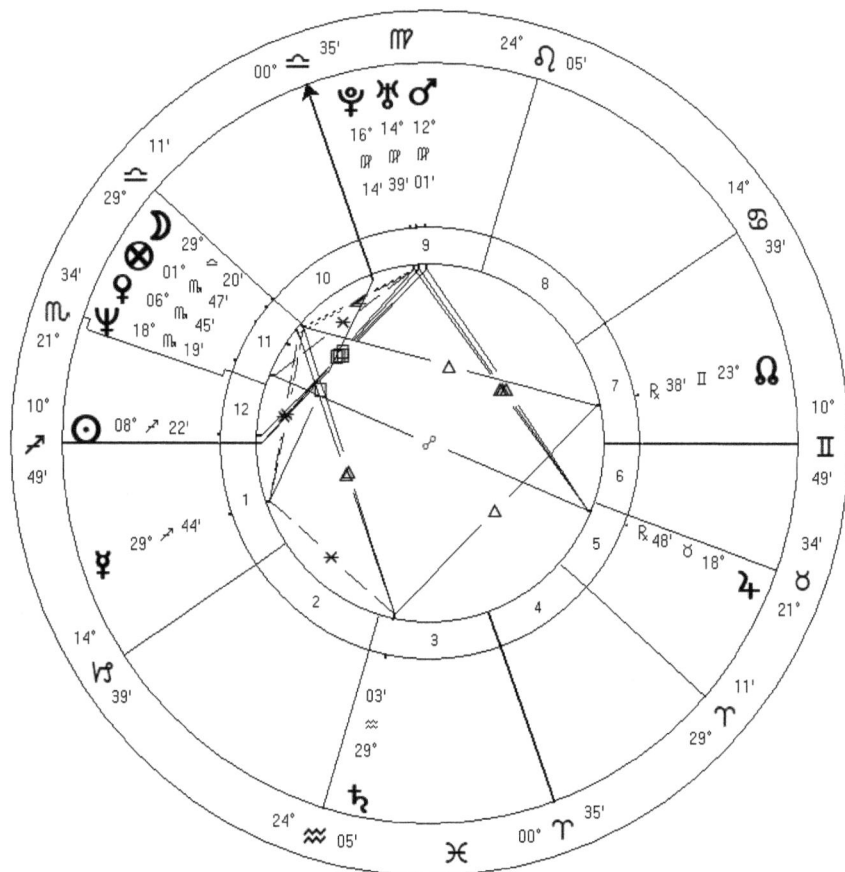

Figure 7-13
Live Cattle futures First Trade Horoscope

Live Cattle futures started trading on the Chicago Mercantile Exchange on November 30, 1964. The horoscope in Figure 7-13 shows planetary placements at the first trade date.

Assuming a first-transaction time of 7:15 a.m., the Ascendant is at 10 Sagittarius – the same as it was in the 1919 Chicago Mercantile natal horoscope. The Mid-Heaven at 0 Libra is the same as the Mid-Heaven point in the Feeder Cattle first trade horoscope. Note also how Node, Saturn, and Moon trace out a triangle pattern in the horoscope wheel. The selection of this date in late November 1964 was not an accident.

In addition to the transits past key points in the 1919 Chicago Mercantile natal horoscope, one must watch transits past key points in the 1971 Live Cattle natal horoscope.

For 2025:

Natal Saturn Transits (29 Aquarius)
✿ Venus will pass natal Saturn January 1 to 6
✿ Sun will pass natal Saturn February 13 to 21

Natal Node Transits (23 Gemini)
✿ Jupiter will pass natal Node May 1 to 18
✿ Sun will pass natal Node June 9 to 18

Natal Jupiter Transits (18 Taurus)
✿ Sun will pass natal Jupiter May 4 to 12
✿ Venus will pass natal Jupiter June 20 to 27

Natal Mars Transits (12 Virgo)
✿ Mars will pass the natal Mars point July 3 to 13
✿ Sun will pass the natal Mars point September 1 to 7

Mid-Heaven Transits (0 Libra)
✿ Mars will pass the natal Mid-Heaven August 1 to 13
✿ Sun will pass the natal Mid-Heaven September 18 to 27
✿ Venus will pass the natal Mid-Heaven October 11 to 17

Natal Moon Transits (29 Libra)

☼ Mars will pass this natal point September 16 to 27

☼ Sun will pass this natal point October 18 to 26

Natal Ascendant / Natal Sun Transits (8-10 Sagittarius)

☼ Mars will pass this natal point November 11 to 22

☼ Sun will pass this natal point November 26 to December 4

☼ Venus will pass this natal point December 4 to 10.

Moon Transits

Using the geocentric Moon data in Appendix A, take note of the dates when Moon transits past the key points mentioned for the Chicago Mercantile Exchange and for Live Cattle futures. Watch for increased volatility and possibly even short-term trend changes on these dates.

Declination

At the 1964 first trade date for Live Cattle futures, Venus was at plus 6- degrees declination. Mars was at plus 20- degrees declination.

For 2025:

☼ **Venus will be at 6-degrees declination March 14 to 18, July 24 to 29, and October 25 to 29**

☼ **Mars will be at 20-degrees declination January 28 to February 23**

☼ **Venus will be at the Chicago Mercantile 1919 natal declination of plus 23 degrees January 11 to February 14, and August 24 to September 27**

☼ **Mars will be at the Chicago Mercantile 1919 natal declination of plus 14-degrees March 17 to February 14.**

Mercury Retrograde

Futures and options traders should pay attention to Mercury retrograde events as they often align to tradeable price moves on Live Cattle futures.

For 2025, Mercury will be:
- ☼ **retrograde from March 15 to April 6**
- ☼ **retrograde from July 18 to August 10**
- ☼ **retrograde from November 9 to November 28.**

Venus Retrograde

Looking at past price data of Live Cattle futures going back many years, it is my opinion that Venus retrograde events do align to significant price trend changes, but not consistently so. Nevertheless, it is worthwhile for futures and options traders to watch for these retrograde events.

- ☼ **For 2025, Venus will be retrograde March 2 to April 12.**

Mars Retrograde

Mars retrograde events show a poor alignment with trend changes on Live Cattle futures prices. Futures and options traders who still wish to anticipate these retrograde events should be aware that:

- ☼ **For 2025, Mars will be retrograde January 1 to February 23.**

Lean Hogs

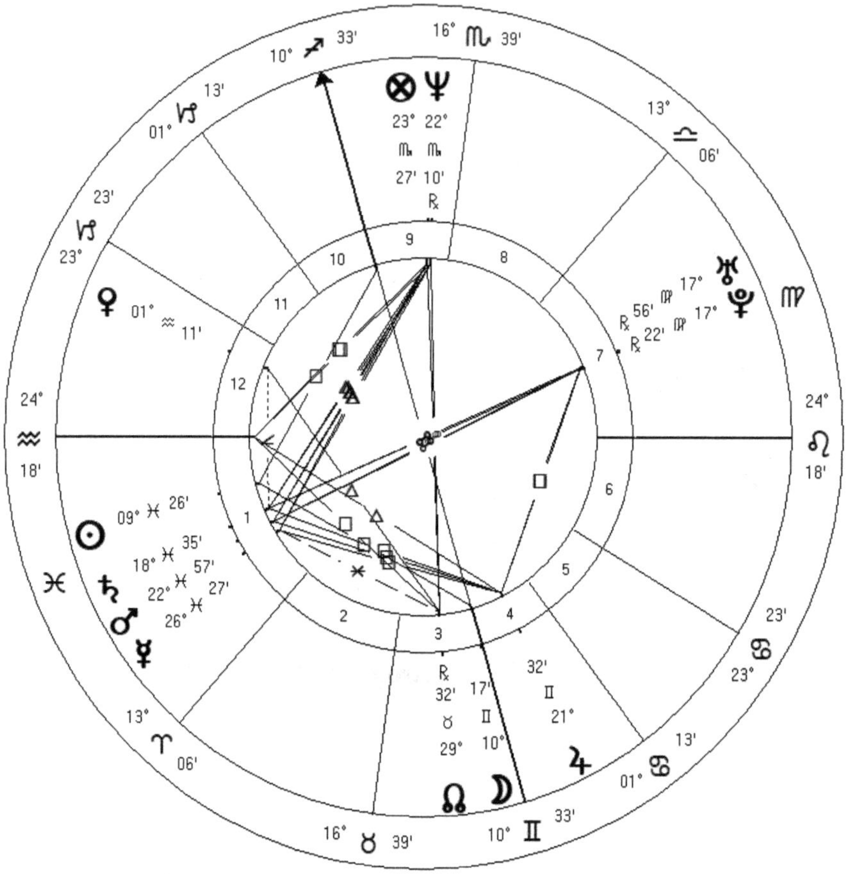

Figure 7-14
Lean Hogs futures First Trade Horoscope

Lean Hog futures started trading on the Chicago Mercantile on February 28, 1966. The horoscope in Figure 7-14 shows planetary placements at the first trade date. Assuming a very early first-trade time of just before 6:00 a.m., the Mid-Heaven is at 10 Sagittarius which is 90-degrees square to the Ascendant point of the 1919 Chicago Mercantile natal horoscope. Pluto, Saturn, and Jupiter can be seen to trace out a triangle

160

pattern in the horoscope wheel. The selection of this first trade date was a deliberate decision, not a random one.

In addition to the transits past key points in the 1919 Chicago Mercantile natal horoscope, one must watch transits past key points in the 1966 Lean Hogs natal horoscope.

For 2025:

Natal Venus Transits (1 Aquarius)
✪ Sun will pass natal Venus January 17 to 24

Natal Ascendant Transits (24 Aquarius)
✪ Sun will pass the natal Ascendant February 8 to 16

Natal Sun Transits (9 Pisces)
✪ Venus will pass the natal Sun point January 9 to 15
✪ Sun will pass the natal Sun point February 23 to March 3

Natal Mars/Saturn Transits (18-22 Pisces)
✪ Venus will pass this natal point January 18 to 29
✪ Saturn will pass this natal point January 27 to February 26
✪ Sun will pass this natal point March 4 to 16

Natal Jupiter Transits (21 Pisces)
✪ Sun will pass natal Jupiter May 4 to 12
✪ Venus will pass natal Jupiter June 20 to 27

Natal Moon Transits (10 Gemini)
✪ Sun will pass the natal Moon point May 27 to June 4
✪ Venus will pass the natal Moon point July 10 to 17

Natal Jupiter Transits (21 Gemini)
○ Jupiter will pass natal Jupiter April 19 to May 10
○ Sun will pass natal Jupiter June 7 to 16
○ Venus will pass natal Jupiter July 20 to 26

Mid-Heaven Transits (10 Sagittarius)
○ Mars will pass the natal Mid-Heaven November 14 to 23
○ Sun passes the natal Mid-Heaven November 28 to December 6
○ Venus will pass the natal Mid-Heaven December 6 to 12.

Moon Transits

Using the geocentric Moon data in Appendix A, take note of the dates when Moon transits past the key points mentioned for the Chicago Mercantile Exchange and for Lean Hogs futures. Watch for increased volatility and possibly even short-term trend changes on these dates.

Declination

At the 1966 first trade date, Venus was at plus 3-degrees declination. Mars was at zero degrees of declination. Moon was very nearly at its maximum declination. Two significant planets practically at the same declination while Moon is nearly at its declination max further suggests this first trade date was not a random selection.

For 2025:
○ **Mars will pass through zero degrees of declination June 6 to 27**
○ **Venus will pass 3-degrees declination March 16 to 23, July 19 to 25, and October 29 to November 3**
○ **Moon will be at maximum declination: January 12, February 9, March 8, April 4, May 1, May 29, June 25, July 22, August 19, September 15, October 12, November 9, and December 6**

- ✡ **Venus will be at the Chicago Mercantile 1919 natal declination of plus 23-degrees January 11 to February 14, and August 24 to September 27**
- ✡ **Mars will be at the Chicago Mercantile 1919 natal declination of plus 14-degrees March 17 to February 14.**

Mercury Retrograde

Futures and options traders should pay attention to Mercury retrograde events as they often align to explosive price moves on Lean Hogs futures.

For 2025, Mercury will be:
- ✡ **retrograde from March 15 to April 6**
- ✡ **retrograde from July 18 to August 10**
- ✡ **retrograde from November 9 to November 28.**

Venus Retrograde

Looking at past price data of Lean Hogs futures going back many years, Venus retrograde events align to significant price trend changes. Futures and options traders definitely must watch for these retrograde events.

- ✡ **For 2025, Venus will be retrograde March 2 to April 12.**

Mars Retrograde

Mars retrograde events show an alignment to significant trend changes on Lean Hogs futures prices, although not a consistent alignment. Futures and options traders who still wish to anticipate these retrograde events should be aware that:

- ✡ **For 2025, Mars will be retrograde January 1 to February 23.**

Chicago Board of Trade

The Chicago Board of Trade started operations on April 3, 1848. Initially the exchange focused on grains futures contracts. However, as time went on, a variety of new contracts were added - including Bond futures. Today, the Chicago Board of Trade is part of the CME Group empire. Bonds, Treasury Notes, Grains, and Oilseed contracts all trade on this exchange.

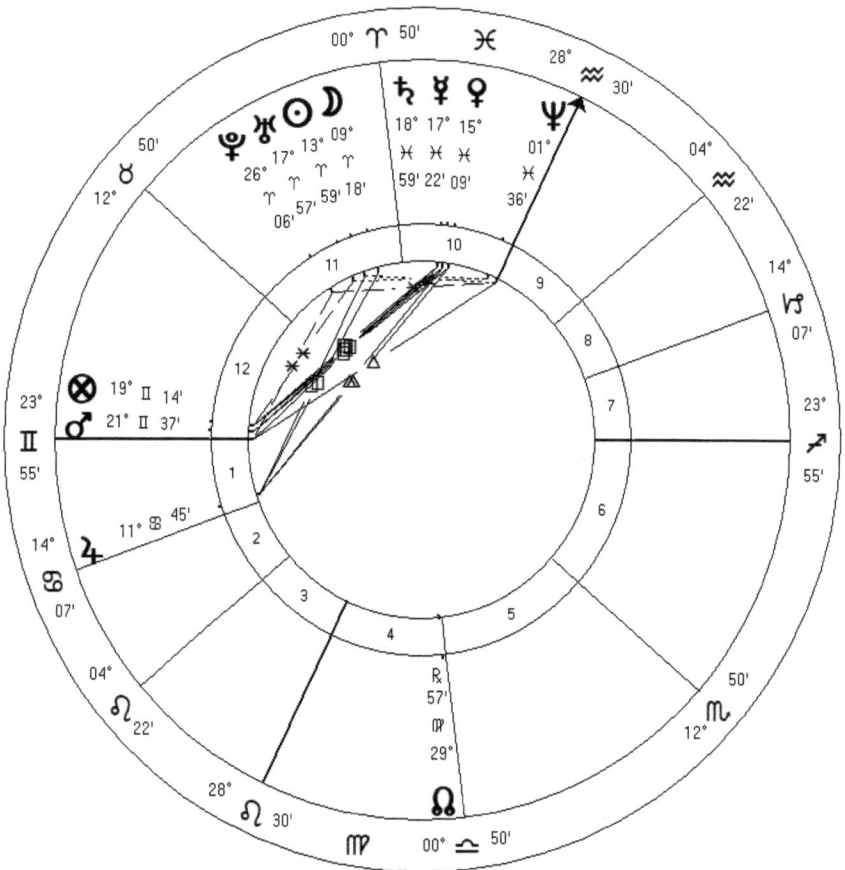

Figure 7-15
First Trade Horoscope for Chicago Board of Trade

The planetary placements at April 3, 1848 are shown in Figure 7-15. Assuming a first-trade time of 9:05 a.m., Sun Mars is positioned exactly at the Ascendant. The Sun is 90-degrees to the 1792 NYSE natal Ascendant.

For 2025, the following are transit dates to watch:

Natal Sun/Natal Moon Transits (9-13 Aries)
- ✿ Venus will pass this 1848 natal point February 13 to March 2
- ✿ Sun will pass this 1848 natal point March 24 to April 5
- ✿ Venus will resume its transit May 9 to 22

Natal Ascendant/Mars Transits (21-23 Gemini)
- ✿ Jupiter will pass this 1848 natal point April 23 to May 20
- ✿ Sun will pass this 1848 natal point June 8 to 18
- ✿ Venus will pass this 1848 natal point July 21 to 28

Natal Jupiter Transits (11 Cancer)
- ✿ Sun will pass natal Jupiter point June 29 to July 7
- ✿ Jupiter will pass natal Jupiter point July 21 to August 12
- ✿ Venus will pass natal Jupiter point August 6 to 13

Mid-Heaven Transits (28 Aquarius)
- ✿ Venus will pass the 1848 Mid-Heaven January 1 to 6
- ✿ Sun will pass the 1848 Mid-Heaven February 12 to 21.

Declination

On April 3, 1848 Mars was at plus 22-degrees of declination and Venus was at minus 22-degrees of declination. This is a contra-parallel setup and very likely explains the choice of April 3 as the launch date for the Exchange.

For 2025:

- ☼ Venus will be at the CBOT 1848 natal declination of plus 22-degrees January 11 to 19, February 8 to 17, August 23 to September 2, and September 20 to 29

- ☼ Mars will be at the CBOT 1848 natal declination of plus 22-degrees January 1 to February 5.

30-Year Bond Futures

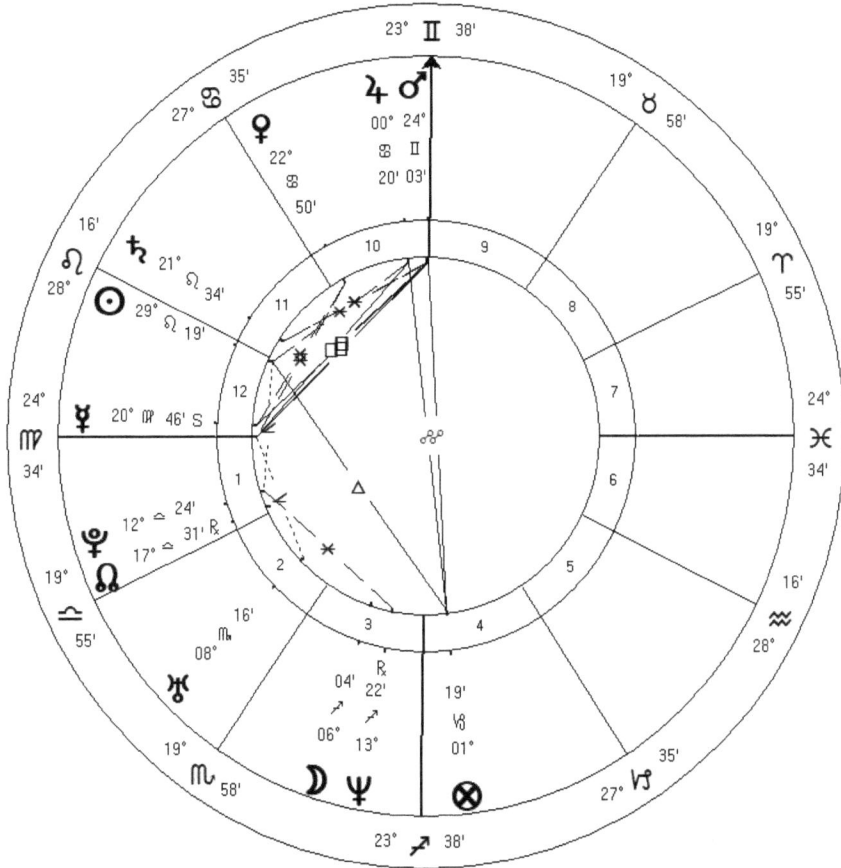

Figure 7-16
First Trade Horoscope for 30-Year Bond futures

30-Year Bond futures started trading on the Chicago Board of Trade on August 22, 1977. Figure 7-16 presents the first trade horoscope for this date. Assuming a first trade time of 8:20 a.m., the Mid-Heaven was at 23 Gemini. This is exactly the position of the Ascendant in the 1848 CBOT natal horoscope. Mercury is positioned right at the Ascendant and is also in the sign of Virgo – an allusion to the goddess Isis. The selection of August 22, 1977 as the start date for this futures contract was not a random selection.

In addition to the transit dates past the CBOT 1848 natal planetary locations, transits of the 1977 first trade natal locations must be watched also

For 2025:

Natal Sun Transits (29 Leo)
- ✿ Mars will pass the 1977 natal Sun point June 9 to 22
- ✿ Sun will pass the natal Sun point August 17 to 26
- ✿ Venus will pass the natal Sun point September 16 to 21

Natal Venus Transits (22 Cancer)
- ✿ Mars will pass natal Venus March 14 to 29

Natal Ascendant/Natal Mercury Transits (20-24 Virgo)
- ✿ Mars will pass this natal point July 21 to August 2
- ✿ Sun will pass this natal point September 12 to 20
- ✿ Mercury will pass this natal point September 13 to 16
- ✿ Venus will pass this natal point October 3 to 11

Natal Jupiter/Mid-Heaven/Mars Transits (23 Gemini – 0 Cancer)
- ✿ Jupiter will pass this natal point April 27 to June 22
- ✿ Sun will pass this natal point June 18 to 24

Natal Moon Transits (6 Sagittarius)
- ✿ Mars will pass the natal Moon November 8 to 17
- ✿ Sun will pass the natal Moon November 24 to Dec 2
- ✿ Venus will pass the natal Moon December 3 to 7.

Moon Transits

Using the geocentric Moon data in Appendix A, take note of the dates when Moon transits past the key points mentioned for the Chicago Board of Trade and for 30-Year Bond futures. Watch for increased volatility and possibly even short-term trend changes on these dates.

Declination

At the August 22, 1977 first trade date Venus was at plus 17-degrees declination and Mars was at plus 16.5-degrees declination. Two significant planets at parallel declination at the first trade date is more than just a little curious. In addition, Moon was within a fraction of a degree of being at minimum declination. This is further evidence that this first trade date was carefully contrived.

For 2025:
- ☼ **Mars will be at plus 16.5-degrees declination February 26 to March 19**
- ☼ **Venus will be at plus 17 degrees declination January 1 to 5, February 21 to 27, August 12 to 17, and October 3 to 8**
- ☼ **Moon will be at minimum declination: January 27, February 23, March 22, April 19, May 16, May 25, June 12, July 9, August 6, September 2, September 29, October 27, November 23, and December 20.**

Mercury Retrograde

In the first trade horoscope in Figure 17-16 note that the position of Mercury (at 24 Virgo) is further delineated by a letter S. This letter denotes stationary. The term stationary refers to the day immediately prior to a planet turning retrograde and starting to move backwards in the zodiac wheel. This first trade date of August 22, 1977 comes one day prior to Mercury turning retrograde. Was this also a factor in selecting this first trade date?

For 2025, Mercury will be:
☼ **retrograde from March 15 to April 6**
☼ **retrograde from July 18 to August 10**
☼ **retrograde from November 9 to November 28.**

Venus Retrograde

Looking at past price data of 30-Year Bond futures going back many years, Venus retrograde events do align to significant price trend changes. Futures and options traders definitely must watch for these retrograde events.

☼ **For 2025, Venus will be retrograde March 2 to April 12.**

Mars Retrograde

Mars retrograde events show an alignment to significant trend changes on 30-Year Bond futures prices. Futures and options traders should anticipate these retrograde events.

☼ **For 2025, Mars will be retrograde January 1 through February 23.**

10-Year Treasury Note Futures

10-Year Treasury Notes started trading in Chicago on May 3, 1982. Figure 7-17 presents the first trade horoscope for this date. Assuming a first-transaction time of 8:09 a.m., the Ascendant at 23 Gemini is conjunct the CBOT 1848 natal Ascendant.

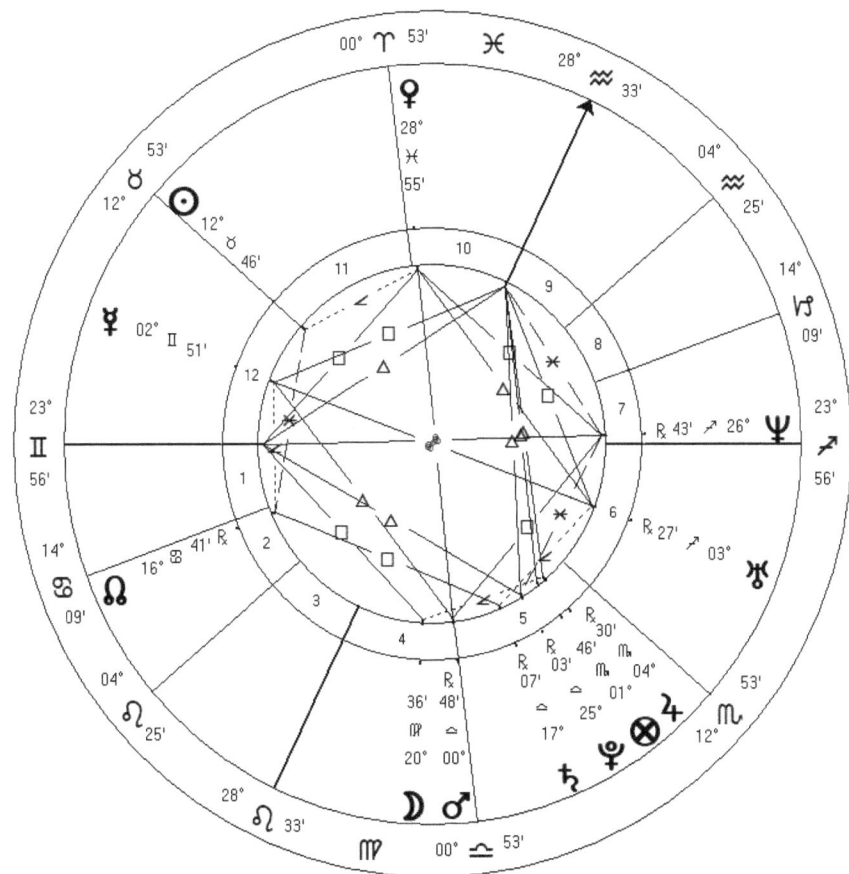

Figure 7-17
First Trade Horoscope for 10-Year Treasury Note futures

In addition to the transit dates past the CBOT 1848 natal planetary locations, transits of the 1982 first trade natal locations must be watched also.

For 2025:

Natal Sun Transits (12 Taurus)
☼ Sun will pass the 1982 natal Sun point April 28 to May 6
☼ Venus will pass the 1982 natal Sun point June 15 to 20

Natal Venus Transits
☼ Venus will pass natal Venus January 29 to February 4
☼ Sun will pass natal Venus March 15 to 21
☼ Venus will resume its passage April 1 to May 2

Natal Mid-Heaven Transits (28 Aquarius)
☼ Venus will pass the natal Mid-Heaven January 1 to 4
☼ Sun will pass the natal Mid-Heaven February 12 to 20

Natal Ascendant Transits (23 Gemini)
☼ Jupiter passes the natal Ascendant April 29 to May 16
☼ Sun will pass the natal Ascendant June 9 to 18
☼ Venus will pass the natal Ascendant July 20 to 27

Natal Mars Transits (0 Libra)
☼ Mars will pass the natal Mars point August 2 to 11
☼ Sun will pass the natal Mars point September 18 to 26
☼ Venus will pass the natal Mars point October 10 to 17

Natal Jupiter Transits (4 Scorpio)
☼ Mars passes natal Jupiter September 24 to October 2
☼ Sun will pass natal Jupiter point October 22 to 31
☼ Venus passes natal Jupiter point November 7 to 13

Natal Moon Transits (20 Virgo)
- ☼ Mars will pass the natal Moon July 18 to 26
- ☼ Sun will pass the natal Moon September 8 to 12
- ☼ Venus will pass the natal Moon October 4 to 8.

Moon Transits

Using the geocentric Moon data in Appendix A, take note of the dates when Moon transits past the key points mentioned for the Chicago Board of Trade and for 10-Year Treasury Note futures. Watch for increased volatility and possibly even short-term trend changes on these dates.

Declination

At the May 3, 1982 first trade date Venus was at minus 24-degrees declination and Mars was at minus 9-degrees declination. Moon was within one day of being at exact maximum declination.

For 2025:
- ☼ **Mars passes minus 9-degrees declination July 28 to Aug 15**
- ☼ **Venus will be at minus 24-degrees declination May 8 to June 5, and December 16 to 31**
- ☼ **Moon will be at maximum declination: January 12, February 9, March 8, April 4, May 1, May 29, June 25, July 22, August 19, September 15, October 12, November 9, and December 6**
- ☼ **Venus will be at the CBOT 1848 natal declination of plus 22-degrees January 11 to 19, February 8 to 17, August 23 to September 2, and September 20 to 29**
- ☼ **Mars will be at the CBOT 1848 natal declination of plus 22- degrees January 1 to February 5.**

Mercury Retrograde

Futures and options traders should pay attention to Mercury retrograde events as they align well to tradeable swing points on 10-Year Treasury Note futures.

> **For 2025, Mercury will be:**
> ☼ **retrograde from March 15 to April 6**
> ☼ **retrograde from July 18 to August 10**
> ☼ **retrograde from November 9 to November 28.**

Venus Retrograde

Looking at past price data of 10-Year Bond futures going back many years, Venus retrograde events do align to significant price trend changes. Futures and options traders definitely must watch for these retrograde events.

> ☼ **For 2025, Venus will be retrograde March 2 to April 12.**

Mars Retrograde

Mars retrograde events show an alignment to significant trend changes on 10-Year Bond futures prices. Futures and options traders should anticipate these retrograde events.

> ☼ **For 2025, Mars will be retrograde January 1 to February 23.**

Wheat, Corn, and Oats

Wheat, Corn, and Oats futures all share the same first trade date of January 2, 1877. The horoscope in Figure 7-18 shows planetary placements at that date.

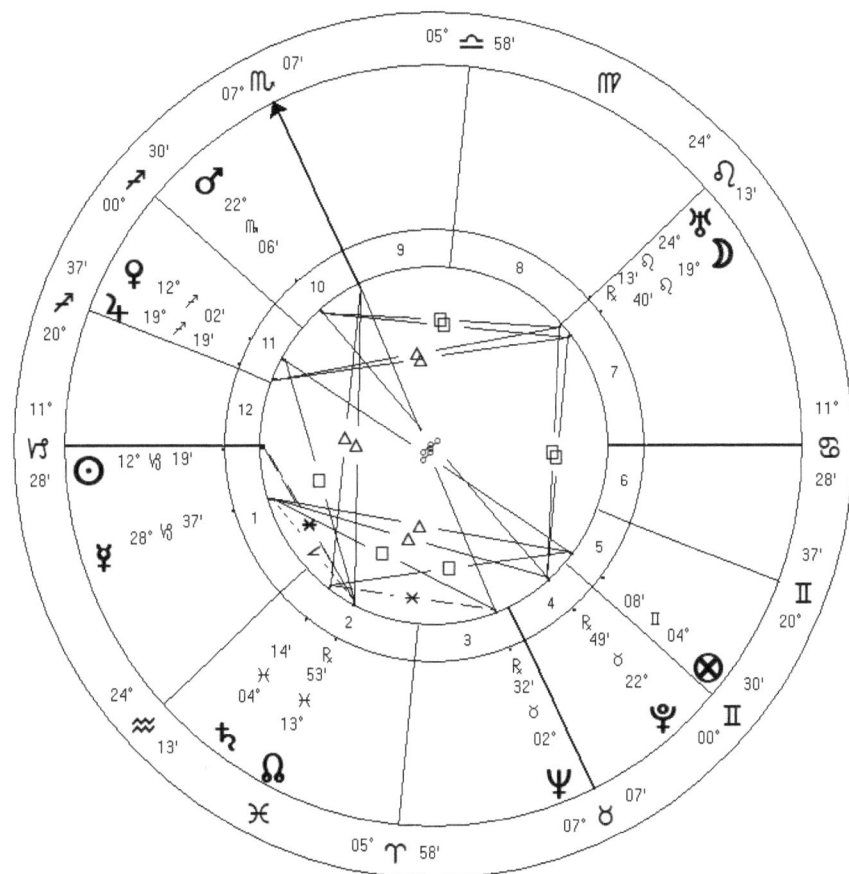

Figure 7-18
First Trade Horoscope for Wheat, Corn, and Oats futures

Assuming a 7:30 a.m. first-transaction time, Venus is 90-degrees square to the Venus location in the CBOT 1848 horoscope. Sun is 90-degrees square to the Sun location in the CBOT 1848 horoscope.

In addition to the transit dates past the CBOT 1848 natal planetary locations, transits of the 1877 first trade natal locations must be watched also.

For 2025:

Natal Sun/Natal Ascendant Transits (11-12 Capricorn)
☼ Sun will pass this 1877 natal point January 1 to 6
☼ Mars will pass this 1877 natal point December 27 to 31

Natal Mid-Heaven Transits (7 Scorpio)
☼ Mars passes the natal Mid-Heaven Sept 26 to Oct 7
☼ Sun passes the natal Mid-Heaven October 26 to Nov 3
☼ Venus will pass the natal Mid-Heaven November 9 to 14

Natal Venus Transits (12 Sagittarius)
☼ Mars will pass natal Venus November 17 to 25
☼ Sun will pass natal Venus November 30 to December 6

Natal Mars Transits (22 Scorpio)
☼ Mars will pass natal Mars October 20 to 29
☼ Sun will pass natal Mars November 10 to 18
☼ Venus passes natal Mars November 21 to 26

Natal Jupiter Transits (19 Sagittarius)
☼ Mars will pass natal Jupiter November 26 to December 4
☼ Sun will pass the natal Jupiter point December 5 to 13
☼ Venus will pass the natal Jupiter point December 13 to 19

Natal Moon Transits (19 Leo)
☼ Mars will pass the 1877 natal Moon May 22 to June 1
☼ Sun will pass the 1877 natal Moon August 7 to 13.

Moon Transits

Using the geocentric Moon data in Appendix A, take note of the dates when Moon transits past the key points mentioned for the Chicago Board of Trade and for the first trade date of January 2, 1877. Watch for increased volatility and possibly even short-term trend changes on these dates.

Declination

At the January 2, 1877 first trade date Venus was at minus - degrees declination and Mars was at minus 8-degrees declination. A first trade date with two significant planets at parallel declination level is not an accidental selection. In addition, Moon was within a couple degrees of being at its declination maximum.

For 2025:
☼ **Mars passes minus 8-degrees declination July 22 to Aug 10**
☼ **Venus will be at minus 8-degrees declination April 4 to 9, July 1 to 5, and November 15 to 19**
☼ **Moon will be at maximum declination: January 12, February 9, March 8, April 4, May 1, May 29, June 25, July 22, August 19, September 15, October 12, November 9, and December 6**
☼ **Venus will be at the CBOT 1848 natal declination of plus 22-degrees January 11 to 19, February 8 to 17, August 23 to September 2, and September 20 to 29**
☼ **Mars will be at the CBOT 1848 natal declination of plus 22-degrees January 1 to February 5.**

Mercury Retrograde

Futures and options traders should pay attention to Mercury retrograde events as they align well to tradeable swing points on Wheat, Corn, and even Oats futures.

For 2025, Mercury will be:
- ☼ **retrograde from March 15 to April 6**
- ☼ **retrograde from July 18 to August 10**
- ☼ **retrograde from November 9 to November 28.**

Venus Retrograde

Looking at past price data of Wheat, Corn, and Oats futures going back many years, Venus retrograde events do align to significant price trend changes. Futures and options traders definitely must watch for these retrograde events.

- ☼ **For 2025, Venus will be retrograde March 2 to April 12.**

Mars Retrograde

Mars retrograde events also show a good alignment to significant trend changes on Wheat, Corn, and Oats futures prices. Futures and options traders should anticipate these retrograde events.

- ☼ **For 2025, Mars will be retrograde January 1 to February 23.**

Soybeans

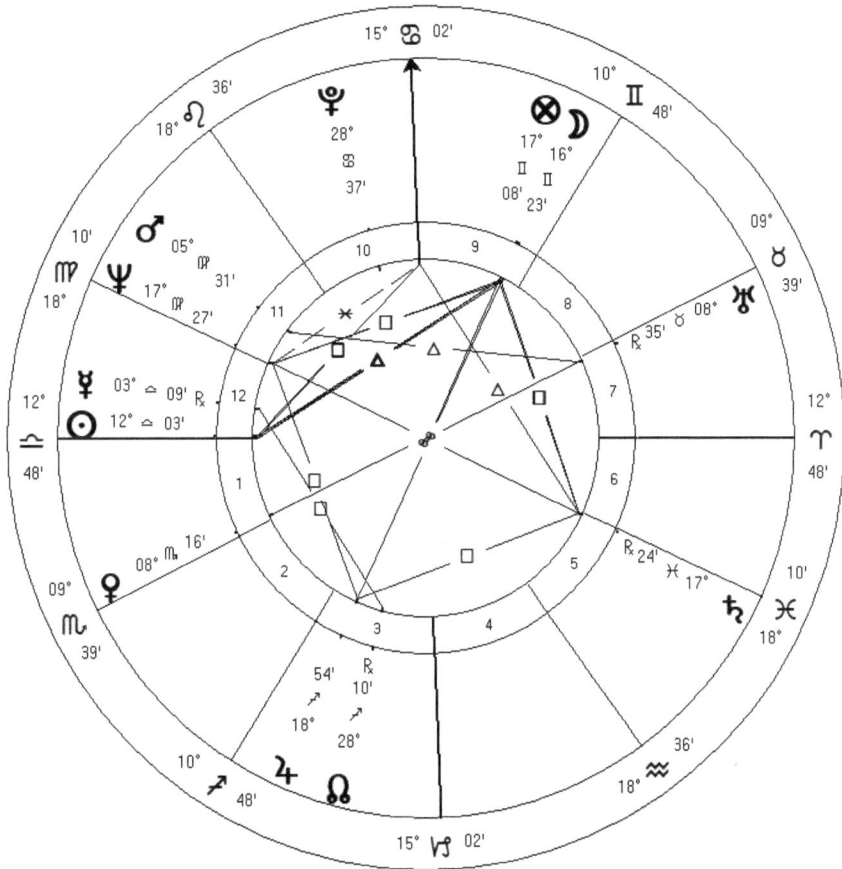

Figure 7-19
Soybean futures First Trade Horoscope

Soybean futures started trading in Chicago on October 5, 1936. The horoscope in Figure 7-19 illustrates the planetary placements at that time. If one makes the reasonable assumption of a 7:00 a.m. first trade, the Mid-Heaven (MH) is at the historically significant point of 14 Cancer. The Sun is situated right at the Ascendant and is 90-degrees square to the CBOT 1848 natal Sun. Moreover, at 7:00 am, the position of the Moon was such that in collaboration with Saturn, Jupiter, and Neptune, a geometric square pattern can be seen in the horoscope wheel.

In addition to the transit dates past the CBOT 1848 natal planetary locations, transits of the 1936 Soybean futures first trade natal locations must be watched also.

For 2025:

Natal Saturn Transits (17 Pisces)
✿ Saturn passes natal Saturn January 1 to February 7
✿ Venus passes natal Saturn January 16 to 23
✿ Sun passes natal Saturn March 3 to 10

Natal Sun/Ascendant Transits (12 Libra)
✿ Mars will pass this 1936 natal point August 21 to 30
✿ Sun will pass this 1936 natal point October 2 to 9
✿ Venus will pass this 1936 natal point October 20 to 26

Natal Mid-Heaven Transits (15 Cancer)
✿ Mars nears natal Mid-Heaven February 24 to March 12
✿ Sun will pass the natal Mid-Heaven July 2 to 11
✿ Venus will pass the natal Mid-Heaven August 10 to 16
✿ Jupiter will pass the Mid-Heaven August 7 to 31

Natal Mars Transits (5 Virgo)
✿ Mars will pass the 1936 natal Mars point June 21 to July 2
✿ Sun will pass the 1936 natal Mars point August 24 to 31

Natal Venus Transits (8 Scorpio)
✿ Sun will pass natal Venus October 28 to November 4
✿ Mars will pass natal Venus September 29 to October 8
✿ Venus will pass the 1936 natal Venus November 10-16

Natal Jupiter Transits (18 Sagittarius)
✿ Mars will pass natal Jupiter November 25 to December 3

✧ Sun will pass natal Jupiter point December 5 to 13
✧ Venus will pass natal Jupiter point December 12 to 17

Natal Moon Transits (16 Gemini)
✧ Jupiter will pass the 1936 natal Moon March 19 to April 17
✧ Sun will pass the 1936 natal Moon June 2 to 10
✧ Venus will pass the 1936 natal Moon July 16 to 21

Natal Neptune Transits (17 Virgo)
✧ Mars passes natal Neptune July 12 to 21
✧ Sun passes natal September 5 to 12.

Moon Transits

Using the geocentric Moon data in Appendix A, take note of the dates when Moon transits past the key points mentioned for the Chicago Board of Trade and for the Soybeans first trade date. Watch for increased volatility and possibly even short-term trend changes on these dates.

Declination

At the October 5, 1936 first trade date Venus was at minus 22-degrees declination and Mars was at plus 18-degrees declination. Moon was at its declination maximum.

For 2025:
✧ **Mars will be at plus 18-degrees declination February 14 to March 8**
✧ **Venus will be at minus 22-degrees declination May 1 to June 10 and again December 10 to 31.**
✧ **Moon will be at maximum declination: January 12, February 9, March 8, April 4, May 1, May 29, June 25, July 22, August 19, September 15, October 12, November 9, and December 6**

☼ Venus will be at the CBOT 1848 natal declination of plus 22 degrees January 11 to 19, February 8 to 17, August 23 to September 2, and September 20 to 29

☼ Mars will be at the CBOT 1848 natal declination of plus 22-degrees January 1 to February 5.

Mercury Retrograde

Mercury retrograde events bear watching when following price action on Soybeans. These events align to pivot swing points and also strong continuation of trend moves.

For 2025, Mercury will be:
☼ retrograde from March 15 to April 6
☼ retrograde from July 18 to August 10
☼ retrograde from November 9 to November 28.

Venus Retrograde

Looking at past price data of Soybean futures going back many years, Venus retrograde events do align to tradeable price trend changes. Futures and options traders definitely must watch for these retrograde events.

☼ For 2025, Venus will be retrograde March 2 to April 12.

Mars Retrograde

Mars retrograde events definitely show a very good alignment to significant trend change points on Soybean futures prices. Futures and options traders must anticipate these retrograde events.

☼ For 2025, Mars will be retrograde January 1 to February 23.

The New York Cotton Exchange

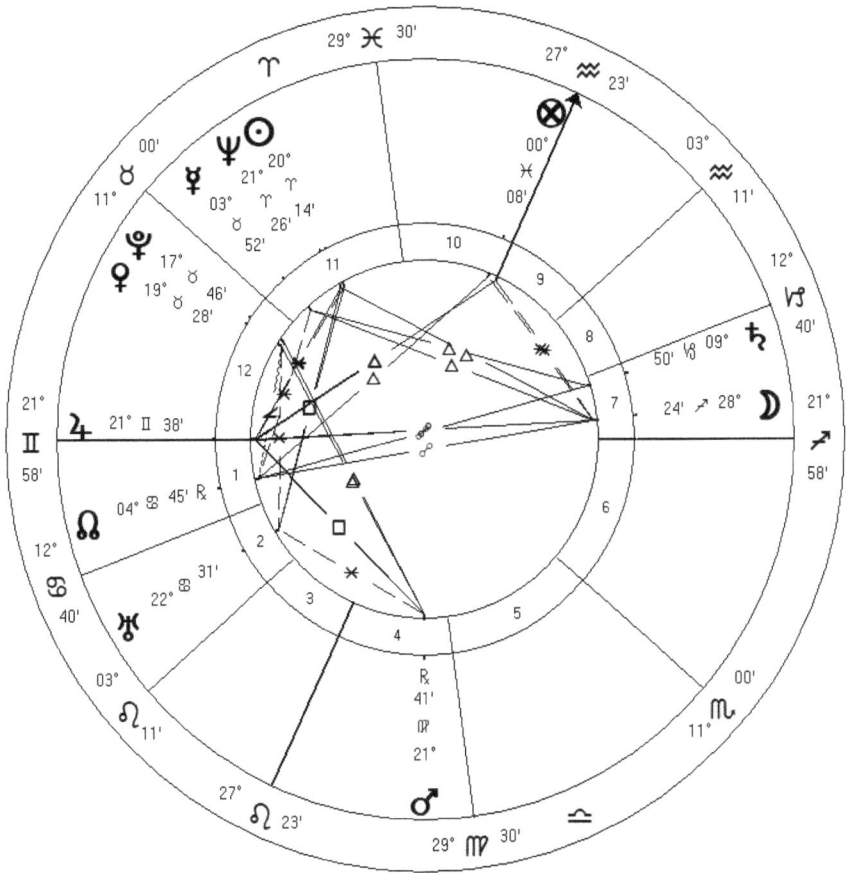

Figure 7-20
Cotton Exchange & Cotton futures First Trade Horoscope

In 1870, the controlling exchange for the global Cotton trade was located in Liverpool, U.K. In early 1870, a group of cotton merchants and brokers doing business in New York decided to create a Cotton trading association that would focus on fair dealing and fair pricing. By late 1870, the operational framework had been created and on April 8, 1871 the New York Cotton Exchange was granted a charter from the State of New York legislature. This date was a Saturday. The Exchange would have opened for trading the following Monday (April 10) to trade one and only one commodity - Cotton.

The horoscope wheel in Figure 7-20 illustrates planetary placements assuming a first-execution time of 8:45 a.m. Notice that Jupiter is positioned right on the Ascendant.

In my opinion, the key points in this horoscope to focus on should be Ascendant/Jupiter, Mid-Heaven, Sun, Mars, Moon, and Venus.

For 2025, watch the following transit dates:

Natal Ascendant/natal Jupiter Transits (21 Gemini)
- ✪ Jupiter will pass this 1870 natal point April 14 to May 13
- ✪ Sun will pass this 1870 natal point June 9 to 15
- ✪ Venus will pass this 1870 natal point July 20 to 26

Natal Mid-Heaven Transits (27 Aquarius)
- ✪ Venus passes natal Mid-Heaven January 29 to February 7
- ✪ Sun will pass natal Mid-Heaven February 11 to 19
- ✪ Venus will complete its transit April 21 to May 2

Natal Mars Transits (21 Virgo)
- ✪ Mars will pass the 1870 natal Mars July 19 to 29
- ✪ Sun will pass the 1870 natal Mars September 9 to 17
- ✪ Venus will pass the 1870 natal Mars October 4 to 10

Natal Venus Transits (19 Taurus)
- ✪ Sun will pass natal Venus May 6 to 13
- ✪ Venus will pass natal Venus June 22 to 27

Natal Sun Transits (20 Aries)
- ✿ Sun will pass the 1870 natal Sun April 6 to 14
- ✿ Venus will pass the 1870 natal Sun May 24 to 30

Natal Moon Transits (28 Sagittarius)
- ✿ Mars will pass natal Moon December 5 to 17
- ✿ Sun will pass natal Moon December 6 to 14
- ✿ Venus will pass natal Moon December 20 to 26.

Moon Transits

Using the geocentric Moon data in Appendix A, take note of the dates when Moon transits past the key points mentioned for the Cotton Exchange first trade date. Watch for increased volatility and possibly even short-term trend changes on these dates.

Declination

At the April 10, 1871 first trade date Venus was at maximum declination (plus 24 degrees). Mars was at minus 2-degrees declination. Moon was at its declination minimum.

For 2025:
- ✿ **Venus will be at its declination maximum January 15 to February 11, and again from August 29 to September 24**
- ✿ **Mars will be at minus 2-degrees of declination June 19 to July 5**
- ✿ **Moon will be at minimum declination: January 27, February 23, March 22, April 19, May 16, May 25, June 12, July 9, August 6, September 2, September 29, October 27, November 23, and December 20.**

Mercury Retrograde

Mercury retrograde events bear watching when following price action on Cotton futures. These events align fairly well to pivot swing points.

For 2025, Mercury will be:
- ✪ **retrograde from March 15 to April 6**
- ✪ **retrograde from July 18 to August 10**
- ✪ **retrograde from November 9 to November 28.**

Venus Retrograde

Looking at past price data of Cotton futures going back many years, Venus retrograde events align to tradeable price trend changes. However, the alignment is somewhat lacking. Futures and options traders who nevertheless wish to watch for Venus retrograde events should note that:

- ✪ **In 2025, Venus will be retrograde March 2 to April 12.**

Mars Retrograde

Mars retrograde events align to tradeable price trend changes. However, as with Venus, the alignment is somewhat lacking. Futures and options traders who wish to watch for Mars retrograde events should note that:

- ✪ **In 2025, Mars will be retrograde January 1 to February 23.**

The New York Mercantile Exchange

In 1872 a group of merchants in New York created the Butter and Cheese Exchange. By 1882, opportunities to add new contracts to its trading floor beckoned. On April 25, 1882 the exchange was renamed the New York Mercantile Exchange.

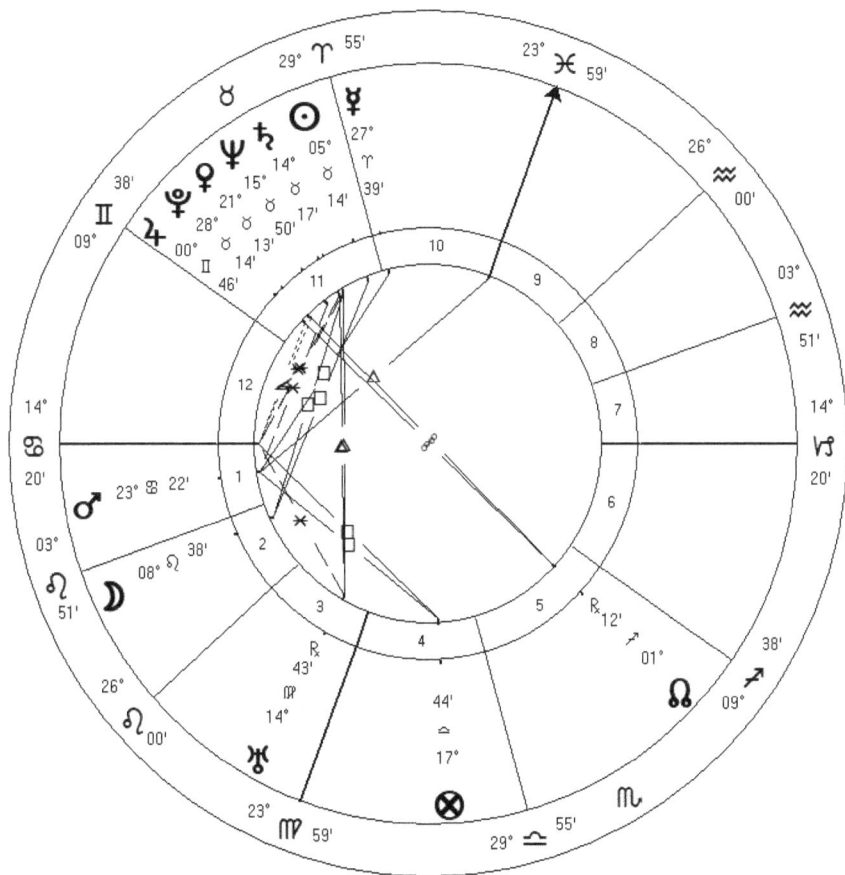

Figure 7-21
New York Mercantile First Trade Horoscope

Assuming a 9:20 a.m. first trade time, the Ascendant can be seen at 14 of Cancer and the Mid-Heaven at 23 Pisces – very similar to the 1792 NYSE natal horoscope.

For 2025:

Natal Ascendant Transits (14 Cancer)
- ☼ Sun will pass the natal Ascendant July 1 to 9
- ☼ Jupiter will pass the natal Ascendant August 4 to 26
- ☼ Venus will pass the natal Ascendant August 9 to 14

Natal Mars Transits (23 Cancer)
- ☼ Mars will pass natal Mars March 19 to April 10
- ☼ Sun will pass natal Mars July 12 to 19
- ☼ Jupiter will pass natal Mars September 20 to October 3

Natal Moon Transits (8 Leo)
Mars will pass natal Moon point April 29 to May 12
Sun will pass natal Moon point July 27 to August 4
Venus will pass natal Moon August 29 to September 4

Natal Mid-Heaven Transits (23 Pisces)
- ☼ Venus will pass natal Mid-Heaven January 23 to 31
- ☼ Sun will pass natal Mid-Heaven March 10 to 16

Natal Sun Transits (5 Taurus)
- ☼ Sun will pass natal Sun April 20 to 29
- ☼ Venus will pass natal Sun June 7 to 14

Natal Venus Transits (21 Taurus)
- ☼ Sun will pass natal Venus May 8 to 15
- ☼ Venus will pass natal Venus June 23 to 29

Natal Jupiter Transits (0 Gemini)
- ☼ Sun will pass natal Jupiter May 17 to 24
- ☼ Venus will pass natal Jupiter July 1 to 8.

Declination

At this trade date, Mars was at plus 13-degrees of declination and Venus was at plus 22-degrees of declination.

For 2025:
- ☼ **Mars will pass plus 13-degrees declination March 25 to April 12**
- ☼ **Venus will be at plus 22-degrees declination January 1 to 8, February 9 to 18, August 22 to 31, and September 21 to October 1.**

Crude Oil

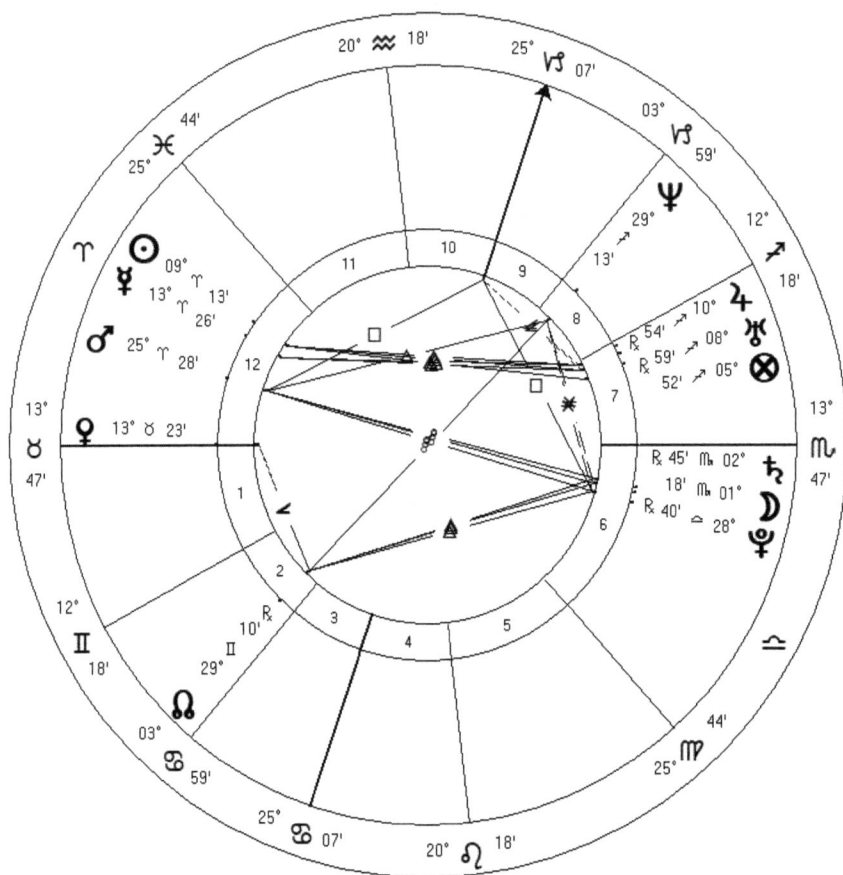

Figure 7-22
Crude Oil futures First Trade Horoscope

West Texas Intermediate Crude Oil futures started trading for the first time on the New York Mercantile on March 30, 1983.

A unique alignment of celestial points can be seen in the horoscope in Figure 7-22. This is assuming a first-trade time of 7:15 a.m. Notice how Mars (25 Aries), North Node (29 Gemini), Saturn/Moon (1 Scorpio), and Neptune (29 Sagittarius) conspire to form what appears to be a rectangle shape. The Mid-Heaven point is 25 of Capricorn and Venus is situated right at the Ascendant point. The choice of this date to commence trading WTI Crude Oil futures was carefully chosen.

Oil can be a complex instrument to analyze using astrology given how easily trader's emotions are disturbed by geopolitical events. However, despite the background noise, paying attention to times when transiting Sun, Mars, and Venus each transit past the four corner points of the rectangle is a valuable strategy. Bear in mind that the tenor of the price reaction as these planets each pass the various corner points will vary from year to year.

For 2025:

Sun Transits
- ☼ Sun will pass the natal Mid-Heaven January 11 to 19
- ☼ Sun will pass natal Sun March 24 to April 2
- ☼ Sun will pass the natal Mars point April 11 to 20
- ☼ Sun will pass the natal Ascendant April 29 to May 7
- ☼ Sun will pass the natal Node from June 15 to 25
- ☼ Sun will pass natal (Saturn/Moon) October 20 to 29
- ☼ Sun will pass natal Neptune December 17 to 21

Venus Transits
- ☼ Venus will pass natal Sun February 12 to March 1
- ☼ Venus will complete its passage of natal Sun May 10 to 19
- ☼ Venus will pass natal Ascendant June 16 to 22
- ☼ Venus will pass natal Node July 28 to August 3
- ☼ Venus will pass natal (Saturn/Moon) November 5 to 12
- ☼ Venus will pass natal Neptune December 21 to 27

Mars Transits
- ☼ Mars will pass natal (Saturn/Moon) September 18 to 30
- ☼ Mars will pass natal Neptune December 9 to 19.

Moon Transits

Using the geocentric Moon data in Appendix A, take note of the dates when Moon transits past the key points mentioned for the New York Mercantile Exchange and for the WTI Crude Oil futures first trade date. Watch for increased volatility and possibly even short-term trend changes on these dates.

Declination

At the 1983 first trade date, Venus was at its maximum declination of plus 24 degrees. Mars was at plus 13-degrees declination. Moon was at zero degrees declination. These degree locations are remarkably similar to the declination levels of Mars and Venus at the 1882 founding of the New York Mercantile Exchange. Further evidence that this 1983 first trade date was carefully contrived.

For 2025:
- ☼ **Venus will be at its declination maximum January 14 to February 14 and August 23 to September 30**
- ☼ **Mars will be at plus 13-degrees of declination March 23 to April 12**
- ☼ **Venus will be at its 1882 natal declination of plus 22-degrees January 1 to 8, February 9 to 18, August 22 to 31, and September 21 to October 1**
- ☼ **Mars will pass its 1882 natal declination of plus 13-degrees March 23 to April 12**
- ☼ **Moon will be at zero degrees declination on January 3, 16 and 30, February 13, March 11, April 7, May 4, June 1 and 28, July 12 and 25, August 8 and 21, September 4 and 18, October 1, 16 and 29, November 11, and December 22.**

Mercury Retrograde

Mercury retrograde events bear watching when following price action on WTI Oil futures. These events align fairly well to pivot swing points.

For 2025, Mercury will be:
- ☼ **retrograde from March 15 to April 6**
- ☼ **retrograde from July 18 to August 10**
- ☼ **retrograde from November 9 to November 28.**

Venus Retrograde

Venus retrograde events do align to tradeable price trend changes on WTO Oil futures. Futures and options traders who wish to watch for Venus retrograde events should note that:

- ☼ **In 2025, Venus will be retrograde March 2 to April 12.**

Mars Retrograde

Likewise, Mars retrograde events also align to tradeable price trend changes.

- ☼ **In 2025, Mars will be retrograde January 1 through February 23.**

Natural Gas

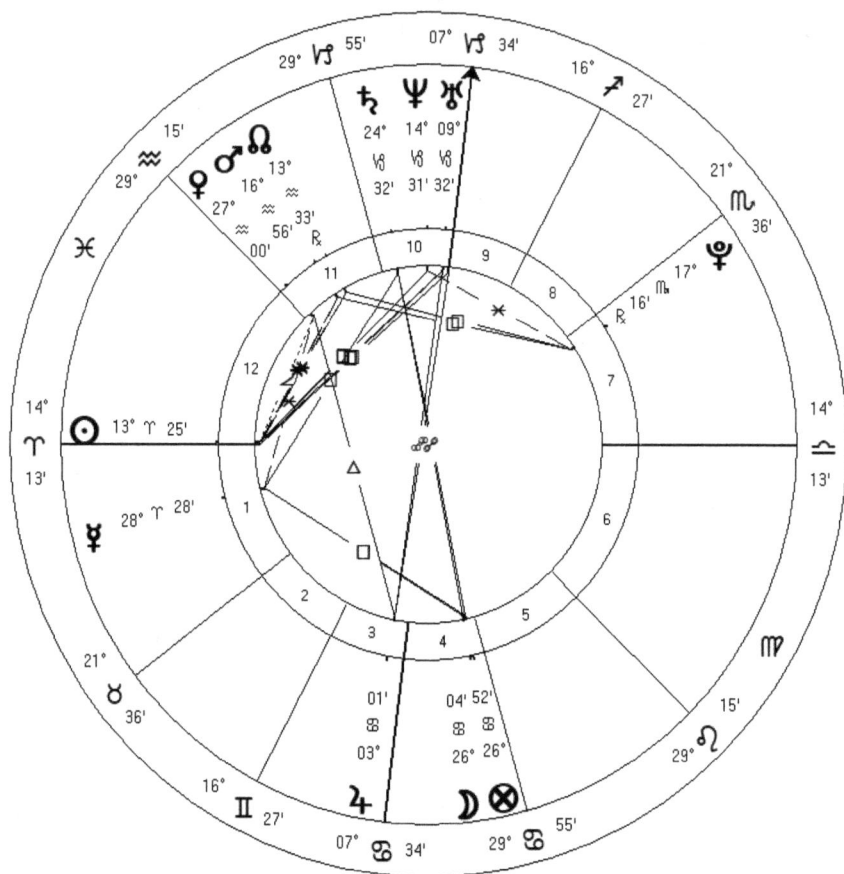

Figure 7-23
Natural Gas futures First Trade Horoscope

Natural Gas futures started trading on the New York Mercantile Exchange on April 3, 1990.

Assuming an early morning first-transaction time of 6:43 a.m., the Ascendant at 14 Aries is 90-degrees square to the 1882 New York Mercantile natal horoscope Ascendant. Sun is at the Ascendant. The choice of this first trade date was not random.

In addition to the transits of key points in the New York Mercantile 1882 natal chart, one must pay attention to transits of key points in the 1990 Natural Gas futures first trade horoscope.

For 2025:

Natal Ascendant/Sun Transits (14 Aries)
- ☼ Sun will pass the natal Ascendant March 30 to April 7
- ☼ Venus will pass the natal Ascendant May 16 to 23

Natal Jupiter Transits (3 Cancer)
- ☼ Jupiter will pass natal Jupiter June 13 to July 5
- ☼ Sun will pass natal Jupiter June 20 to 28
- ☼ Venus will pass natal Jupiter July 30 to August 5

Natal Moon Transits (26 Cancer)
- ☼ Mars will pass natal Moon April 1 to 16
- ☼ Venus will pass natal Moon August 20 to 26

Natal Mid-Heaven Transits (7 Capricorn)
- ☼ Mars will pass the natal Mid-Heaven December 20 to 28
- ☼ Sun will pass the natal Mid-Heaven December 24 to 31
- ☼ Venus will pass the natal Mid-Heaven December 24 to 31

Natal Mars Transits (16 Aquarius)
- ☼ Sun will pass the natal Mars point February 1 to 7

Natal Venus Transits (27 Aquarius)
- ☼ Venus will pass the natal Venus point January 1 to 4
- ☼ Sun will pass the natal Venus point February 12 to 18.

Moon Transits

Using the geocentric Moon data in Appendix A, take note of the dates when Moon transits past the key points mentioned for the New York Mercantile Exchange and for the Natural Gas futures first trade date. Watch for increased volatility and possibly even short-term trend changes on these dates.

Declination

At April 3, 1990 Moon was withing one degree of its declination maximum. Mars was at its declination minimum at minus 24-degrees. Venus was at minus 19-degrees declination. Moon and Mars both at their declination extremes further suggests this first trade date was not a random selection.

For 2025:
- ☼ **Venus will be at -19 degrees declination April 22 to 30, June 9 to 17, and December 5 to 13**
- ☼ **Mars will be at minus 24-degrees declination from November 1 to December 31**
- ☼ **Moon will be at its declination maximum January 23, February 19, March 18, April 13, May 11, June 7, July 5, August 1, August 28, September 24, October 21, November 18, and December 16.**

Mercury Retrograde

Mercury retrograde events bear watching when following price action on Natural Gas futures. These events align fairly well to pivot swing points.

For 2025, Mercury will be:
- ☼ **retrograde from March 15 to April 6**

- ✿ **retrograde from July 18 to August 10**
- ✿ **retrograde from November 9 to November 28.**

Venus Retrograde

Venus retrograde events align very well to pivotal price trend changes on Natural Gas futures. Futures and options traders anticipating Venus retrograde events should note that:

- ✿ **In 2025, Venus will be retrograde March 2 through April 12.**

Mars Retrograde

Likewise, Mars retrograde events also align well to tradeable price trend changes. Futures and options traders who wish to watch for Mars retrograde events should note that:

- ✿ **In 2025, Mars will be retrograde January 1 to February 23.**

New York Coffee Exchange

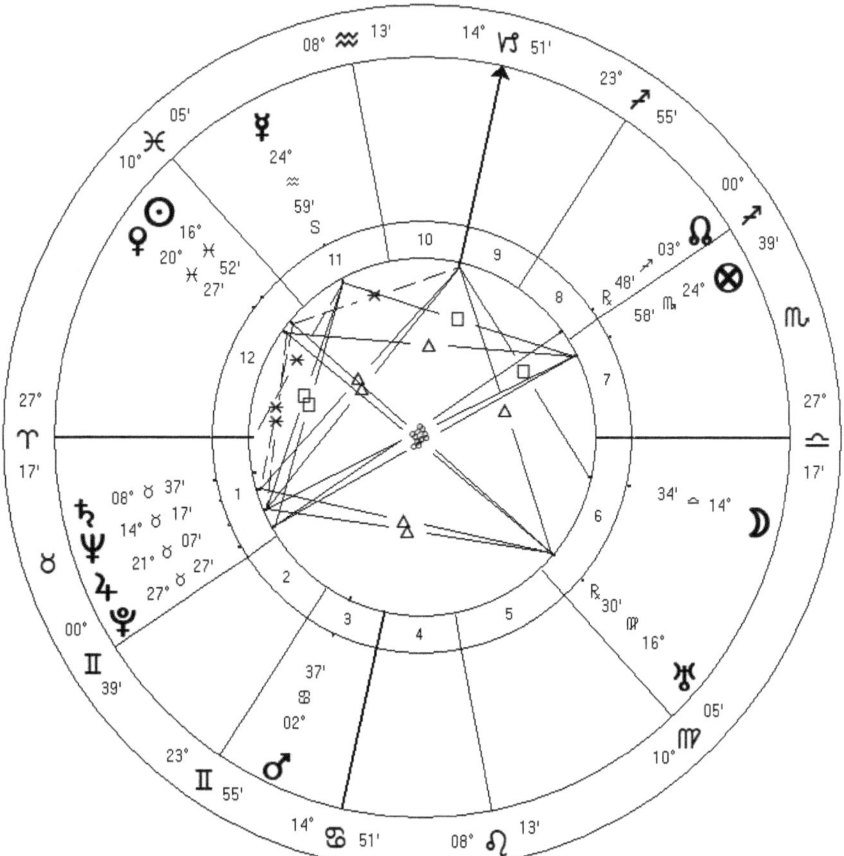

Figure 7-24
Coffee Exchange & Coffee futures First Trade Horoscope

During the U.S. Civil War, Washington was a major buyer of coffee beans. Coffee imports in those years came via Dutch and British suppliers. Following the war, demand for coffee dropped as did prices. Several years of adverse weather around the globe then created speculative fervor and prices traded wildly up and down.

To gain control over pricing, a group of coffee importing merchants established a coffee exchange in New York.

Coffee futures contracts started trading on the newly formed New York Coffee Exchange on March 7, 1882.

The horoscope wheel in Figure 7-24 illustrates planetary placements at that time. The Mid-Heaven at 14 Capricorn is 90-degrees square to the Ascendant in the 1792 natal horoscope for the NYSE.

The 1882 Coffee horoscope chart has a kite-shaped geometric pattern in it. The points of this triangle are: 14 Capricorn (Mid-Heaven), 16 Pisces, 14 Taurus (Neptune), and 16 Virgo (Uranus). The Ascendant is at 27 Aries. This is assuming an 8:00 a.m. first trade start time.

Traders of coffee futures or investors in coffee retail type stocks should pay attention to transits of key points in the 1882 horoscope.

For 2025:

Natal Ascendant Transits (27 Aries)
✿ Sun passes natal Ascendant April 13 to 20
✿ Venus passes natal Ascendant May 30 to June 7

Natal Jupiter Transits (21 Taurus)
✿ Sun passes natal Jupiter May 7 to 15
✿ Venus passes natal Jupiter June 23 to July 1

Natal Mars Transits (2 Cancer)
✿ Jupiter passes natal Mars June 15 to 26
✿ Sun passes natal Mars June 19 to 27
✿ Venus passes natal Mars July 29 to August 4

Natal Moon Transits (14 Libra)
- ☼ Mars passes natal Moon August 26 to September 3
- ☼ Sun passes natal Moon October 3 to 11
- ☼ Venus passes natal Moon October 22 to 28

Natal Mid-Heaven Transits (14 Capricorn)
- ☼ Sun passes the natal Mid-Heaven January 1 to 8
- ☼ Mars begins to pass the natal Mid-Heaven December 28

Natal Sun/Venus Transits (16-20 Pisces)
- ☼ Venus passes this natal point January 15 to 27.

Moon Transits

Using the geocentric Moon data in Appendix A, take note of the dates when Moon transits past the key points mentioned for the New York Coffee Exchange. Watch for increased volatility and possibly even short-term trend changes on these dates.

Declination

On March 7, 1882 Venus was at minus 5-degrees declination. Mars was at plus 20-degrees declination.

In 2025:
- ☼ **Mars will be at plus 20-degrees January 31 to February 20**
- ☼ **Venus will be at minus 5-degrees declination March 31 to April 4, July 6 to 11, and November 11 to 16.**

Mercury Retrograde

Mercury retrograde events bear watching when following price action on Coffee futures. These events align very well to pivot swing points.

For 2025, Mercury will be:
- ✿ **retrograde from March 15 to April 6**
- ✿ **retrograde from July 18 to August 10**
- ✿ **retrograde from November 9 to November 28.**

Venus Retrograde

Venus retrograde events align to times of increased volatility on Coffee futures. However, the alignment to pivotal price trend changes is lacking in consistency. Futures and options traders who wish to watch for Venus retrograde events should note that:

- ✿ **In 2025, Venus will be retrograde March 2 to April 12.**

Mars Retrograde

Mars retrograde events align well to tradeable price trend changes on Coffee futures. Looking back over many years of price data, Mars retrograde events can be seen aligning to several incidents of pivot swing trend changes. Futures and options traders who wish to watch for Mars retrograde events should note that:

- ✿ **In 2025, Mars will be retrograde January 1 to February 23.**

New York Coffee and Sugar Exchange

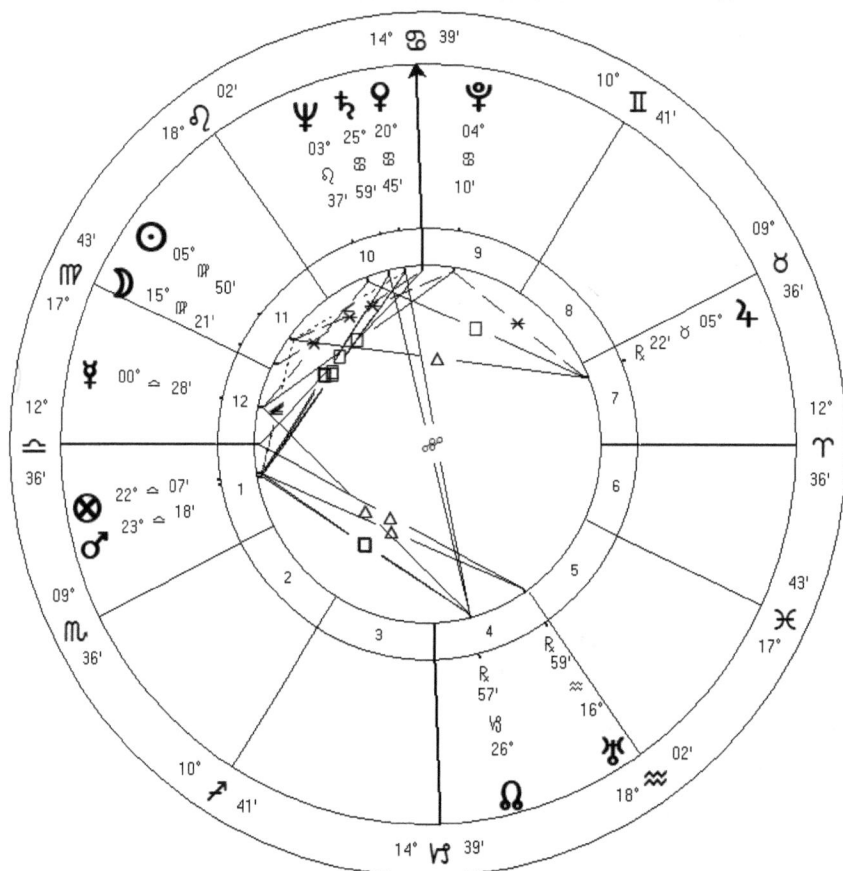

Figure 7-25
Sugar futures First Trade Horoscope

Sugar as a bulk commodity started trading in New York as early as 1881. However, at that time the majority of Sugar trades were done in Hamburg and London. The New York Exchange saw little business.

After WW I hostilities ceased, the decision was made to start trading Sugar contracts in New York. On August 29, 1916, the New York Coffee Exchange changed its name to the New York Coffee and Sugar Exchange. With that, Sugar futures began trading.

Assuming a first trade time of 8:20 a.m., the Moon is at the Ascendant which is 90-degrees square to 14 of Cancer–a reference to the Ascendant point of the New York Stock Exchange. Sun and Moon are in the sign of Virgo – a reference to the goddess Isis. Furthermore, Mars, Node, and Venus trace out a triangular pattern in the horoscope wheel.

For 2025:

Natal Jupiter Transits (5 Taurus)
- ☼ Sun passes the natal Jupiter point April 21 to 28
- ☼ Venus passes the natal Jupiter point June 8 to 14

Natal Mid-Heaven Transits (14 Cancer)
- ☼ Sun passes the natal Mid-Heaven July 1 to 9
- ☼ Jupiter passes the natal Mid-Heaven August 2 to 23
- ☼ Venus passes the natal Mid-Heaven August 10 to 15

Natal Venus Transits (20 Cancer)
- ☼ Mars passes the natal Venus point March 8 to 30
- ☼ Sun passes the natal Venus point July 9 to 15

Natal Mars Transits (23 Libra)
- ☼ Mars passes natal Mars September 6 to 16
- ☼ Sun passes natal Mars October 13 to 19
- ☼ Venus passes natal Mars October 30 to November 4

Natal Moon Transits (15 Virgo)
- ☼ Mars passes natal Moon July 8 to 18
- ☼ Sun passes the natal Moon September 3 to 11

Natal Sun Transits (5 Virgo)
- ☼ Mars passes natal Sun June 21 to 29
- ☼ Sun passes natal Sun August 24 to September 1
- ☼ Venus passes natal Sun September 21 to 27

Natal Ascendant Transits (12 Libra)
- ☼ Mars passes natal Ascendant August 22 to September 1
- ☼ Sun passes natal Ascendant October 1 to 9
- ☼ Venus passes natal Ascendant October 21 to 26.

Moon Transits

Using the geocentric Moon data in Appendix A, take note of the dates when Moon transits past the key points mentioned for the 1916 natal chart. Watch for increased volatility and possibly even short-term trend changes on these dates.

Declination

At the August 1916 founding date of the New York Coffee Exchange, Mars was at minus 18-degrees of declination. Venus was at plus 1-degree of declination.

In 2025:
- ☼ **Venus will be at plus 1-degree of declination March 23-27, July 16-22, and November 1-6**
- ☼ **Mars will be at minus 18-degrees declination September 19-October 7**
- ☼ **Moon will be at zero degrees declination: January 6 and 19, February 2 and 15, March 1, 15, and 29, April 11 and 25, May 8 and 22, June 5 and 19, July 2, 16, and 29, August 12 and 25, September 8 and 22, October 6 and 19, November 3, 15, and 30, and December 13 and 27.**

Mercury Retrograde

Mercury retrograde events bear watching when following price action on Sugar futures. These events align very well to pivot swing points.

For 2025, Mercury will be:
- ☼ **retrograde from March 15 to April 6**
- ☼ **retrograde from July 18 to August 10**
- ☼ **retrograde from November 9 to November 28.**

Venus Retrograde

Venus retrograde events align to times of increased volatility on Sugar futures. However, the alignment to pivotal price trend changes is lacking in consistency. Futures and options traders who wish to watch for Venus retrograde events should note that:

- ☼ **In 2025, Venus will be retrograde March 2 to April 12.**

Mars Retrograde

Mars retrograde events align well to tradeable price trend changes on Sugar futures. Looking back over many years of price data, Mars retrograde events can also be seen aligning to times of trend continuation and acceleration. Futures and options traders who wish to watch for Mars retrograde events should note that:

- ☼ **In 2025, Mars will be retrograde January 1 to February 23.**

New York Cocoa Exchange

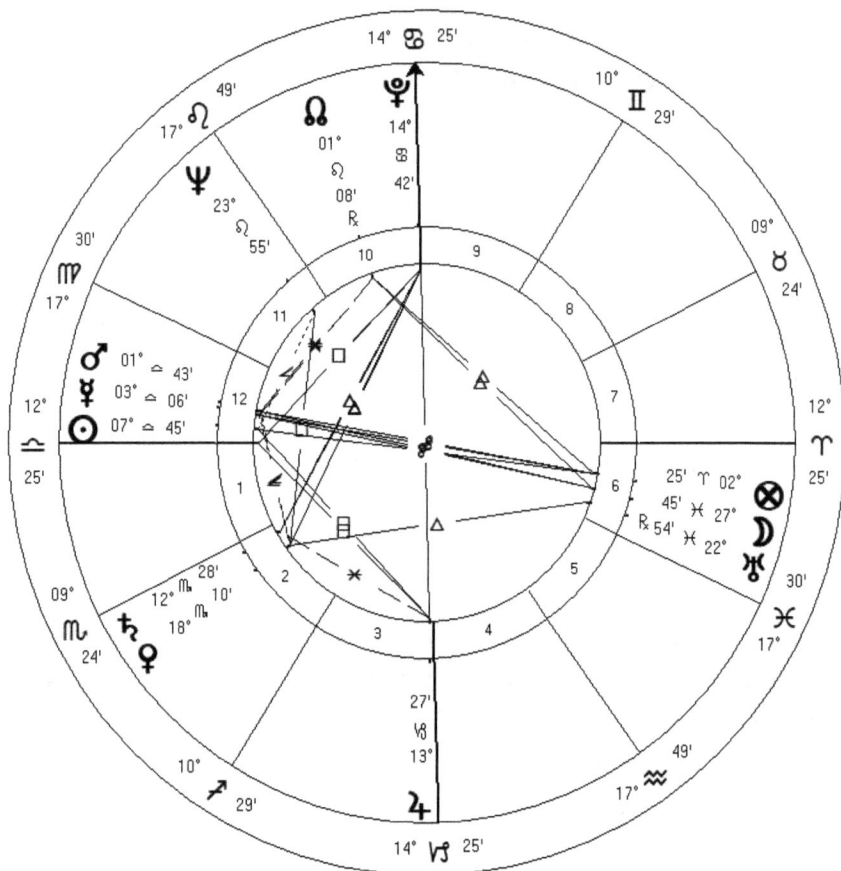

Figure 7-26
First Trade Horoscope Cocoa futures

As early as the US War of Independence, cocoa was being imported into the American colonies. However, it would not be until 1925 that a formal futures exchange would be established in New York to handle Cocoa futures.

Cocoa futures contracts started trading in New York on October 1, 1925. The horoscope in Figure 7-26 shows planetary placements at the first trade date. Assuming a 6:20 a.m. first trade time, the Mid-

Heaven point located at 14 of Cancer, the same point that defines the Ascendant in the natal horoscope of the New York Stock Exchange. Sun is positioned just a few degrees from the Ascendant.

For 2025:

Natal Moon Transits (27 Pisces)
- ✿ Venus will pass natal Moon January 28 to February 4
- ✿ Sun will pass natal Moon March 14 to 21

Mid-Heaven Transits (14 Cancer)
- ✿ Sun passes the natal Mid-Heaven July 3 to 10
- ✿ Jupiter will pass the natal Mid-Heaven August 2 to 27
- ✿ Venus will pass the natal Mid-Heaven August 10 to 15

Sun/Ascendant Transits (7-12 of Libra)
- ✿ Mars will pass this natal grouping August 19 to 31
- ✿ Sun will pass this natal grouping October 1 to 9
- ✿ Venus will pass this natal grouping October 21 to 26

Natal Venus Transits (18 Scorpio)
- ✿ Mars will pass natal Venus October 14 to 23
- ✿ Sun will pass natal Venus November 6 to 13
- ✿ Venus will pass natal Venus November 18 to 24

Natal Mars Transits (1 Libra)
- ✿ Mars will pass natal Mars August 3 to 13
- ✿ Sun will pass September 19 to 27
- ✿ Venus will pass natal Mars October 12 to 17

Natal Jupiter Transits (13 Capricorn)
- ✿ Sun will pass natal Jupiter January 1 to 5
- ✿ Mars will pass natal Jupiter December 29 to 31.

Moon Transits

Using the geocentric Moon data in Appendix A, take note of the dates when Moon transits past the key points mentioned for the 1925 natal chart. Watch for increased volatility and possibly even short-term trend changes on these dates.

Declination

On the date the Cocoa Exchange opened, Mars was at plus 2-degrees declination, Venus was at minus 23-degrees declination, and. Moon was at zero degrees declination.

In 2025:
- ☼ **Mars will be at plus 2-degrees declination May 27 to June 12**
- ☼ **Venus will be at minus 23-degrees declination May 4 to June 6, and December 15-31**
- ☼ **Moon will be at zero declination: January 6 and 19, February 2 and 15, March 1, 15, and 29, April 11 and 25, May 8 and 22, June 5 and 19, July 2, 16, and 29, August 12 and 25, September 8 and 22, October 6 and 19, November 3, 15, and 30, and December 13 and 27.**

Mercury Retrograde

Calendar year 2024 saw a dramatic surge higher in Cocoa prices. The two Mercury retrograde events that have occurred so far in 2024 (at this time of writing) bear strong alignment to powerful price trend changes.

For 2025, Mercury will be:
- ☼ **retrograde from March 15 to April 6**
- ☼ **retrograde from July 18 to August 10**
- ☼ **retrograde from November 9 to November 28.**

Venus Retrograde

Venus retrograde events align to times of increased volatility on Cocoa futures. However, the alignment to pivotal price trend changes is lacking in consistency. Futures and options traders who wish to watch for Venus retrograde events should note that:

☼ **In 2025, Venus will be retrograde March 2 to April 12.**

Mars Retrograde

Mars retrograde events align well to tradeable price trend changes on Cocoa futures. However, the alignment to pivotal price trend changes is lacking in consistency. Futures and options traders who wish to watch for Mars retrograde events should note that:

☼ **In 2025, Mars will be retrograde January 1 to February 23.**

FMX Exchange

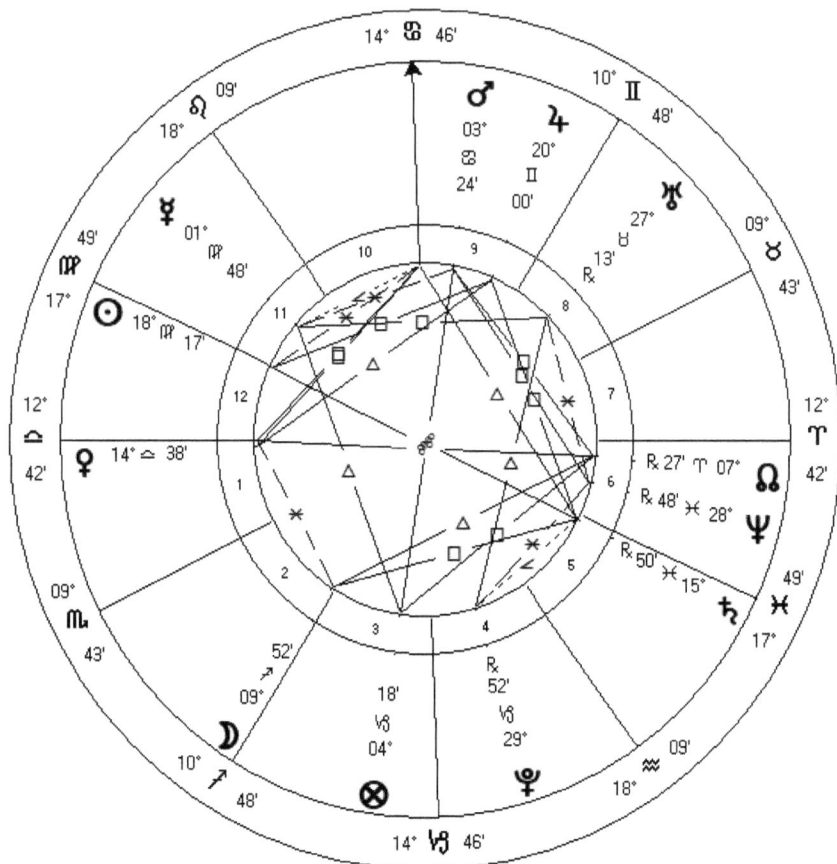

Figure 7-27
FMX Exchange First Trade Horoscope

On September 10, 2024 New York-based investment banker Cantor Fitzgerald launched a new exchange called the FMX Exchange. This upstart exchange will trade interest rate futures contracts. Cantor CEO Howard Lutnick has expressed grand plans to one day rival the established exchanges in size and market penetration.

Figure 7-27 illustrates the natal horoscope for this new Exchange. Assuming a first trade execution time of 8:40 a.m., Venus is positioned right at the Ascendant. The Mid-Heaven is at 14 of Cancer. The choice of September 10 as a first trade date was carefully thought out. In addition, this first trade date comes one day before the anniversary of the events of 9-11 in which Cantor Fitzgerald lost hundreds of employees in the World Trade Center disaster.

Furthermore, Sun and Mercury are in the sign of Virgo. Saturn is 120-degrees trine to the Mid-Heaven. Jupiter is within orb of being 120-degrees trine to the Ascendant. Sun is within orb of being a favorable 30-degrees to the Ascendant. Sun is a favorable 60-degrees to the Mid-Heaven.

On a questionable note, Moon is 90-degrees square to Saturn, Sun is 90-degrees square to Jupiter, and Jupiter is 90-degrees square to Saturn.

It will be interesting to see if this upstart Exchange thrives or not given the three negative aspects present in the natal horoscope.

CHAPTER EIGHT

Quantum Science

Quantum Lines Math

Quantum Price Lines are based on Einstein's quantum theory. The notion of Quantum Lines posits that the price of a stock, index or commodity can be thought of as a light particle or electron that can occupy different energy levels or orbital shells.

Author and market researcher, Fabio Oreste, combined the notion of quantum price lines with Einstein's theory that the planets can cause the fabric of space-time to bend. Picture a group of people holding the edges of a large blanket. They pull on the edges until the blanket is stretched tight. Next, someone places a ball on the tight blanket. The weight of the ball causes a slight sag in the blanket fabric. Next the ball is moved to a different location on the blanket, where the weight of the ball once again causes a sag. The two points of sag are then joined by a line that is sketched onto the blanket. Oreste says the line joining these two points where the ball has caused the blanket to sag is akin to a Quantum Price Line. In his book entitled *Quantum Trading,* [1] Oreste details his formula for Quantum Price Line calculation:

Quantum Line = (N x 360) + PSO ;

Where N is the harmonic level = 1,2,3,4,5,6,8,... (Always think of harmonics in terms of even whole number divisions of a circle. A 3rd harmonic (N=3) is 120-degrees, a 5th harmonic (N=5) is 360/5 =72 degrees, and so on).

Where PSO = heliocentric planetary longitude x Conversion Scale

Where Conversion Scale = 2^n ; 1,2,4,8,16,...; with n=0,1,2,3,4,....

When dealing with prices less than 360, the inverse variation of the formula is used.

Quantum Line = (1/N x 360) + PSO

Oreste's technique can be parsed into sub-divisions of these Quantum Lines. For example, if one calculated the values of a 3rd harmonic and a 4th harmonic quantum line, one could then calculate the ¼, ½, and ¾ sub-divisions of the distance between the lines.

Note the use of *heliocentric* planetary data in these Quantum Line calculations. There are websites that will provide you with this data such as **www.astro.com/swisseph**. You can also purchase a Heliocentric Ephemeris book such as *The American Heliocentric Ephemeris, 2001-2050.*

To assist you with calculating Quantum Lines, consider the following example:

On a given date, suppose the following heliocentric planetary positions are noted: Mars 306 degrees, Jupiter 307 degrees, Neptune 324 degrees, Pluto 271 degrees.

In this example, let N=1 and let the conversion scale be set to CS=1. PSO will be the planetary longitude x CS.

The Oreste point of maximum curvature for these planets is then:

Mars: (N x 360) + PSO; which is (1 x360) + 306 = 666
Jupiter: 360 + 307 = 667
Neptune: 360 + 324 = 684
Pluto: 360 + 271 = 631

If you were to take another date in the future and calculate the points of maximum curvature, you could then join the two points for each planet. By definition two points joined equals a straight line. You could then extend these lines out into the future. These lines are the *Quantum Lines* (or QLs).

If the above maximum curvature numbers seem vaguely familiar, think back to early 2009 and consider: The S&P 500 at the March 6, 2009 low delivered an intra-day price of 665.7 and the close for the day was 687. Indeed, Mars, Jupiter and Neptune all acted in concert on March 6, 2009 to provide a floor of support under the US equity market. Such is the elegance of Quantum Lines.

More recently, in mid-July 2024, the S&P 500 reached an intra-day high of 5688. Using the data in the tables on the following pages, one can quickly identify that at this time the Saturn 6th harmonic quantum line (CS=8) was at 5720. The Neptune 6th harmonic quantum line (CS=8) was at 5760. Both these planets were imposing overhead resistance on human emotion and the market could push no higher.

As an example with prices below 360, consider that in March 2024, Crude Oil reached an intra-day peak of $87.63. The Saturn quantum line (CS=1/4) was at $87.25. Price tried to surpass this resistance level and failed to succeed.

Calculating Quantum Lines is onerous initially. However, with practice the task becomes easier. What follows is a suggested list of some points of maximum curvature you can apply to various indices and commodities for 2025.

These various points are based on the following heliocentric planetary positions at January 1, July 1, and December 30, 2025.

As 2025 begins, sketch the Jan 1 and July 1 points on your charts. Join the points with a line. Later in 2025, add the December 30 point and extend your lines.

HELIOCENTRIC DEGREE POSITION			
Planet	Jan 1, 2025	July 1, 2025	Dec 30, 2025
Jupiter	78	93	106
Saturn	349	355	359
Neptune	359	360	360
Uranus	55	57	59
Pluto	301	302	303

2025 Quantum Levels

JUPITER CS=1

PLANET & HARMONIC	JAN 1	JULY 1	DEC 30
Jupiter 1st	438	453	466
Jupiter 2nd	798	813	826
Jupiter 3rd	1158	1173	1186
Jupiter 4th	1518	1533	1546
Jupiter 5th	2238	2253	2266
Jupiter 6th	2958	2973	2986

JUPITER CS=2

PLANET & HARMONIC	JAN 1	JULY 1	DEC 30
Jupiter 1st	516	546	572
Jupiter 2nd	876	906	932
Jupiter 3rd	1236	1266	1292
Jupiter 4th	1596	1626	1652
Jupiter 5th	2316	2346	2372
Jupiter 6th	3036	3066	3092

JUPITER CS=4

PLANET & HARMONIC	JAN 1	JULY 1	DEC 30
Jupiter 1st	672	732	784
Jupiter 2nd	1032	1092	1144
Jupiter 3rd	1392	1452	1504
Jupiter 4th	1752	1812	1864
Jupiter 5th	2472	2532	2584
Jupiter 6th	3036	3252	3302

JUPITER CS=8

PLANET & HARMONIC	JAN 1	JULY 1	DEC 30
Jupiter 1st	984	1104	1208
Jupiter 2nd	1344	1464	1568
Jupiter 3rd	1704	1824	1928
Jupiter 4th	2064	2184	2288
Jupiter 5th	2784	2904	3008
Jupiter 6th	3504	3624	3728

JUPITER CS=16

PLANET & HARMONIC	JAN 1	JULY 1	DEC 30
Jupiter 1st	1608	1848	2056
Jupiter 2nd	1968	2208	2416
Jupiter 3rd	2328	2568	2776
Jupiter 4th	2688	2928	3136
Jupiter 5th	3408	3648	3856
Jupiter 6th	4128	4368	4576

JUPITER CS=32

PLANET & HARMONIC	JAN 1	JULY 1	DEC 30
Jupiter 1st	2856	3336	3752
Jupiter 2nd	3216	3696	4112
Jupiter 3rd	3576	4056	4472
Jupiter 4th	3936	4416	4832
Jupiter 5th	4656	5136	5552
Jupiter 6th	5376	5856	6272

JUPITER CS=64

PLANET & HARMONIC	JAN 1	JULY 1	DEC 30
Jupiter 1st	5352	6312	7272
Jupiter 2nd	7712	6672	7632
Jupiter 3rd	6072	7032	7992
Jupiter 4th	6432	7392	8352
Jupiter 5th	7152	8112	9072
Jupiter 6th	7872	8832	9792

JUPITER CS=128

PLANET & HARMONIC	JAN 1	JULY 1	DEC 30
Jupiter 1st	9704	12392	14952
Jupiter 2nd	10064	12752	15312
Jupiter 3rd	10424	13112	15672
Jupiter 4th	10784	13472	16032
Jupiter 5th	11504	14192	16752
Jupiter 6th	12224	14912	17472

SATURN CS=1

PLANET & HARMONIC	JAN 1	JULY 1	DEC 30
Saturn 1st	709	715	719
Saturn 2nd	1069	1075	1079
Saturn 3rd	1429	1435	1439
Saturn 4th	1789	1795	1799
Saturn 5th	2509	2515	2519
Saturn 6th	3229	3235	3239

SATURN CS=2

PLANET & HARMONIC	JAN 1	JULY 1	DEC 30
Saturn 1st	1058	1070	1078
Saturn 2nd	1419	1430	1438
Saturn 3rd	1778	1790	1798
Saturn 4th	2138	2150	2158
Saturn 5th	2858	2870	2878
Saturn 6th	3578	3590	3598

SATURN CS=4

PLANET & HARMONIC	JAN 1	JULY 1	DEC 30
Saturn 1st	1756	1780	1796
Saturn 2nd	2116	2140	2156
Saturn 3rd	2476	2500	2526
Saturn 4th	2836	2860	2876
Saturn 5th	3556	3580	3596
Saturn 6th	4276	4300	4316

SATURN CS=8

PLANET & HARMONIC	JAN 1	JULY 1	DEC 30
Saturn 1st	3152	3200	3232
Saturn 2nd	3512	3560	3592
Saturn 3rd	3872	3920	3952
Saturn 4th	4232	4280	4312
Saturn 5th	4952	5000	5032
Saturn 6th	5672	5720	5752

SATURN CS=16

PLANET & HARMONIC	JAN 1	JULY 1	DEC 30
Saturn 1st	5944	6040	6104
Saturn 2nd	6304	6400	6464
Saturn 3rd	6664	6760	6824
Saturn 4th	7024	7120	7184
Saturn 5th	7744	7840	7904
Saturn 6th	8464	8560	8624

SATURN CS=32

PLANET & HARMONIC	JAN 1	JULY 1	DEC 30
Saturn 1st	11528	11720	11848
Saturn 2nd	11888	12080	12208
Saturn 3rd	12248	12440	12568
Saturn 4th	12608	12800	12928
Saturn 5th	13328	13520	13648
Saturn 6th	14048	14420	14368

URANUS CS=1

PLANET & HARMONIC	JAN 1	JULY 1	DEC 30
Uranus 1st	415	417	419
Uranus 2nd	775	777	779
Uranus 3rd	1135	1137	1139
Uranus 4th	1495	1497	1499
Uranus 5th	2215	2217	2219
Uranus 6th	2935	2937	2939

URANUS CS=2

PLANET & HARMONIC	JAN 1	JULY 1	DEC 30
Uranus 1st	470	474	478
Uranus 2nd	830	834	838
Uranus 3rd	1190	1194	1198
Uranus 4th	1550	1554	1558
Uranus 5th	2220	2274	2278
Uranus 6th	2990	2994	2998

URANUS CS=4

PLANET & HARMONIC	JAN 1	JULY 1	DEC 30
Uranus 1st	580	588	596
Uranus 2nd	940	948	956
Uranus 3rd	1300	1308	1316
Uranus 4th	1660	1668	1676
Uranus 5th	2380	2388	2396
Uranus 6th	3100	3108	3116

URANUS CS=8

PLANET & HARMONIC	JAN 1	JULY 1	DEC 30
Uranus 1st	800	816	832
Uranus 2nd	1160	1176	1192
Uranus 3rd	1520	1536	1552
Uranus 4th	1880	1896	1912
Uranus 5th	2600	2616	2632
Uranus 6th	3320	3336	3352

URANUS CS=16

PLANET & HARMONIC	JAN 1	JULY 1	DEC 30
Uranus 1st	1240	1272	1304
Uranus 2nd	1600	1632	1664
Uranus 3rd	1960	1992	2024
Uranus 4th	2320	2352	2384
Uranus 5th	3040	3072	3104
Uranus 6th	3760	3792	3824

URANUS CS=32

PLANET & HARMONIC	JAN 1	JULY 1	DEC 30
Uranus 1st	2120	2184	2248
Uranus 2nd	2480	2544	2608
Uranus 3rd	2840	2904	2968
Uranus 4th	3200	3264	3328
Uranus 5th	3920	3984	4048
Uranus 6th	4640	4704	4768

URANUS CS=64

PLANET & HARMONIC	JAN 1	JULY 1	DEC 30
Uranus 1st	3880	4008	4136
Uranus 2nd	4240	4368	4496
Uranus 3rd	4600	4728	4856
Uranus 4th	4960	5088	5216
Uranus 5th	5680	5808	5936
Uranus 6th	6400	6528	6656

URANUS CS=128

PLANET & HARMONIC	JAN 1	JULY 1	DEC 30
Uranus 1st	7400	7656	7912
Uranus 2nd	7760	8016	8272
Uranus 3rd	8120	8376	8632
Uranus 4th	8480	8736	8992
Uranus 5th	9200	9456	9712
Uranus 6th	9920	10176	10432

URANUS CS=256

PLANET & HARMONIC	JAN 1	JULY 1	DEC 30
Uranus 1st	14440	14952	15464
Uranus 2nd	14800	15312	15824
Uranus 3rd	15160	15672	16184
Uranus 4th	15520	16032	16544
Uranus 5th	16240	16752	17264
Uranus 6th	16960	17472	17984

NEPTUNE CS=1

PLANET & HARMONIC	JAN 1	JULY 1	DEC 30
Neptune 1st	719	720	721
Neptune 2nd	1079	1080	1081
Neptune 3rd	1439	1440	1441
Neptune 4th	1799	1800	1801
Neptune 5th	2519	2520	2521
Neptune 6th	3239	3240	3241

NEPTUNE CS=2

PLANET & HARMONIC	JAN 1	JULY 1	DEC 30
Neptune 1st	1078	1080	1082
Neptune 2nd	1438	1440	1442
Neptune 3rd	1798	1800	1802
Neptune 4th	2158	2160	2162
Neptune 5th	2878	2880	2882
Neptune 6th	3598	3600	3602

NEPTUNE CS=4

PLANET & HARMONIC	JAN 1	JULY 1	DEC 30
Neptune 1st	1796	1800	1804
Neptune 2nd	2156	2160	2164
Neptune 3rd	2516	2520	2524
Neptune 4th	2876	2880	2884
Neptune 5th	3596	3600	3604
Neptune 6th	4316	4320	4324

NEPTUNE CS=8

PLANET & HARMONIC	JAN 1	JULY 1	DEC 30
Neptune 1st	3232	3240	3248
Neptune 2nd	3592	3600	3608
Neptune 3rd	3952	3960	3968
Neptune 4th	4312	4320	4328
Neptune 5th	5032	5040	5048
Neptune 6th	5752	5760	5768

NEPTUNE CS=16

PLANET & HARMONIC	JAN 1	JULY 1	DEC 30
Neptune 1st	6104	6120	6136
Neptune 2nd	6464	6480	6496
Neptune 3rd	6824	6840	6856
Neptune 4th	7184	7200	7216
Neptune 5th	7904	7920	7936
Neptune 6th	8624	8640	8656

NEPTUNE CS=32

PLANET & HARMONIC	JAN 1	JULY 1	DEC 30
Neptune 1st	11848	11880	11912
Neptune 2nd	12208	12240	12272
Neptune 3rd	12568	12600	12632
Neptune 4th	12928	12960	12992
Neptune 5th	13648	13680	13712
Neptune 6th	14368	14400	13432

PLUTO CS=1

PLANET & HARMONIC	JAN 1	JULY 1	DEC 30
Pluto 1st	661	662	663
Pluto 2nd	1021	1022	1023
Pluto 3rd	1381	1382	1383
Pluto 4th	1741	1742	1743
Pluto 5th	2461	2462	2463
Pluto 6th	3181	3182	3183

PLUTO CS=2

PLANET & HARMONIC	JAN 1	JULY 1	DEC 30
Pluto 1st	962	964	966
Pluto 2nd	1322	1324	1326
Pluto 3rd	1682	1684	1686
Pluto 4th	2042	2044	2046
Pluto 5th	2762	2764	2766
Pluto 6th	3482	3484	3486

PLUTO CS=4

PLANET & HARMONIC	JAN 1	JULY 1	DEC 30
Pluto 1st	1564	1568	1572
Pluto 2nd	1924	1928	1932
Pluto 3rd	2284	2288	2292
Pluto 4th	2644	2648	2652
Pluto 5th	3364	3368	3372
Pluto 6th	4084	4088	4092

PLUTO CS=8

PLANET & HARMONIC	JAN 1	JULY 1	DEC 30
Pluto 1st	2768	2776	2784
Pluto 2nd	3128	3136	3144
Pluto 3rd	3488	3496	3504
Pluto 4th	3884	3856	3864
Pluto 5th	4568	4576	4584
Pluto 6th	5288	5296	5304

PLUTO CS=16

PLANET & HARMONIC	JAN 1	JULY 1	DEC 30
Pluto 1st	5176	5192	5208
Pluto 2nd	5536	5552	5568
Pluto 3rd	5896	5912	5928
Pluto 4th	6256	6272	6288
Pluto 5th	6976	6992	7008
Pluto 6th	7696	7712	7728

PLUTO CS=32

PLANET & HARMONIC	JAN 1	JULY 1	DEC 30
Pluto 1st	9992	10024	10056
Pluto 2nd	10352	10384	10416
Pluto 3rd	10712	10744	10776
Pluto 4th	11072	11104	11136
Pluto 5th	11792	11824	11856
Pluto 6th	12512	12544	12576

JUPITER CS=1/2

PLANET & HARMONIC	JAN 1	JULY 1	DEC 30
Jupiter 1st	39.00	46.50	53.00
Jupiter 24th	39.06	45.56	53.06

JUPITER CS=1/4

PLANET & HARMONIC	JAN 1	JULY 1	DEC 30
Jupiter 1st	19.50	23.25	26.50
Jupiter 24th	19.56	23.31	26.56

JUPITER CS=1/8

PLANET & HARMONIC	JAN 1	JULY 1	DEC 30
Jupiter 1st	9.75	11.62	13.25
Jupiter 24th	9.81	11.69	13.31

JUPITER CS=1/16

PLANET & HARMONIC	JAN 1	JULY 1	DEC 30
Jupiter 1st	4.87	5.81	6.62
Jupiter 24th	4.94	5.88	6.69

JUPITER CS=1/32

PLANET & HARMONIC	JAN 1	JULY 1	DEC 30
Jupiter 1st	2.44	2.90	3.31
Jupiter 24th	2.50	2.97	3.37

JUPITER CS=1/64

PLANET & HARMONIC	JAN 1	JULY 1	DEC 30
Jupiter 1st	1.22	1.45	1.65
Jupiter 24th	1.28	1.51	1.72

JUPITER CS=1/128

PLANET & HARMONIC	JAN 1	JULY 1	DEC 30
Jupiter 1st	0.612	0.729	0.830
Jupiter 12th	0.642	0.759	0.861
Jupiter 24th	0.676	0.793	0.894

SATURN CS=1/2

PLANET & HARMONIC	JAN 1	JULY 1	DEC 30
Jupiter 1st	174.50	177.50	179.50
Jupiter 24th	174.56	177.56	179.56

SATURN CS=1/4

PLANET & HARMONIC	JAN 1	JULY 1	DEC 30
Jupiter 1st	87.25	88.75	89.25
Jupiter 24th	87.31	88.81	89.81

SATURN CS=1/8

PLANET & HARMONIC	JAN 1	JULY 1	DEC 30
Jupiter 1st	43.62	44.37	44.87
Jupiter 24th	43.69	44.44	44.94

SATURN CS=1/16

PLANET & HARMONIC	JAN 1	JULY 1	DEC 30
Jupiter 1st	21.81	22.19	22.44
Jupiter 24th	21.87	22.25	22.50

SATURN CS=1/32

PLANET & HARMONIC	JAN 1	JULY 1	DEC 30
Saturn 1st	10.90	11.09	11.22
Saturn 24th	10.97	11.16	11.28

SATURN CS=1/64

PLANET & HARMONIC	JAN 1	JULY 1	DEC 30
Saturn 1st	5.45	5.49	5.61
Jupiter 24th	5.52	5.61	5.67

SATURN CS=1/128

PLANET & HARMONIC	JAN 1	JULY 1	DEC 30
Saturn 1st	2.72	2.77	2.80
Saturn 24th	2.79	2.84	2.87

SATURN CS=1/256

PLANET & HARMONIC	JAN 1	JULY 1	DEC 30
Saturn 1st	1.36	1.38	1.40
Saturn 24th	1.42	1.45	1.47

SATURN CS=1/512

PLANET & HARMONIC	JAN 1	JULY 1	DEC 30
Saturn 1st	0.683	0.695	0.702
Saturn 12th	0.713	0.725	0.733
Saturn 24th	0.747	0.759	0.766

URANUS CS=1/2

PLANET & HARMONIC	JAN 1	JULY 1	DEC 30
Uranus 1st	27.50	28.50	29.50
Uranus 24th	27.56	28.56	29.56

URANUS CS=1/4

PLANET & HARMONIC	JAN 1	JULY 1	DEC 30
Uranus 1st	13.75	14.25	14.75
Uranus 24th	13.81	14.31	14.81

URANUS CS=1/8

PLANET & HARMONIC	JAN 1	JULY 1	DEC 30
Uranus 1st	6.87	7.12	7.37
Uranus 24th	6.94	7.19	7.44

URANUS CS=1/16

PLANET & HARMONIC	JAN 1	JULY 1	DEC 30
Uranus 1st	3.44	3.56	3.69
Uranus 24th	3.50	3.62	3.75

URANUS CS=1/32

PLANET & HARMONIC	JAN 1	JULY 1	DEC 30
Uranus 1st	1.72	1.78	1.84
Uranus 24th	1.78	1.84	1.91

URANUS CS=1/64

PLANET & HARMONIC	JAN 1	JULY 1	DEC 30
Uranus 1st	0.862	0.893	0.924
Uranus 12th	0.892	0.923	0.955
Uranus 24th	0.926	0.957	0.988

NEPTUNE CS=1/2

PLANET & HARMONIC	JAN 1	JULY 1	DEC 30
Neptune 1st	179.50	180	180.50
Neptune 24th	179.56	180.06	180.56

NEPTUNE CS=1/4

PLANET & HARMONIC	JAN 1	JULY 1	DEC 30
Neptune 1st	89.75	90	90.25
Neptune 24th	89.81	90.06	90.31

NEPTUNE CS=1/8

PLANET & HARMONIC	JAN 1	JULY 1	DEC 30
Neptune 1st	44.87	45	45.12
Neptune 24th	44.94	45.06	45.20

NEPTUNE CS=1/16

PLANET & HARMONIC	JAN 1	JULY 1	DEC 30
Neptune 1st	22.44	22.50	22.56
Neptune 24th	22.50	22.56	22.63

NEPTUNE CS=1/32

PLANET & HARMONIC	JAN 1	JULY 1	DEC 30
Neptune 1st	11.22	11.25	11.28
Neptune 24th	11.28	11.31	11.34

NEPTUNE CS=1/64

PLANET & HARMONIC	JAN 1	JULY 1	DEC 30
Neptune 1st	5.61	5.62	5.64
Neptune 24th	5.67	5.69	5.70

NEPTUNE CS=1/128

PLANET & HARMONIC	JAN 1	JULY 1	DEC 30
Neptune 1st	2.80	2.81	2.82
Neptune 24th	2.87	2.89	2.90

NEPTUNE CS=1/256

PLANET & HARMONIC	JAN 1	JULY 1	DEC 30
Neptune 1st	1.402	1.406	1.410
Neptune 12th	1.433	1.437	1.441
Neptune 24th	1.466	1.47	1.474

NEPTUNE CS=1/512

PLANET & HARMONIC	JAN 1	JULY 1	DEC 30
Neptune 1st	0.702	0.704	0.706
Neptune 12th	0.733	0.735	0.737
Neptune 24th	0.766	0.768	0.770

PLUTO CS=1/2

PLANET & HARMONIC	JAN 1	JULY 1	DEC 30
Pluto 1st	150.5	151	151.50
Pluto 24th	150.56	151.06	151.56

PLUTO CS=1/4

PLANET & HARMONIC	JAN 1	JULY 1	DEC 30
Pluto 1st	75.25	75.50	75.75
Pluto 24th	75.31	75.56	75.81

PLUTO CS=1/8

PLANET & HARMONIC	JAN 1	JULY 1	DEC 30
Pluto 1st	37.62	37.75	37.87
Pluto 24th	37.69	37.81	37.94

PLUTO CS=1/16

PLANET & HARMONIC	JAN 1	JULY 1	DEC 30
Pluto 1st	18.81	18.87	18.94
Pluto 24th	18.87	18.94	19.00

PLUTO CS=1/32

PLANET & HARMONIC	JAN 1	JULY 1	DEC 30
Pluto 1st	9.40	9.44	9.47
Pluto 24th	9.47	9.50	9.59

PLUTO CS=1/64

PLANET & HARMONIC	JAN 1	JULY 1	DEC 30
Pluto 1st	4.70	4.72	4.73
Pluto 24th	4.76	4.78	4.80

PLUTO CS=1/128

PLANET & HARMONIC	JAN 1	JULY 1	DEC 30
Pluto 1st	2.35	2.36	2.37
Pluto 12th	2.38	2.39	2.40
Pluto 24th	2.41	2.42	2.44

PLUTO CS=1/256

PLANET & HARMONIC	JAN 1	JULY 1	DEC 30
Pluto 1st	1.17	1.18	1.185
Pluto 12th	1.207	1.211	1.215
Pluto 24th	1.24	1.244	1.248

PLUTO CS=1/512

PLANET & HARMONIC	JAN 1	JULY 1	DEC 30
Pluto 1st	0.589	0.591	0.593
Pluto 12th	0.620	0.622	0.624
Pluto 24th	0.653	0.655	0.657

FINAL WORDS

I have taken you on a wide-ranging journey to acquaint you with the mathematical links between planetary activity and market price behavior. I sincerely hope you will embrace planetary cycles as a valuable tool to assist you in your trading and investing activity. I hope you will pause often to contemplate the price action you see unfolding on stocks, commodities, and indices. Are these ups and downs in price strictly an emotional reaction of market participants to events in the cosmos, or are traders at large investment institutions anticipating planetary events and exacerbating price volatility? Or, is it a combination of both?

If you decide to embrace financial astrology as a tool to help you navigate the markets, I encourage you to stick with it. At first it might seem daunting, but fight the urge to give up. Soon enough, trading and investing will take on a new meaning.

To encourage you, I will leave you with the words of Neil Turok from his 2012 book, *The Universe Within*:[1]

"Perseverance leads to enlightenment. And the truth is more beautiful than your wildest dreams."

NOTES

&

RECOMMENDED

READING

Introduction

1) McWhirter, L. (1938) *McWhirter Theory of Stock Market Forecasting*. Astro Book Company, USA.
2) Bradley, D. (1948) *Stock Market Prediction*. Llewellyn Publishers, USA.

Chapter 1

Figure 1-1: Loes Ten Kate, I. (2006) *Organics on Mars -Laboratory studies of organic material under simulated Martian conditions*. Ph.D. Thesis.

Figure 1-2: **www.wikimediacommons.com**. File: Earth's orbit and ecliptic.PNG

Figure 1-3: **https://www.elsaelsa.com/astrology/zodiac-sign-glyphs**

Figure 1-4: **http://mysticaltransformations.com**

Figure 1-5: **https://serc.carleton.edu/mel/teaching_resources/**

moon_mel.html
Figure 1-7: **http://www.astronomy.ohio-state.edu/ ~pogge/ Ast161/Unit2**
1) Read, B. (1970) Fibonacci Series in the Solar System. The Fibonacci Quarterly. October issue, p. 428.
2) Seddon, C. (2021) Mercury: Elusive Messenger of the Gods. Glanville Press, USA.
3) Ebertin, R. (1972) *Applied Cosmobiology*. AFA Inc, USA.

Chapter 3

1) McWhirter, L. (1938) *McWhirter Theory of Stock Market Forecasting*. Astro Book Company, USA.

Chapter 4

1) Cahn, J. (2011) *The Harbinger*. Charisma Media, USA.
2) Cahn, J. (2016) *The Book of Mysteries*. Charisma Media, USA.
3) Cahn, J. (2017) *The Paradigm*. Charisma Media, USA.
4) Wong, M.(2005) Tunnel Through the Air. *Traders World*. Issue 39, p.46.

Chapter 5

1) Long, J. (1992) *Basic astrotech: A new technique for trading commodities using geocosmic energy fields with technical analysis.* 6th ed. Professional Astrology Service Inc. USA.
2) Bradley, D. (2004) *Stock Market Prediction: The Historical and Future Siderograph Charts*. Books Work. USA.
3) Kramer, J. (1995) *Astrology Really Works*. Hay House, USA.
4) Gann, W.D. (1927) *Tunnel Through the Air*. Pantainos Classics, USA.

Chapter 6

1) McWhirter, L. (1938) *McWhirter Theory of Stock Market Forecasting*. Astro Book Company, USA.

Chapter 8

1) Oreste, F. (2011) *Quantum Trading*. J. Wiley & Sons, USA.

Final Words

1) Turok, N. (2012) *The Universe Within*. House of Anansi Press, Canada.

GLOSSARY

Ascendant: one of four cardinal points on a horoscope, the Ascendant denotes the constellation visible at a given time on the eastern horizon

Aspect: the angular relationship between two planets measured in degrees

Autumnal Equinox (see Equinox): the time of year when Sun is at zero-degrees Libra

Conjunct: an angular relationship of zero-degrees between two planets

Cosmo-biology: changes in human emotion caused by changes in cosmic energy

Declination: the amount (in degrees) that a planet wanders above or below the ecliptic plane as measured using heliocentric data

Descendant: one of four cardinal points on a horoscope, the Descendant denotes the constellation visible at a given time on the western horizon

Ecliptic Plane: the plane of motion traveled by the planets as they orbit the Sun

Elongation: the angle between a planet and the Sun, based on an observer's position on Earth

Ephemeris: a daily tabular compilation of planetary and lunar positions

Equinox: an event occurring twice annually that marks the time when the tilt of the Earth's axis is neither toward nor away from the Sun

Fibonacci Sequence: a recursive mathematical sequence in which a given term is the sum of the two preceding terms. (The infinite sequence is as follows: 0,1,1,2,3,5,8,13,21,34,55,89…)

First Trade chart: a zodiac chart depicting the positions of the planets at the time a company's stock or a commodity future commenced trading on a recognized financial exchange

First Trade date: the date a stock or commodity futures contract first began trading on a recognized exchange

Full Moon: from a vantage point situated on Earth, when the Moon is seen to be 180-degrees to the Sun

Gann Master Cycle: the 19.86-year time span from heliocentric Saturn and Jupiter being conjunct to once again being conjunct

Geocentric: planetary location system in which the vantage point for determining planetary aspects is the Earth

Heliocentric: planetary location system in which the vantage point for determining planetary aspects is the Sun

Horoscope: an image of the zodiac overlaid with the positions of the planets

House: a 1/12th portion of the zodiac. Portions are not necessarily equal depending on the mathematical formula used to calculate the divisions

Lunar Month: (see Synodic Month)

Lunation: (see New Moon)

McWhirter Cycle: The 18.6-year time span in which the North Node progresses around the 12 zodiac signs

Mid-Heaven: one of four cardinal points on a horoscope, situated in the South

Natal: the position of a planet at the time of creation of a futures contract, or the IPO of a stock

New Moon: when the Moon is seen to be zero-degrees to the Sun.

North Node of Moon: the intersection points between the Moon's plane and Earth's ecliptic are termed the *North* and *South* nodes (Astrologers tend to focus on the North node and Ephemeris tables list the zodiacal position of the North Node for each calendar day.)

Orb: the amount of flexibility or tolerance given to an aspect

Quantum Point: a mathematical construct that refers to the point of maximum distortion of the time-space fabric due to the presence of a planet

Retrograde motion: the apparent backwards motion of a planet through the zodiac signs when viewed from a vantage point on Earth

Sidereal Month: the Moon orbits Earth with a slightly elliptical pattern in approximately 27.3 days, relative to a fixed frame of reference

Sidereal Orbital Period: the time required for a planet to make one full orbit of the Sun as viewed from a fixed vantage point on the Sun.

Siderograph: a mathematical equation developed by astrologer Donald Bradley in 1946. (By plotting the output of the equation against the date, inflection points can be seen on the plotted curve. It is at these inflection points that human emotion is most apt to change resulting in a trend change on the Dow Jones or S&P 500 Index.)

Solstice: occurring twice annually, a solstice event marks the time when the Sun reaches its highest or lowest altitude above the horizon at noon

Synodic Month: from a moving frame of reference, the 29.5-day time span for the Moon to orbit the Earth

Synodic Orbital Period: the time required for a planet to make one full orbit of the Sun as viewed from a fixed vantage point on Earth

Transiting: the action of a planet moving past a selected point of the zodiac wheel

Vernal Equinox: the time of the year when Sun is at zero-degrees Aries

Zodiac: an imaginary band encircling the 360-degrees of the planetary system divided into twelve equal portions of 30-degrees each

Zodiac Wheel: a circular image broken into 12 portions of 30-degrees each. Each portion represents a different astrological sign

ABOUT THE AUTHOR

Malcolm Bucholtz, B.Sc, MBA, M.Sc., is a graduate of Queen's University (Faculty of Engineering) in Canada and Heriot Watt University in Scotland (where he received an MBA degree and a M.Sc. degree). After working in Canadian industry for far too many years, Malcolm followed his passion for the financial markets by becoming an Investment Advisor/Commodity Trading Advisor with an independent brokerage firm in western Canada. Today, he resides in Saskatchewan, Canada where he trades the financial markets using technical chart analysis, esoteric mathematics, and the planetary principles outlined in this book.

Malcolm is the author of several books. His first book, T*he Bull, the Bear and the Planets*, offers the reader an introduction to financial astrology and makes the case that there are esoteric and astrological phenomena that influence the financial markets. His second book, *The Lost Science*, takes the reader on a deeper journey into planetary events and unique mathematical phenomena that influence financial markets. His third book, *De-Mystifying the McWhirter Theory of Stock Market Forecasting* seeks to simplify and illustrate the McWhirter methodology. *The Cosmic Clock* follows from the *Lost Science* and helps the reader become better acquainted with planetary events that influence markets. Malcolm has been writing the *Financial Astrology Almanac* each year since 2014. In 2023, he also released *Follow the Trend*, a book to assist traders and investors in identifying price trend changes on indices, stocks, and commodity futures.

Malcolm maintains a website (**www.investingsuccess.ca**) where he provides traders and investors with astrological insights into the financial markets. He also offers the *Astrology Letter* where subscribers receive twice-monthly previews of pending astrological events that stand to influence markets.

RECOMMENDED READING

Follow the Trend, M.G, Bucholtz, (Canada 2023).

The Cosmic Clock, M.G. Bucholtz (Canada, 2016).

Stock Market Forecasting – The McWhirter Method De-Mystified, M.G. Bucholtz, (Canada, 2014).

A Theory of Continuous Planet Interaction, *NCGR Research Journal*, T. Waterfall, Volume 4, Spring 2014, pp 67-87.

The Bull, the Bear and the Planets, M.G. Bucholtz, (USA, 2013).

The Lost Science, M.G. Bucholtz, (USA, 2013)

Financial Astrology, Giacomo Albano, (U.K., 2011)

The Universal Clock, J. Long, (USA, 1995)

OTHER BOOKS BY THE AUTHOR

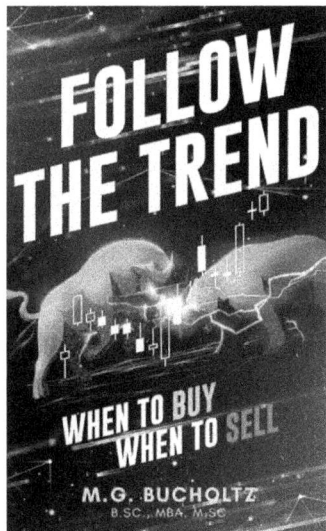

Follow The Trend

Geopolitical unrest, increasing inflation and interest rates, financial blogs and media channels with rock-star status fund managers touting the latest, greatest investment idea. The emotions of traders and investors are continually being pulled in multiple directions at once. What to buy? When to buy? When to sell? At times the noise can be deafening.

This book introduces the reader to the concept of the *trend*; the direction of price movement. Is price moving in a bullish direction or bearish direction? Is the trend changing? Paying attention to changes of trend on a stock, an index, an ETF, or a commodity futures contract can help traders and investors tune out the noise and re-gain a sense of clarity.

The trend is seldom mentioned in financial media. Instead, the media serves up a constant stream of angst and drama. The trend is also ignored by individual financial advisors who prefer to promote the strategy of buying and holding for the long term. This book pushes back against the angst, drama, and passive complacency that pervades our investment decision making. There was a time when the trend *was* followed. In the 1930s, H.M. Gartley taught investors how to use major and intermediate trend lines to make better buying and selling decisions. W.D. Gann also focused on the trend, using swing points to delineate buying and selling opportunities. The 1980s and 1990s heralded computer algorithms and chart technical indicators to more effectively demarcate changes in trend.

Follow The Trend shows the reader how to apply trend lines and swing points to make buy and sell decisions. This book goes on to examine a number of chart technical indicators and answers the following questions: How are they mathematically structured? What do they reveal about the trend? How should they be interpreted? Are some better than others? Follow The Trend – When to Buy and When to Sell offers a fresh way to look at trading and investing, giving the reader the knowledge to answer the two critical questions: When to Buy? When to Sell?

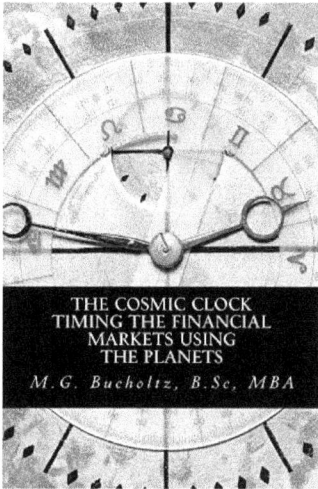

The Cosmic Clock

Are price swings on Crude Oil, Soybeans, the British pound and other financial instruments a reflection of planetary placements?

Can the movements of the Moon affect the stock market?

THE COSMIC CLOCK
TIMING THE FINANCIAL
MARKETS USING
THE PLANETS
M.G. Bucholtz, B.Sc, MBA

The answer to these questions is YES. Changes in price trends on the markets are in fact related to our changing emotions. Our emotions, in turn, are impacted by the changing events in our cosmos.

In the early part of the 20th century, many successful traders on Wall Street, including the venerable W.D. Gann and the mysterious Louise McWhirter, understood that emotion was linked to the forces of the cosmos. They used astrological events and esoteric mathematics to predict changes in price trend and to profit from the markets.

However, by the latter part of the 20th century, the investment community had become more comfortable in relying on academic financial theory and the opinions of colorful television media personalities, all wrapped up in a buy and hold mentality.

The Cosmic Clock has been written for traders and investors who are seeking to gain an understanding of the cosmic forces that influence emotion and the financial markets.

This book will acquaint you with an extensive range of astrological and mathematical phenomena-from the Golden Mean and Fibonacci Sequence through planetary transit lines, quantum lines, the McWhirter method, planetary conjunctions and market cycles. The numerous illustrated examples show how these unique phenomena can deepen your understanding of the financial markets with the goal of making you a better trader and investor.

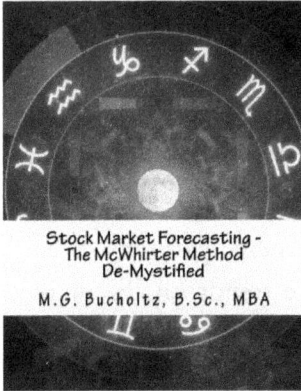

Stock Market Forecasting -
The McWhirter Method
De-Mystified

M.G. Bucholtz, B.Sc., MBA

Stock Market Forecasting: The McWhirter Method De-Mystified

Very little is known about Louise McWhirter, except that in 1937 she wrote the book, *McWhirter Theory of Stock Market Forecasting*.

In my travels to places as far away as the British Library in London, England to research financial Astrology, not once did I come across any other books by McWhirter. Nor did I find any other book from her era that even mentioned her name. I find all of this to be deeply mysterious. Whoever she was, she wrote only one book. It is a powerful one that is as accurate today as it was back in 1937. The purpose of writing this book is suggested by the title itself – to de-mystify McWhirter's methodology.

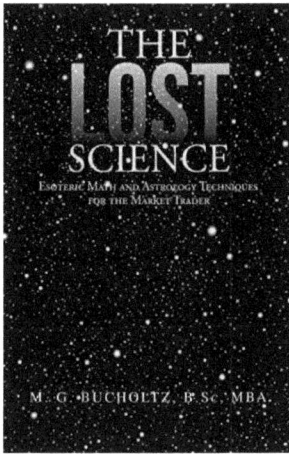

The Lost Science

The financial markets are a reflection of the psychological emotions of traders and investors. These emotions ebb and flow in harmony with the forces of nature.

Scientific techniques and phenomena such as square root mathematics, the Golden Mean, the Golden Sequence, lunar events, planetary transits and planetary aspects have been used by civilizations dating as far back as the ancient Egyptians in order to comprehend the forces of nature.

The emotions of traders and investors can fluctuate in accordance with these forces of nature. Lunar events can be seen to align with trend changes on financial markets. Significant market cycles align with planetary transits and aspects. Price patterns on stocks, commodity futures and market indices can be seen to conform to square root and Golden Mean mathematics.

In the early years of the 20th century, the most successful traders on Wall Street, including the venerable W.D. Gann, used these scientific techniques and phenomena to profit from the markets. However, over the ensuing decades as technology has advanced, the science has been lost.

The Lost Science acquaints the reader with an extensive range of astrological and mathematical phenomena. From the Golden Mean and Fibonacci Sequence, to planetary transit lines and square roots through to an examination of lunar and planetary aspects, the numerous illustrated examples in this book show the reader how these unique scientific phenomena impact the financial markets.

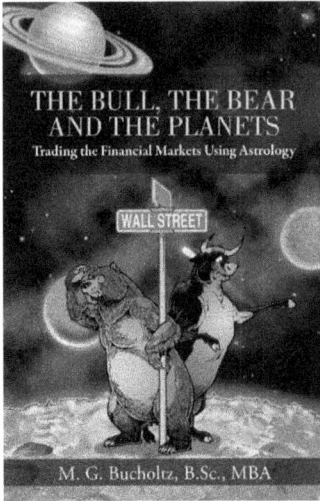

The Bull, The Bear and The Planets

Once maligned by many, the subject of financial astrology is now experiencing a revival as traders and investors seek deeper insight into the forces that move the financial markets.

The markets are a dynamic entity fueled by many factors, some of which we can easily comprehend, some of which are esoteric. *The Bull, The Bear and the Planets* introduces the reader to the notion that astrological phenomena can influence price action on financial markets and create trend changes across both short and longer term time horizons. From an introduction to the historical basics behind astrology through to an examination of lunar astrology and planetary aspects, the numerous examples in this book will introduce the reader to the power of astrology and its impact on both equity markets and commodity futures markets.

APPENDIX A

DATE	MOON	DATE	MOON
Jan 1 2025	26°Cp43'	Feb 1 2025	17°Pi56'
Jan 2 2025	10°Aq18'	Feb 2 2025	02°Ar17'
Jan 3 2025	24°Aq02'	Feb 3 2025	16°Ar36'
Jan 4 2025	07°Pi53'	Feb 4 2025	00°Ta51'
Jan 5 2025	21°Pi49'	Feb 5 2025	14°Ta59'
Jan 6 2025	05°Ar50'	Feb 6 2025	28°Ta59'
Jan 7 2025	19°Ar54'	Feb 7 2025	12°Ge51'
Jan 8 2025	04°Ta00'	Feb 8 2025	26°Ge33'
Jan 9 2025	18°Ta09'	Feb 9 2025	10°Cn05'
Jan 10 2025	02°Ge17'	Feb 10 2025	23°Cn24'
Jan 11 2025	16°Ge22'	Feb 11 2025	06°Le31'
Jan 12 2025	00°Cn20'	Feb 12 2025	19°Le23'
Jan 13 2025	14°Cn07'	Feb 13 2025	02°Vi01'
Jan 14 2025	27°Cn39'	Feb 14 2025	14°Vi25'
Jan 15 2025	10°Le53'	Feb 15 2025	26°Vi36'
Jan 16 2025	23°Le47'	Feb 16 2025	08°Li36'
Jan 17 2025	06°Vi22'	Feb 17 2025	20°Li29'
Jan 18 2025	18°Vi40'	Feb 18 2025	02°Sc18'
Jan 19 2025	00°Li43'	Feb 19 2025	14°Sc07'
Jan 20 2025	12°Li36'	Feb 20 2025	26°Sc02'
Jan 21 2025	24°Li25'	Feb 21 2025	08°Sg07'
Jan 22 2025	06°Sc14'	Feb 22 2025	20°Sg27'
Jan 23 2025	18°Sc09'	Feb 23 2025	03°Cp07'
Jan 24 2025	00°Sg16'	Feb 24 2025	16°Cp10'
Jan 25 2025	12°Sg37'	Feb 25 2025	29°Cp37'
Jan 26 2025	25°Sg18'	Feb 26 2025	13°Aq29'
Jan 27 2025	08°Cp20'	Feb 27 2025	27°Aq43'
Jan 28 2025	21°Cp44'	Feb 28 2025	12°Pi16'
Jan 29 2025	05°Aq27'		
Jan 30 2025	19°Aq26'		
Jan 31 2025	03°Pi38'		

DATE	MOON
Mar 1 2025	27°Pi00'
Mar 2 2025	11°Ar48'
Mar 3 2025	26°Ar34'
Mar 4 2025	11°Ta10'
Mar 5 2025	25°Ta34'
Mar 6 2025	09°Ge40'
Mar 7 2025	23°Ge29'
Mar 8 2025	07°Cn01'
Mar 9 2025	20°Cn15'
Mar 10 2025	03°Le13'
Mar 11 2025	15°Le58'
Mar 12 2025	28°Le29'
Mar 13 2025	10°Vi49'
Mar 14 2025	22°Vi58'
Mar 15 2025	05°Li00'
Mar 16 2025	16°Li55'
Mar 17 2025	28°Li46'
Mar 18 2025	10°Sc34'
Mar 19 2025	22°Sc25'
Mar 20 2025	04°Sg20'
Mar 21 2025	16°Sg25'
Mar 22 2025	28°Sg43'
Mar 23 2025	11°Cp18'
Mar 24 2025	24°Cp15'
Mar 25 2025	07°Aq37'
Mar 26 2025	21°Aq25'
Mar 27 2025	05°Pi40'
Mar 28 2025	20°Pi19'
Mar 29 2025	05°Ar15'
Mar 30 2025	20°Ar22'
Mar 31 2025	05°Ta30'

DATE	MOON
Apr 1 2025	20°Ta29'
Apr 2 2025	05°Ge13'
Apr 3 2025	19°Ge35'
Apr 4 2025	03°Cn32'
Apr 5 2025	17°Cn05'
Apr 6 2025	00°Le14'
Apr 7 2025	13°Le02'
Apr 8 2025	25°Le32'
Apr 9 2025	07°Vi49'
Apr 10 2025	19°Vi55'
Apr 11 2025	01°Li53'
Apr 12 2025	13°Li46'
Apr 13 2025	25°Li37'
Apr 14 2025	07°Sc26'
Apr 15 2025	19°Sc17'
Apr 16 2025	01°Sg11'
Apr 17 2025	13°Sg10'
Apr 18 2025	25°Sg18'
Apr 19 2025	07°Cp37'
Apr 20 2025	20°Cp11'
Apr 21 2025	03°Aq03'
Apr 22 2025	16°Aq17'
Apr 23 2025	29°Aq56'
Apr 24 2025	14°Pi01'
Apr 25 2025	28°Pi31'
Apr 26 2025	13°Ar24'
Apr 27 2025	28°Ar33'
Apr 28 2025	13°Ta48'
Apr 29 2025	29°Ta00'
Apr 30 2025	13°Ge58'

DATE	MOON	DATE	MOON
May 1 2025	28°Ge34'	Jun 1 2025	18°Le13'
May 2 2025	12°Cn43'	Jun 2 2025	01°Vi03'
May 3 2025	26°Cn23'	Jun 3 2025	13°Vi30'
May 4 2025	09°Le35'	Jun 4 2025	25°Vi40'
May 5 2025	22°Le22'	Jun 5 2025	07°Li38'
May 6 2025	04°Vi48'	Jun 6 2025	19°Li29'
May 7 2025	16°Vi58'	Jun 7 2025	01°Sc17'
May 8 2025	28°Vi57'	Jun 8 2025	13°Sc07'
May 9 2025	10°Li49'	Jun 9 2025	25°Sc02'
May 10 2025	22°Li38'	Jun 10 2025	07°Sg04'
May 11 2025	04°Sc26'	Jun 11 2025	19°Sg15'
May 12 2025	16°Sc17'	Jun 12 2025	01°Cp35'
May 13 2025	28°Sc13'	Jun 13 2025	14°Cp06'
May 14 2025	10°Sg13'	Jun 14 2025	26°Cp48'
May 15 2025	22°Sg22'	Jun 15 2025	09°Aq40'
May 16 2025	04°Cp38'	Jun 16 2025	22°Aq44'
May 17 2025	17°Cp05'	Jun 17 2025	06°Pi02'
May 18 2025	29°Cp44'	Jun 18 2025	19°Pi35'
May 19 2025	12°Aq38'	Jun 19 2025	03°Ar24'
May 20 2025	25°Aq49'	Jun 20 2025	17°Ar30'
May 21 2025	09°Pi21'	Jun 21 2025	01°Ta53'
May 22 2025	23°Pi15'	Jun 22 2025	16°Ta29'
May 23 2025	07°Ar31'	Jun 23 2025	01°Ge15'
May 24 2025	22°Ar10'	Jun 24 2025	16°Ge04'
May 25 2025	07°Ta06'	Jun 25 2025	00°Cn46'
May 26 2025	22°Ta12'	Jun 26 2025	15°Cn14'
May 27 2025	07°Ge19'	Jun 27 2025	29°Cn22'
May 28 2025	22°Ge17'	Jun 28 2025	13°Le05'
May 29 2025	06°Cn57'	Jun 29 2025	26°Le21'
May 30 2025	21°Cn11'	Jun 30 2025	09°Vi12'
May 31 2025	04°Le56'		

DATE	MOON	DATE	MOON
Jul 1 2025	21°Vi42'	Aug 1 2025	05°Sc43'
Jul 2 2025	03°Li54'	Aug 2 2025	17°Sc35'
Jul 3 2025	15°Li53'	Aug 3 2025	29°Sc29'
Jul 4 2025	27°Li45'	Aug 4 2025	11°Sg32'
Jul 5 2025	09°Sc35'	Aug 5 2025	23°Sg45'
Jul 6 2025	21°Sc28'	Aug 6 2025	06°Cp14'
Jul 7 2025	03°Sg27'	Aug 7 2025	18°Cp59'
Jul 8 2025	15°Sg36'	Aug 8 2025	02°Aq01'
Jul 9 2025	27°Sg58'	Aug 9 2025	15°Aq21'
Jul 10 2025	10°Cp32'	Aug 10 2025	28°Aq57'
Jul 11 2025	23°Cp19'	Aug 11 2025	12°Pi45'
Jul 12 2025	06°Aq20'	Aug 12 2025	26°Pi44'
Jul 13 2025	19°Aq33'	Aug 13 2025	10°Ar51'
Jul 14 2025	02°Pi57'	Aug 14 2025	25°Ar02'
Jul 15 2025	16°Pi31'	Aug 15 2025	09°Ta16'
Jul 16 2025	00°Ar16'	Aug 16 2025	23°Ta29'
Jul 17 2025	14°Ar10'	Aug 17 2025	07°Ge40'
Jul 18 2025	28°Ar14'	Aug 18 2025	21°Ge46'
Jul 19 2025	12°Ta27'	Aug 19 2025	05°Cn45'
Jul 20 2025	26°Ta47'	Aug 20 2025	19°Cn35'
Jul 21 2025	11°Ge10'	Aug 21 2025	03°Le14'
Jul 22 2025	25°Ge33'	Aug 22 2025	16°Le38'
Jul 23 2025	09°Cn50'	Aug 23 2025	29°Le47'
Jul 24 2025	23°Cn56'	Aug 24 2025	12°Vi39'
Jul 25 2025	07°Le45'	Aug 25 2025	25°Vi16'
Jul 26 2025	21°Le14'	Aug 26 2025	07°Li37'
Jul 27 2025	04°Vi22'	Aug 27 2025	19°Li46'
Jul 28 2025	17°Vi10'	Aug 28 2025	01°Sc45'
Jul 29 2025	29°Vi38'	Aug 29 2025	13°Sc39'
Jul 30 2025	11°Li50'	Aug 30 2025	25°Sc30'
Jul 31 2025	23°Li50'	Aug 31 2025	07°Sg24'

DATE	MOON	DATE	MOON
Sep 1 2025	19°Sg26'	Oct 1 2025	22°Cp08'
Sep 2 2025	01°Cp40'	Oct 2 2025	04°Aq54'
Sep 3 2025	14°Cp10'	Oct 3 2025	18°Aq04'
Sep 4 2025	26°Cp59'	Oct 4 2025	01°Pi39'
Sep 5 2025	10°Aq10'	Oct 5 2025	15°Pi41'
Sep 6 2025	23°Aq43'	Oct 6 2025	00°Ar07'
Sep 7 2025	07°Pi37'	Oct 7 2025	14°Ar53'
Sep 8 2025	21°Pi50'	Oct 8 2025	29°Ar52'
Sep 9 2025	06°Ar16'	Oct 9 2025	14°Ta55'
Sep 10 2025	20°Ar50'	Oct 10 2025	29°Ta52'
Sep 11 2025	05°Ta26'	Oct 11 2025	14°Ge37'
Sep 12 2025	19°Ta59'	Oct 12 2025	29°Ge02'
Sep 13 2025	04°Ge24'	Oct 13 2025	13°Cn05'
Sep 14 2025	18°Ge37'	Oct 14 2025	26°Cn45'
Sep 15 2025	02°Cn36'	Oct 15 2025	10°Le03'
Sep 16 2025	16°Cn20'	Oct 16 2025	23°Le02'
Sep 17 2025	29°Cn49'	Oct 17 2025	05°Vi44'
Sep 18 2025	13°Le03'	Oct 18 2025	18°Vi12'
Sep 19 2025	26°Le02'	Oct 19 2025	00°Li29'
Sep 20 2025	08°Vi49'	Oct 20 2025	12°Li38'
Sep 21 2025	21°Vi23'	Oct 21 2025	24°Li40'
Sep 22 2025	03°Li45'	Oct 22 2025	06°Sc36'
Sep 23 2025	15°Li57'	Oct 23 2025	18°Sc29'
Sep 24 2025	28°Li00'	Oct 24 2025	00°Sg20'
Sep 25 2025	09°Sc56'	Oct 25 2025	12°Sg11'
Sep 26 2025	21°Sc48'	Oct 26 2025	24°Sg04'
Sep 27 2025	03°Sg38'	Oct 27 2025	06°Cp03'
Sep 28 2025	15°Sg31'	Oct 28 2025	18°Cp12'
Sep 29 2025	27°Sg31'	Oct 29 2025	00°Aq33'
Sep 30 2025	09°Cp42'	Oct 30 2025	13°Aq13'
		Oct 31 2025	26°Aq15'

DATE	MOON	DATE	MOON
Nov 1 2025	09°Pi43'	Dec 1 2025	16°Ar27'
Nov 2 2025	23°Pi39'	Dec 2 2025	01°Ta06'
Nov 3 2025	08°Ar04'	Dec 3 2025	16°Ta08'
Nov 4 2025	22°Ar55'	Dec 4 2025	01°Ge24'
Nov 5 2025	08°Ta04'	Dec 5 2025	16°Ge44'
Nov 6 2025	23°Ta24'	Dec 6 2025	01°Cn57'
Nov 7 2025	08°Ge41'	Dec 7 2025	16°Cn50'
Nov 8 2025	23°Ge45'	Dec 8 2025	01°Le18'
Nov 9 2025	08°Cn28'	Dec 9 2025	15°Le15'
Nov 10 2025	22°Cn43'	Dec 10 2025	28°Le43'
Nov 11 2025	06°Le30'	Dec 11 2025	11°Vi42'
Nov 12 2025	19°Le49'	Dec 12 2025	24°Vi18'
Nov 13 2025	02°Vi44'	Dec 13 2025	06°Li35'
Nov 14 2025	15°Vi18'	Dec 14 2025	18°Li39'
Nov 15 2025	27°Vi36'	Dec 15 2025	00°Sc34'
Nov 16 2025	09°Li42'	Dec 16 2025	12°Sc25'
Nov 17 2025	21°Li41'	Dec 17 2025	24°Sc15'
Nov 18 2025	03°Sc35'	Dec 18 2025	06°Sg07'
Nov 19 2025	15°Sc27'	Dec 19 2025	18°Sg02'
Nov 20 2025	27°Sc19'	Dec 20 2025	00°Cp03'
Nov 21 2025	09°Sg11'	Dec 21 2025	12°Cp11'
Nov 22 2025	21°Sg05'	Dec 22 2025	24°Cp25'
Nov 23 2025	03°Cp03'	Dec 23 2025	06°Aq47'
Nov 24 2025	15°Cp07'	Dec 24 2025	19°Aq19'
Nov 25 2025	27°Cp18'	Dec 25 2025	02°Pi03'
Nov 26 2025	09°Aq40'	Dec 26 2025	15°Pi02'
Nov 27 2025	22°Aq17'	Dec 27 2025	28°Pi18'
Nov 28 2025	05°Pi12'	Dec 28 2025	11°Ar54'
Nov 29 2025	18°Pi31'	Dec 29 2025	25°Ar52'
Nov 30 2025	02°Ar15'	Dec 30 2025	10°Ta13'
		Dec 31 2025	24°Ta54'